D1204144

CHARLES H. DOW: ECONOMIST

CHARLES H. DOW: ECONOMIST

A Selection of His Writings on Business Cycles

Edited, with comments, by

GEORGE W. BISHOP, JR.

DOW JONES BOOKS
Princeton — New Jersey

5/9/85

Third Printing

Library of Congress Catalog Number: 67-18137

To

Helen

Georgelen

and

George III

PREFACE

The lexicon of Wall Street includes the name of Charles H. Dow in the terms "Dow Theory" and the "Dow-Jones Averages," and practically all books written on investments since Dow's death in 1902 devote some space to this original thinker. In contrast, he is not mentioned in those volumes concerned with business cycles, and his pioneering work in this field has been overlooked by economists. Dow's name is missing as well from standard histories of economic thought.

Considering the advances made in the state of knowledge since Dow's time, it might appear rather superfluous, at this late date, to print a selection of his writings on business cycles. However, it seems only fitting that the work of every man should receive the recognition it deserves. While the state of knowledge of business-cycle thought may not be advanced by this book, a certain perspective is gained so that men and economic theories may be viewed in a new and different light.

I wish to acknowledge my indebtedness to Mr. Bernard Kilgore, Chairman of the Board of Dow Jones & Company, for his kindness and encouragement over the years.

I am also indebted to my former colleague at the University of Tennessee, Mrs. Winifred Goehring Simmons, Business Administration Librarian, who was of inestimable assistance. Her aid was invaluable, as she provided advice and furnished many volumes for study.

For their careful typing and preparation of the manuscript, I wish to thank Mrs. Kay Cafferky, Mrs. Eileen Duffy, Mrs. Betsy Snyder Roberts, and my daughter, Miss Georgelen Bishop, who also aided me in research and editorial matters.

George W. Bishop, Jr.

Northern Illinois University
DeKalb, Illinois

INTRODUCTION

Charles Henry Dow, the financial journalist, was born in Sterling, Connecticut on November 6, 1851. His father was a farmer, born in Sterling in 1816. The family traced their ancestry to Henry Dow, who arrived in Boston in 1637.

Dow's father died when he was six years old, leaving the farm to the widowed mother. Little is known of Dow's early life and nothing of his schooling. He left the farm when he was quite young and turned his hand to several kinds of work. However, in 1872, having decided upon a career in journalism, he joined the staff of the *Springfield Republican* of Springfield, Massachusetts. This was at the time a newspaper of national repute under the editorship of Samuel Bowles III, one of the newspaper giants of all time.

Dow remained with the *Springfield Republican* until 1875 and left, a trained newspaperman, for Providence, Rhode Island. Here he was first employed by the *Providence Star,* and it is reported that he also wrote for the *Providence Evening Press.* In 1877 he joined the *Providence Journal* as a reporter and worked for this paper from 1877 through 1879. While with the *Providence Journal,* Dow wrote a number of articles which established his reputation as a historian of the local scene.

In the summer of 1879 Dow accompanied a party of capitalists to Leadville, Colorado, in the capacity of special correspondent for the *Providence Journal.* He covered the silver mining boom, and his graphic articles, entitled "The Leadville Letters," appeared in both the *Providence Journal* and the (Providence) *Evening Bulletin.* They were also reprinted in full in the Appendix to the author's *Charles H. Dow and the Dow Theory* (Appleton-Century-Crofts, Inc., New York, 1960).

Dow moved to New York City in 1880, where he was employed as a financial reporter by the Kiernan News Agency. In November, 1882, with a fellow worker, Edward D. Jones, Dow left the Kiernan News Agency and formed Dow Jones & Company, the financial news service. From December 24, 1885, until April 30, 1891, Dow was a member of the New York Stock Exchange and a partner in the brokerage firm of Goodbody, Glyn & Dow.

Dow Jones & Company first published *The Wall Street Journal* on July 8, 1889, with Dow as editor. His work on this famous newspaper established his reputation as an outstanding financial journalist. Dow's many paragraphs appeared in *The Wall Street Journal* until a short time before he died on December 4, 1902. In conformity with prevailing newspaper practice, Dow did not sign his articles. However, it is possible to establish the identity of his writings for the period April 21, 1899, to October 25, 1902, inclusive. These consisted of editorials that appeared in the column of *The Wall Street Journal*, "Review and Outlook," which Dow authored.

These editorials covered many subjects, and the selected editorials that follow illustrate the caliber and depth of Dow's writings on business cycles.

CONTENTS

CHAPTER ONE

April 21, 1899 — June 19, 1899

THESE selected editorials from the pen of Charles H. Dow were published in *The Wall Street Journal* during the first half of the year 1899. They appeared in the special column entitled "Review and Outlook" which Dow authored from April 21, 1899, until shortly before his death on December 4, 1902.

These early editorials show that Dow held an advanced view of business cycles for the time. It is apparent that he was vitally concerned with business activity in the broadest sense of the term. In the editorials Dow presents a similarity of thought with that of Thorstein Veblen and Wesley Clair Mitchell, who followed him in writing on business cycles.

During the period April 21, 1899, through June 30, 1899, there were several occasions of disturbance on the New York Stock Exchange, but in the main a spirit of buoyancy prevailed in the province of financial and economic affairs. However, the American investor was hard pressed to keep abreast of the happenings on many fronts—both foreign and domestic.

Early in April a financial reporter on *The New York Times,* writing about April anticipations in the stock market, referred to Daniel Drew's picturesque quotation on April markets. "When the sap is rising in the trees, then stocks must go a-rising too."

As the writer viewed the then current economic situation, he was so impressed by the general air of well-being that he advised his readers: ". . . in no springtime for a decade or more have there been features in the business situation comparable in their inspiriting character to what now predominate. Staple products of the country are demanding better prices. Capital in every department reaps profits. Labor is employed, satisfied, not threatening or incumbering any enterprise. Business men almost universally prosper. Money is plenty and money is cheap. Not only confidence, but even the adventurous spirit shows in the industrial and commercial world. Coincident with the appearance of all these inspiring factors, there disappear other almost numerous factors that for years have been restrictive and discouraging."

In closing, the journalist warned: "Markets run by the almanac do not always prove to be what their prophets promise, however, and because in preceding Aprils good times have come to Wall Street, can hardly be taken as a safe guarantee that this April shall be similarly satisfactory."

This shows that writers on the stock market have long followed the practice of the oracle of ancient Delphi in the manner in which they present their predictions.

The New York Stock Exchange suffered a decline on April 7, 1899, with volume reaching 1,267,927 shares, and almost panic conditions prevailed. On the following day another decline was witnessed, with volume reaching 1,268,000 shares. The industrial section of the list was particularly depressed by waves of heavy selling.

The prominent brokerage firm of Dimock and Company failed, with the result that Julian A. Dimock followed in his father's footsteps, since speculation in Atlantic Mail caused the firm of A. W. Dimock & Company to founder in 1869.

Therefore, at the time of writing his April editorials Dow was surveying a period of general business prosperity coupled with a stock market which had recently undergone a severe reaction, with the more speculative stocks showing declines extending from five to twenty-five points.

In the Pacific the troops of Aguinaldo were defeated by MacArthur on April 1, 1899, and the Filipinos retreated as the American flag was raised over Malolos in the Philippines. General Lawton captured Santa Cruz early in April.

There was trouble in Samoa as the warriors of Mataafa attacked American and British naval personnel. A naval buildup by Germany, Great Britain, and the United States was a disturbing feature of the international situation.

Dow, no doubt, had noticed the death of Horace A. W. Tabor on April 10, 1899, in Denver, as well as that of Professor O. C. Marsh of Yale University the month previously. Dow and Marsh were members of the party of capitalists that visited Leadville, Colorado in 1879 during the silver boom, when Dow had served the *Providence Journal* as a special correspondent on the trip. Tabor joined the capitalists on their arrival in Leadville, and Dow also made his acquaintance. In the articles entitled "The Leadville Letters," which he wrote for the *Providence Journal,* Dow described both Marsh and Tabor. Tabor's fortune, which had its start with the "Little Pittsburg" silver mine, was at one time estimated at $9,000,000, but he died penniless. Marsh was professor of paleontology at Yale University and the nephew and heir of George Peabody, the great American-English merchant and banker; Professor Marsh was largely responsible for the establishment of the Peabody Museum at Yale.

Late in April, Amalgamated Copper was incorporated with a capital of $75,000,000. It was a Standard Oil production, with Henry H. Rogers, William G. Rockefeller, Marcus Daly, Frederick P. Olcott, James Stillman, Roswell P. Flower, Robert Bacon, and Albert C. Burrage as directors. Offered to the public at one hundred dollars per share, it was one of the many large-scale combinations that characterized the year. Such enormous industrial combinations were the order of the day.

Two other matters were in the news. The *Figaro* in Paris published evidence given in secret before the Court of Cassation in the Dreyfus case which caused comment in Paris, London, and New York and revived interest in the case.

The other affair, which made the front pages of the American press, was the question of whether or not our troops in Cuba had been served "embalmed beef." The testimony of the experts could not be said to be in full agreement. General Adna R. Chaffee pronounced: "I consider this much-maligned beef very good food. The soldiers in Cuba have it regularly. . . . There is complaint if they do not get it."

On the other hand, General Shafter remarked that "the beef was not appetizing but I ate it every day." This is probably the only record of a general in the army attesting to the fact that he followed an unappetizing menu on a daily basis.

Orators, then as now, were busy. Bryan talked on "Democracy," and Booker T. Washington on "Race Problems." Governor Theodore Roosevelt regaled his listeners on "The Strenuous Life." Professor John D. Quackenbos of Columbia University proposed hypnotism to regenerate the human race by reforming criminals and "removing crime and moral obliquity from this terraqueous sphere."

There was a reaction in the stock market when former Governor Roswell P. Flower died suddenly on the evening of May 12, 1899, at Eastport, Long Island, New York. On the following day the "Flower panic" occurred, with many stocks suffering drastic declines. New York Air Brake sold as low as 125 after closing on May 12th at 185. Flower had returned to Wall Street after his term of office as Governor of New York and was a stock manipulator of the first rank. Henry Clews called him the leader of the boom in stocks that took place in 1899.

In the month of June the industrial stocks continued their decline, although the rails improved on the prospects of heavy crop shipments and increased earnings. On the first day of the month the immortal Anna Pavlova made her debut at the Marinsky Theater in St. Petersburg.

April 21, 1899

We have occasionally called attention to the fact that during the present generation, at least, the great swing of the market up or down has in no case been completed in less than four years. The proof on this point is obtained by taking the average price of a considerable number of stocks and finding the low point and then following the movement of averages until the high point has been reached. Reversing the operation gives the low point.

A high point in the market, determined by this process, was reached in September, 1872. The next low point was in April, 1877; the next high point, May, 1881; and the next low, June, 1886. The succeeding high point presented unusual features. A high point was made in May, 1890, but the rising tendency was checked by the development of the Baring panic, after which the market recovered, establishing a point about as high in the spring of 1892 as that occurring in the spring of 1890.[1] From this point, the market went down until August, 1896, since which time prices have been rising.

This suggests that the high point of the present period will not be due until 1900 or 1901. The time involved in these turns is determined by natural causes. The cause is that the stock market reflects general conditions, and it takes several years for such a change for the better or for the worse to work its way through the community; so that the mass of people are either optimistic or pessimistic in their views. Some people foresee changes in the situation much quicker than others, but it takes a change of opinion on the part of millions of people to produce a well-defined sentiment throughout the country.[2]

The action of the market is entirely consistent with the idea that we are in a bull swing of four or five years. It has usually occurred that bullish sentiment was more pronounced in the third and fourth years of such a period than in the first and second. On the other hand, the fluctuations in prices during the third and fourth years have been much greater than in those preceding. This has been partly because the level of prices has been higher, partly because high prices have tempted a large manufacture of stocks, producing an increase in the supply of securities as compared with a decrease in the supply of money available for carrying them.[3]

There are two unfavorable factors in the situation at present. The first is the great increase in industrial stocks, calling for increased employment of money as these stocks become distributed. The second is the condition of winter wheat, which is comparatively unfavorable, although perhaps not as much damaged as would be suggested by current reports.

Offsetting these factors is the general prosperity and the inertia of the buying movement which has been and is still lifting prices. It is the experience of practically all operators in stocks that they do not wait long enough for profits. This is due to the fact that the public buying or the public selling which, in the end, determines the movement of stocks, is much slower and also much more persistent than is expected.

The confidence of the public in the market has been illustrated by the break in prices occurring early in the present month. Under some conditions that decline would have brought a succeeding volume of selling. Under existing conditions, it has brought very little selling, showing [that] the mass of people feel confident of higher prices. This sentiment if it holds will go far towards bringing about this result and rounding out the bull market of the period in something like its normal time.

April 22, 1899

We have received some inquiries in regard to the figures referred to yesterday as representing the high and the low points in stocks in recent years. We give, today, these figures showing the low points and the high points of the market periods since 1872. It may be added that the general character of the market has been the same since 1857, but the comparatively small number of active stocks during the war period makes that average less significant than it has been since.

There was a low point in the market in 1867–68, following which prices rose to the high point of 1872. This advance reflected the inflation and the development following the war and led to the 1873 panic. The high point represented by the average of sixty stocks in September, 1872, was 76.57. The panic and the resulting liquidation carried the average in 1877 of practically the same stocks back to 36.33, an average decline of 40.24.

The bull period extending from April, 1877, to May, 1881, could very properly be called the era of railway expansion. The Granger stocks rose in that time from prices below 20 to prices above par. The average of sixty stocks rose from 36.33 to 99.80, an average gain of 63.47.

The next important move was the decline lasting up to 1885. This was essentially the period of the trunk-line war, the great fight growing out of the construction of West Shore, Nickel Plate, and the Lackawanna extension. It carried Lake Shore from 136 to 51 and affected other stocks proportionately. This period included the great bear campaign made against Mr. Gould, culminating in the Stock Exchange panic of 1884.[4] The fall in prices was from 99.80 to 41.28, an average decline of 58.52. The acquisition of West Shore by New York Central was the turning point. The market had a rapid advance in 1886 and 1887, followed by quite an important decline culminating in the spring of 1888, followed, however, by another advance, carrying prices to their best average in May, 1890. The high point of twenty stocks in May, 1890, was 78.03, an advance of 36.75.

The decline culminating in August, 1896, was due to the free-trade agitation and the anxiety in regard to the currency. The average of twenty stocks fell from 78.03 in May, 1890, to 41.82 in August, 1896, a decline of 56.21. [The figure 56.21 is in error and should be 36.21.]

Since August, 1896, the advance has been comparatively steady. The average of twenty railroad stocks has risen from 41.82 to 87.04, a gain of 45.22. The average of twelve industrial stocks has risen in the same time from 28.48 to 76.04, an average advance of 47.56. It is noticeable that industrials and rails have risen in the present period almost exactly the same amount.

There has been a disposition to compare the present period with that of 1879. If the comparison holds good, the average must go considerably higher. An advance in sixty stocks of over 63 points each in 1879 calls for a rise of over 45 points in twenty stocks now if the comparison is to hold good.

This is pre-eminently the period of industrial speculation, yet the creation of industrial stocks has become pronounced only within a year. It is impossible that any large portion of the industrial stocks created in the last six months should have been marketed. As it is the intention of the promoters of industrial combinations to sell a portion, at least, of the stocks which they have made, it follows that there must be a very strong body of capitalists prepared at present to resist anything like collapse in the industrial market and to promote by every means in their power firm or advancing prices for the market as a whole. And this effort on their part is being powerfully supported by the excellent condition of practically all branches of trade.[5]

April 24, 1899

There is a pronounced difference between bull markets that are made by manipulation and those that are made by the public. The former represent[s] the effort of a small number of persons; the latter reflects the sense of the country on values. It is possible to create a limited public sentiment by manipulation, but the sentiment that endures and sweeps away the strongest interests which oppose it is invariably founded upon general conditions which are sufficiently universal and sufficiently potent to affect the opinions of practically everybody.

The growth of public opinion in regard to values is necessarily slow. The low point in the stock market is generally reached at a time when commodities are well down to the cost of production, when manufacturing interests are depressed, when railroad earnings are small, and when general business is unprofitable. People have sold their investments because the proceeds were needed in their lines of business or for living purposes. Everybody buys from hand to mouth because the experience of the years preceding has been that everything grew cheaper.

At such a time, some one industry begins to improve. Others gradually follow. There are usually some great causes like unusually high prices for crops, which exert an influence.[6] People find themselves to be making money instead of losing it, and that the raw materials or half-finished products which they consume are advancing in price. Merchants and manufacturers begin to increase stocks. People who have money begin to make investments. During this period of advance everybody makes money and grows confident that whatever is undertaken will prove sucessful. A man who would hardly dare to put in his winter stock of coal one year will be found two years later quite willing to buy a coal mine, with a view of supplying the wants of the community. It takes two or three years for this change to occur, because millions of people have to experience in their own fortunes the change of conditions before they are willing to accept them as genuine.

The effect of a change on the part of a nation of 75,000,000 of people from feeling discouraged and doubtful to being confident and enterprising, is stupendous in its results upon all lines of business, including the stock market. It shows clearly how irresistible such a force becomes when it is focused upon speculative markets. It shows, too, why bull and bear markets persist as they do.

When the public mind has a well-defined tendency, either bullish or bearish, it is not easily changed. Scores or hundreds of people may change, but the mass press on in the same direction. The public mind, when it, as at present, favors the long side of the market, is not likely to alter that opinion until one of several things have occurred. The public may lose its confidence in stocks as the result of some national calamity which arrests attention and creates alarm. It may change on account of such a wave of selling of newly created stocks as prevents advance in prices and creates so many losses or permits so few profits as to tire out the public buyer. It may be checked by such an exhaustion of the supply of money as makes the carrying cost of stocks excessive, and thereby discourages trading.[7]

The public interest in the market of 1872 was checked partly by dear money and partly by apprehensions that the policy of contracting the greenbacks would make a great scarcity of funds throughout the country. This apprehension was well founded, as the panic of 1873 was essentially a money panic. The bull market of 1879 was checked largely by the creation of new railway securities growing out of the expansion in that period of western and southwestern roads. Money was a factor in the case, but it was not the main one. The bull period in 1890 was checked by the selling of American securities from London and was due especially to the Baring panic.

It seems reasonably certain that the present bull market will be checked, when the time comes, by the creation of a greater supply of industrial stocks than the public will be able to absorb. Vast as the surplus fund is, it is no match for the printing presses of the country. We think, however, that while the character of the end of the bull market is tolerably clear, the time is, at least, a year away.[8] It may be considerably more than that.

The evidence on this point is that to which we have frequently referred. The creation of new securities has not been very large until this year. There has not been time to get them distributed. The public hardly knows the names of many of the new industrials. Before the public will absorb these stocks, there must be a period during which they are made popular and profitable. The public must see them quoted and must learn more or less about them before it will buy. To assume that the bull market is to end this spring is to assume that many of the ablest financiers in the country are going to be left with large lines of new stocks on their hands. Somebody will undoubtedly be left with more stocks than are wanted, but the fact that bankers and syndicates are still willing to take the new stocks of industrial enterprises is evidence that they believe the tide of public interest in securities to be flowing with unabated force.

April 25, 1899

The bull market has been under way nearly three years. It began with the prices of stocks and commodities at a low point. The lowest average of stocks and the lowest average of commodities were reached at practically the same time. Railroad earnings were at a minimum and general business was depressed. As a result the supply of money was more than abundant. The past three years have seen an entire change in the character of general business, a pronounced advance in the price of most commodities and a large advance in stocks. The supply of money, on the other hand, has been gradually absorbed until surplus reserves are no longer excessive.

The situation at present is clear. There is no abatement in the volume of business.[9] Clearings show steady expansion. The iron trade is exceedingly prosperous. Manufactures generally are in demand. Railroad tonnage is the largest on record, and the earnings on stocks are as good or better than they were last year. The crop outlook as far as winter wheat is concerned is not as favorable as it was a year ago, but the damage is not considered as serious as it was thought to be at the beginning of the month. The money market has been unfavorably affected by the spring demand, but a period of fair supplies is likely to last until the crop movement makes fresh demands later in the year. The price of securities is in the main justified by existing conditions.

When it comes to considering the future, there is, of course, uncertainty as to the result, but the factors which enter into the case are not difficult to locate. The first great factor must be the supply of money. The advance in prices has absorbed money. The increased volume of business in all lines over the country has absorbed money, and the creation of new securities has been a further draft upon the surplus fund of the country. There will certainly come a time when the supply of money will not be adequate to sustain prices at the level which they will have reached. It is not apparent that this time has come yet.

The second factor in determining the duration of the bull market will be the prosperity of general business. As long as the profits in great staple industries continue large, so long will there be sustained or increased values for the securities entitled to share in that prosperity. As long as general business thrives, railroad earnings will be large enough for that portion belonging to stocks to justify sustained advanced prices. There will come a time, however, when production will outrun consumption, and then there will be a check in the prosperity of one industry after another resulting in contraction and later in the loss of profits.[10] This is a point to be watched with special care, but it does not appear that any such check or interruption has yet been felt.

A third factor in estimating the duration of the bull market is the condition of public sentiment. That sentiment is the best indication of the condition of the thousands of lines of business in which the public is engaged. When men begin to find their own line of business less profitable, they will begin to suspect that other lines are experiencing similar conditions. This will bring a check in outside buying and will lead to a disposition to take profits or to stop losses. In other words, the weight of the public business in stocks will shift over from the buying to the selling side. This will not all come at once, but the tendency will gradually appear. It seems safe to say that there is thus far no decided evidence that the public is losing confidence in the market.

If this reasoning is sound, it seems fair to conclude that we are in the second half of a bull period, but that the conditions which have supported the advance show no signs of immediate exhaustion, and the market bids fair to have further advance.

April 27, 1899

The bull market of 1879 witnessed the creation and the first great development of speculation in railroad stocks in this market. The bull period of 1899 witnesses the development and the first great speculation in industrial shares. There is some reason for thinking that these periods will show a certain amount of similarity, because the forces which bear upon each are in many respects similar. It is more likely than not that the present industrial period will have its rise and fall quite in keeping with the rise and fall in newly created railroad stocks twenty years ago.

A brief look at the 1879 development is, therefore, not without interest. That market sprang out of the dull period of 1876 and 1877. Mr. Keene was the first great bull, taking a large proportion of Mr. Gould's stocks. Mr. Gould became a bear in the fall of 1878 and fought the market in the spring of 1879. He turned bull in the late spring of that year, and a considerable proportion of his fortune was made on the bull side of the last half of 1879 and the year 1880.[11] Mr. Vanderbilt, Mr. Keene, and Mr. Woerishoffer were prominent factors in the advance.

Stocks which began the period selling below 20, ended it selling about 115, and stocks which were beyond the possibilities of dividends sold in 1880 between 50 and 70. The ability to sell securities encouraged railway building greatly in excess of requirements, and this fact made the succeeding bear market a certainty. It was perfectly evident in the year 1881 that many roads could not hope to earn enough to justify prices then existing for their stocks, and this fact led some of the ablest operators to take the bear side on the disaster to the corn crop in the summer of 1881. It took until 1885 to finish the bear market, and, while the trunk lines were the special objects of attack, the Granger, Pacific and southwestern stocks had steady and large declines.

The creation of industrial securities is proceeding at a rate more rapid than was possible with railway stocks because the present capitalization is of established industries, while the railroads had to be built. The marketing of these securities, which is not unlikely to be the feature of the current and the coming year, may witness some extraordinary advances in prices and very unusual opportunities for profit.

In the end, however, prices are likely to reach a point not justified by profits. This will be known to insiders, who, in many cases, will strive to add to the profits made on the long side of their stocks a series of profits obtained on the short side. When this time comes, the industrial list will have its period of severe trial. Combinations launched with high hopes and strong professions of confidence will have to be reorganized within a few years on a level of capitalization based upon hard times.

The point of importance for those who deal in industrial stocks is whether the capitalization of the companies into which they propose to buy is moderate or excessive, when compared with the aggregate earnings of the various concerns forming the combination in a period of depression. It is probable that consolidated companies will be able to earn as much in the next period of low prices as the companies forming the combine were able to earn in the last one; hence the very foundation of investments in industrials should be knowledge of what these companies earned, say in 1893 to 1896, making, perhaps, reasonable allowance for economies under consolidation. Where the earnings so shown would have provided dividends for industrials now active, the fact must be regarded as a very strong point in favor of those stocks.

It will, of course, be difficult for investors in many cases to acquire this information, and this leads to a matter which the managers of industrial corporations ought to consider. The time will come when industrial companies in which the public is a large owner, will be required to make frequent reports of earnings, as the railroad companies have been gradually compelled to do. The Tennessee Coal and Iron Co. sets an excellent example in this respect. It does not appear that this business has ever suffered from the publicity regularly given to its gross and net earnings.

Nothing would do more toward the establishment of confidence in an industrial stock now than for the company to publish monthly statements of income and expense. The companies which could do this with credit to themselves have an excellent opportunity to win public favor. It is for the interests of those which could not make a good showing to withhold all information. This, however, deprives the other companies of an advantage to which they are fairly entitled and which they could easily gain.

The investor who in 1880 selected the best stocks for either speculation or investment obtained a fair share of the profits of the rise. When, however, the period of decline came, his advantage was much more pronounced. This will be found just as true in dealing in industrials during the next few years.

May 13, 1899

. . . .

. . . The stock market is in the nature of a barometer which reflects the rise and fall in general conditions. The stock market is made by outside business. Stocks getting dividends, instead of fixed interest, get the surplus profits of good times and are the first to feel the loss of profits in bad times. As long as general business is prosperous, the surplus earnings [earnings available for dividend payment on common stock] which are the stay and support of prices of stocks will continue.

There is no evidence thus far of any essential falling off in this volume of profits. The testimony of the largest men in practically all lines of business is not only that their particular business is still good, but that there is enough in sight to insure good trade and good profits for months to come. The fact that some of the strongest men in the country are bringing out new enterprises shows that they foresee no serious halt in the march of prosperity.

They will see it as soon as anybody, and they will show this apprehension by curtailment of undertakings as soon as reasons satisfactory to their minds exist. As long as this does not appear and as long as there are many clear proofs of continued prosperity of a kind bearing directly upon stock values, it seems unlikely that operators for a rise will find themselves lastingly wrong on the market.

May 20, 1899

The market is working along the lines expected. The views of the large operators happen to be in sympathy with a moderate decline. Their part in bringing this about has been, in the main, the withdrawal of supporting orders, leaving an opening for room attack.[12] The speed of the decline has perhaps been accelerated by Mr. Keene, who believes that the bull market has culminated, and that selling on rallies will be judicious for some time to come.

This position taken by so prominent an operator may result in carrying prices lower than they otherwise would have gone, and it will certainly make fluctuations more violent than they would have been without strong interests on each side of the account. It is probable that attempts will be made from time to time to put the market up on shorts and to put it down on weak holders.[13]

Both bull and bear leaders rely upon the situation to sustain their position. Neither proposes to go against the current of events. The question, therefore, is whether the great factors which cause advance or decline have changed from the bull to the bear side. This is something which can be discerned more or less clearly by all who watch the business situation, but when, as at present, there are facts on both sides, judgment becomes a matter of more difficulty.

The facts which are less favorable are the damage to winter wheat, the less favorable condition of foreign trade, the overcreation of securities and the large advance in prices.

The strongest factors on the bull side are the ease of money, the fact that general business continues profitable, the continued large excess of exports over imports, the continued large yearly additions to the stock of gold, the continued increase in railroad earnings, the continued large investment demand for bonds at prices which show a large fund still seeking investment, and the well-defined position on the bull side of the strongest financial interests of the country.

The trade reports for the week show no abatement in general prosperity. The iron trade is as influential a factor as any. Consumption continues to reduce surplus stocks. Returns show that stocks of coke and anthracite May 1 were less than a week's supply. A considerable percentage of furnaces have sold three-quarters of their production for the second half of the current year. The week has brought another advance in foundry and Bessemer pig. The steel mills are oversold, and the great steel companies have orders materially in excess of their ability to fill. It has happened in the past that one of the first signs of a check to prosperity has appeared in the falling off in a demand for iron. Such a falling off would exert a considerable influence now, but no such sign has appeared.

The winter wheat reports are admittedly unfavorable, but there is a wide difference of opinion as to the extent of the damage. What loss in tonnage there is will be felt by Atchison, Rock Island, Missouri Pacific and roads in the Central belt. It is significant, however, that with most of those properties wheat furnishes a very small percentage of the tonnage. Atchison officials estimate that admitting the damage to be 25 per cent, the loss in the company tonnage would not amount to more than 2½ per cent, which it is estimated would be made up by gain in Pacific coast business and from new railway connections. It is probable that the damage would be more serious in its curtailment of buying power in the year to come than in its effect upon earnings from wheat transportation this year.

A feature in the situation which has not attracted much attention, but which may become important, is the increased London buying. London was a steady seller on the advance, but has been a buyer on the decline. Advices from the other side say there is a disposition to trade in Americans at a fair level of prices. The loss of profits in Americans last year was regretted, and some rather important interests are alleged to have signified their intention to take hold of Americans this year if prices declined. The recent buying seems to be a fulfillment of this purpose.

May 22, 1899

The market continues to make progress in the direction of lower prices. This was to have been expected as far as the immediate market is concerned; the decline should go further. The relapse has not borne its proper ratio to the rally which culminated the middle of last week. It is noticeable, however, that the decline is meeting little or no resistance from the bulls. It is not to be supposed that the powerful bull interest has gone out of business. The inference therefore is that it is permitting decline in the belief that lower prices temporarily will be [to] the advantage of the market in the long run. The extent of the decline will be governed considerably by the amount of liquidation that may grow out of the fall. The more liquidation, the lower prices will go. Without liquidation, short sellers will soon find themselves without ammunition. The market itself, therefore, will be the best indication of the duration of the decline.

The bank statement was unexpectedly favorable both in the increase in reserve and in the decrease in loans. Whatever influence is exerted by easy money is now secure on the long side. *In the long run there is no one factor more potent than easy money.* [Italics supplied.] The condition of money elsewhere is indicated by the fact that out-of-town banks continue to be bidders for paper, without any material increase in offerings.

The strength in exchange was partly due to Baltimore & Ohio settlements.[14] It brought some talk of gold going out, but the probabilities are that there will be liberal offerings of commercial futures before long. Clearings outside of New York continue to show a large gain, about 30 per cent over May last year, while failures are the smallest ever reported.[15] Nothing could speak more eloquently as to the general conditions.

An examination of trade conditions shows an unprecedented condition of the iron trade. Practically no decrease appears in the demand for finished products. Tin is slightly higher, copper a shade easier, and lead quiet. The coal trade continues quiet as the result of a small retail demand. Coke production continues in excess of any previous record. Shipments of boots and shoes continue the largest known, and the advance in prices, instead of checking demand, has resulted in an increase. The leather trade is better than heretofore, although hides are a shade easier.

Wool prices continue firm, although the manufacturing demand is only moderate. The week brought a general advance in cotton goods. The production is above normal, but stocks do not increase. A good demand exists for export. Trade in woolen goods has been somewhat disappointing.

The grain movement shows a distinct fall off. Western receipts last week were 2,110,300 bushels, against 5,876,716 bushels for the same days last year. Receipts for three weeks have been 6,523,593 bushels, against 14,581,002 bushels. Western receipts for the crop year have been 241,610,390 bushels, against 213,596,843 bushels for the previous year. Exports of merchandise from New York for the week were $8,389,281 against $11,382,103 for the same week last year. For two weeks the result was better, showing exports of $17,432,171 against $18,258,976.

Gross earnings in recent weeks show increases of about 6½ per cent over last year. The best results are given by the Grangers and the eastern roads, which were materially above the average. The poorest results are shown by the trunk lines. Tonnage at Chicago and St. Louis shows an increase in the car movement over last year, while Indianapolis does not make as good an exhibit.

There is little in the foregoing analysis of trade conditions to cause uneasiness. In some cases, the record is not quite up to the best, but in a majority of instances the reports covering the past week make as good an exhibit as those of any week since the tide turned. Such conditions must have an effect upon speculative temper all over the country. They are likely to prevent the sacrifice of stocks and to encourage a moderate amount of buying as prices decline.

June 12, 1899

Last week brought a distinct improvement in the general situation as expressed by the relation between supply and demand. It is seldom that a week sees such advances in staple commodities, as iron products rose nearly 9 per cent, pig iron nearly 5 per cent, cotton goods 1½ per cent, woolen goods about 1 per cent, and boots and shoes 1 per cent. Advances in wages were made in over twenty important cases. Clearings showed a gain of about 30 per cent outside of New York. Failures were nearly the lowest on record. Railway earnings showed an average gain of 7.4 per cent over last year and 24 per cent over the largest earnings of 1892.

With such a record, it is not surprising that the stock market advanced. Nor is it unreasonable, under such conditions, to look for improvement in weeks to come. *Nothing is more certain* [*than*] *that the permanent course of the stock market depends upon the condition of general business, as shown by the profitable employment of capital and labor with the resulting increase in the surplus fund for investment.*

People are certainly making money and will therefore have money to invest. [Italics supplied.]

The supply of money determines the return on investments as a class, and prices are governed thereby.[16] Of course, the value of particular stocks is controlled by the particular return, but in the mass it is apparent that the conditions which make higher prices for stocks are in full force and effect.

This is not saying that the market will go up today or this week. It means simply that the tide is coming in instead of going out and that holders of securities have in a sense the whole country working to enhance the value of their properties.

Something can be said in favor of nearly all groups of stocks. The northwestern roads have the spring wheat promise. The southwestern roads are less favorably situated but have a very large volume of general business in sight. The coal stocks are not unlikely to be affected by very important combinations at an early day. Indications are that the sugar-trade war is nearer settlement than insiders are willing to admit.[17] The steel stocks never had such conditions before, and their dullness is almost suspicious.

The bank statement was better than had been expected. The gold exports did not show very fully in the decrease in cash.[18] With the banks holding over 200 millions of specie, there is no cause for anxiety, because a moderate amount of gold goes out of the country at midsummer. The market is quite likely to get reactions on account of the bear interest, but indications are that on such reactions stocks deserving confidence can be bought.

June 19, 1899

The coming week bids fair to offer little more than a midsummer trading market. The forces for and against prices are potent enough to check decisive action on each side of the account. Each side [bull or bear] is clear enough as to what is in its favor but sees and fears the strength equally apparent on the other side. It looks as though the market might not move materially until a preponderating weight was put on one side of the scale or the other. It is natural to suppose that the spring wheat or corn situation might be that weight. In any event some little time must elapse before the facts will be clear enough to be fully utilized.

A factor in the situation which may become important later is the condition of the labor market. In many large lines of industry, wages are still at the level established during hard times. In other cases, there have been voluntary advances in wages, and in a few instances important strikes have recently occurred.[19] It is not unlikely that labor will seek its share of current prosperity and quite possible that its demands may be enforced by strikes on a scale large enough to exert some speculative influence.[20]

Clearings show a decrease compared with recent weeks, but this must be regarded as due to the season. The gain compared with last year is about 34 per cent, and about 100 per cent compared with 1894.

Railroad earnings for the first week in June increased about 9.4 per cent, compared with 15 per cent for the fourth week in May, 8 per cent for the third, and 4 per cent for the second. The most favorable exhibit continues to be made by the Granger and southern roads. The east-bound tonnage from Chicago shows a falling off compared with last year, but the car movement at St. Louis and at Minneapolis exhibits an increase.

As the month draws to a close, it is possible that money may become slightly dearer. Many of the large railroad and industrial corporations are heavy lenders of money on call in New York. This money, to an extent large in the aggregate, will be called in to meet July payments of interest and dividends. It is not unlikely, however, that the effect will be for more than a few days.

The bank statement reflected conditions of the previous week in part, and the situation at the close was probably rather better than that indicated by the statement. The expansion in loans implied that large operations were still under way, especially as the increase was only partly reflected in deposits. The interior currency movement is still in favor of New York banks, and should be during the remainder of the month. Outside of New York, call money is, as a rule, lower than at this time last year. Pittsburg is the only eastern city where the rate is up to 6 per cent, and the Pacific coast is the only place where money is reported dear.

The outward movement of gold continues, apparently against real conditions. The strengthening of the gold reserve of the Bank of England has made the discount rate a shade easier in London. The industrial speculation at Berlin is carrying rates up there under conditions which suggest that the Berlin money market may soon become a factor in international speculation.

Throughout the staple trades there is little which can be considered unfavorable. The condition of the iron and steel trade is well known.

Wool sales continue very heavy, notwithstanding the fact that mills seem to be buying chiefly on orders. The demand for dry goods is fully up to the average of the year. Woolen goods are improving in prices, while cotton goods hold firm. Hemlock leather is in steady demand, while hides are a shade easier.

Western receipts of wheat continue heavy in spite of crop damage. Receipts of wheat at western points for the week were 5,152,995 bushels, against 1,217,475 bushels for the same week last year. Receipts for two weeks have been 10,202,189 bushels against 2,684,541 the previous year. It is astonishing that farmers should continue to deliver wheat in such quantity if the crop damage is anything like what the figures seem to denote.

NOTES

[1] The great English firm of Baring Brothers was forced to default on £21,000,000 home liabilities on November 20, 1889. It was saved by the Bank of England and other financial institutions in London, but the failure disturbed the financial world.

[2] Cf. William Stanley Jevons, *Primer of Political Economy* (New York, n.d.), pp. 115–116. Jevons writes of seasonal "tides" in business and continues: "There is also a much longer kind of tide in business, which usually takes somewhere about ten years to rise and fall."

[3] In this passage Dow shows that there are *two* stages, or phases, of a bull market in stocks. In the second stage "bullish sentiment" is more pronounced, and stock prices fluctuate over a greater amplitude due to the reasons given. Compare the position of William Peter Hamilton that a bull market consists of three phases, in his editorials in *The Wall Street Journal* under date of June 21, 1923, and in *Barron's* dated June 25, 1923. Both editorials may be found in the appendix of Robert Rhea, *The Dow Theory* (New York, 1932), pp. 202–203. Also see Robert Rhea, *Dow's Theory Applied to Business and Banking* (New York, 1938), pp. 30–31.

[4] Dow often quoted Jay Gould in his editorials. For an account of an interesting interview of Gould by Dow, see Sereno S. Pratt, *The Work of Wall Street,* rev. ed. (New York, 1912), p. 366. Pratt writes that during the interview Gould gave stock market orders to a number of brokers without attempting to conceal from Dow what he was doing. Dow possessed a "remarkable memory," and when the interview was over he noted the orders in regular order on paper. From this he tried to discover if Gould was bullish or bearish at the time. However, "so skillfully had Gould covered his real purpose in a labyrinth of orders" that Dow was unable to solve the problem.

[5] For a study of business cycles during the period covered in this editorial, see Rendigs Fels, *American Business Cycles, 1865–1897* (Chapel Hill, N.C., 1959).

[6] Cf. Thorstein Veblen, *The Theory of Business Enterprise* (New York, 1904), p. 194: "A period of prosperity is no more a matter of course than a crisis. It has its beginning in some specific combination of circumstances. It takes its rise from some traceable favorable disturbance of the course of business. In such a period the potent factor which serves as incentive to the acceleration of business is a rise of prices. This rise of prices

presently becomes general as prosperity progresses and becomes an habitual fact, but it takes its start from some specific initial disturbance of prices. That is to say, prices rise first in some one industry or line of industries." Also cf. Wesley C. Mitchell, *Business Cycles* (Berkeley, Calif., 1913), p. 452: "The conspicuous agent in rousing business from its partial lethargy has often been some propitious event. For example, highly profitable crops of grain served as occasions for the American revivals of 1891 and 1897; President Cleveland's contract with the Morgan-Belmont syndicate for the defense of the gold reserve started the revival of 1895. . . ."

[7] Dow's psychological theory of business cycles was clearly stated in 1899 in this editorial. In the following year Edward D. Jones, *Economic Crises* (New York, 1900), dealt at some length with the psychological theory of business cycles. See Paul Barnett, *Business-Cycle Theory in the United States, 1860–1900* (Chicago, 1941), pp. 12–24, for an evaluation of the contribution of Jones in this regard. The Edward D. Jones referred to above was not the Edward D. Jones (1856–1920) of Dow Jones & Company.

[8] Dow's forecast was correct. A slight recession was witnessed in the spring of 1900. The stock market advance was checked at this time.

[9] It is apparent from the items cited that by "the volume of business" Dow means the physical output of industry and agriculture.

[10] Cf. Mitchell, p. 575: "As prosperity approaches its height, then, a sharp contrast develops between the business prospects of different enterprises. Many, probably the majority, are making more money than at any previous stage of the business cycle. But an important minority, at least, face the prospect of declining profits. The more intense prosperity becomes, the larger grows the threatened group. It is only a question of time when these conditions, bred by prosperity, will force some radical readjustment." Also see Mitchell, p. 503, for a similar view.

Cf. Veblen, *Theory,* p. 199: "Only so long as the selling price of the output realizes such a differential gain over the expenses of production, is the putative increased rate of earnings realized; and so soon as such differential advantage ceases, the era of prosperity enters on its closing phase." Veblen claims the differential advantage is mainly due to the slow advance in wages and the position of the line of industry with respect to the "initial disturbance" which started the revival. He recognizes that the initial disturbance may be of a "progressive or recurring character."

[11] For an account of Gould's business transactions during the period see Julius Grodinsky, *Jay Gould: His Business Career, 1867–1892* (Philadelphia, 1957), pp. 160 ff.

[12] Short sales by floor traders constitute a "room attack."

[13] "To put the market up on shorts and to put it down on weak holders" means to bring about short covering, causing the market to rise, and to bring about liquidation of margin accounts, causing the market to decline.

[14] In February 1896 the Baltimore and Ohio went into receivership. A

plan of reorganization was drawn up in June 1898 and the plan received court approval on May 15, 1899. Securities began to be distributed on May 22, 1899 through the Mercantile Trust Company of New York and the London Westminster Bank. There is no summary available as to how much in securities traveled across the Atlantic, but the plan called for raising $36,092,500 to pay off the floating debt. Naturally this would have its effect on foreign exchange. The plan was a great success and almost all security holders immediately turned in their old securities for the new issues.

[15] Note that as early as 1899 Dow used "clearings outside of New York," illustrating that he was aware of the distortion in the New York clearing figures caused by security transactions. See Dow's editorial of May 26, 1900, in this respect.

[16] In 1964 Beryl W. Sprinkel set forth an elaborate presentation of the relationship between the supply of money and stock prices. See *Money and Stock Prices* (Homewood, Ill., 1964), passim.

[17] The American Sugar Refining Company, Arbuckle Brothers, the Doscher interests, and other refineries cut prices during a period of overcapacity in the industry. Henry Havemeyer of the American Sugar Refining Company stated at the time that his company could supply the entire demand of the country for sugar "and twenty thousands tons more." By the end of June the difference between raw and refined sugar advanced to 59 cents from a low of 38 cents per hundred pounds, increasing profits and ending the war.

[18] The weekly bank statement of the New York Clearing House gave the condition of the member banks as to loans, net deposits, specie holdings, and circulation (legal tenders). Reports were made by the banks to the New York Clearing House on the basis of the "average for the week." For example, specie holdings would be added for the number of banking days in the week and divided by the number of banking days to give an average figure. This figure could be substantially different from the actual specie holdings on the last day of the week. A large withdrawal of gold for export on Friday would only show as a loss for one day in the "week's average."

[19] Cf. Mitchell, pp. 464–466.

[20] See Mitchell, p. 476: "The average rise in the rate of wages is slow in the first year or two of a trade revival, but it becomes more rapid in the later stages when employers have difficulty in finding sufficient hands to fill their orders."

Also see Veblen, *Theory,* p. 212: "As noted above, much of the business advantage gained in an era of prosperity is due to the fact that wages advance more tardily than the prices of goods."

Burton also noted that wages responded more slowly than prices. See Theodore E. Burton, *Financial Crises and Periods of Industrial and Commercial Depression* (New York, 1902), p. 47. Veblen wrote a highly critical review of Burton's volume, *Journal of Political Economy,* XI (March, 1903), pp. 324–326.

CHAPTER TWO

July 17, 1899 — December 23, 1899

THE last half of the year 1899 witnessed a sagging rail market, and although the industrials recovered from their May lows, the market could at best be described as "fairly steady" until December when another wave of panic selling hit the industrial shares.

Guerrilla warfare continued in the Philippines, and although it was apparent that the insurrection of Aguinaldo could have but one ending, the fierce fighting fully engaged an American army of 60,000 men.

During August an epidemic of yellow fever occurred in New Orleans. Soon Mississippi suffered an outbreak of the disease, and in October an epidemic prevailed in Key West and other Florida cities.

In October the Boer War began, and the Boers at the outset had the advantage of numbers, since the British had about 25,000 men available in Africa for combat duty. The Boers were armed with the latest artillery purchased from European manufacturers, principally Krupp, and the war proved surprisingly prolonged. It was difficult for those not conversant with military operations to visualize the problem of defeating the Boer forces and maintaining communications over thousands of miles amid a hostile population.

The Boer forces were victorious at Laing's Nek and after suffering defeat at Elandslaagte defeated the British at Nicholson's Nek and occupied Ladysmith by November 2, 1899. The British under General Methuen beat the Boers at the Modder River, but in December the news of the British defeats at Magersfontein and Colenso, when General Buller failed to force a crossing of the Tugela River, staggered London. The reverses were regarded as the most serious losses for British army units since the Indian Mutiny of 1857.

During the period the principal preoccupation of the British was with the conflict. The government was spending more than one million dollars a day, and much of it was spent in the United States. The flow of African gold was cut off, and to attract gold to London the Bank of

England raised the discount rate to 6 per cent late in November. This was the highest rate since the Baring panic of 1890.

December saw financial trouble in Boston due to a decline in copper shares on the Boston Stock Exchange. Within the first three weeks of the month Anaconda declined from 45½ to 31½; Calumet and Hecla fell from 765 to 710; Butte declined from 70 to 40, and Utah Consolidated lost ground from 37 to 22½.

The New York Stock Exchange witnessed a decline on December 11th and panic conditions prevailed on December 18th. The day of the panic opened under gloomy conditions, since the London Stock Exchange was lower due to the news of General Buller's defeat at the Tugela River. The Boston financial difficulties had attracted attention. Throughout the period British investors liquidated American securities, and a tight money market in New York at the time of the panic saw call money rise to 186 per cent representing a commission of one-half of one per cent a day in addition to the regular rate of 6 per cent. To add to the confusion the Produce Exchange Trust Company of New York closed its doors on the day of the panic.

"The squall has come and gone, and the situation is the better for it now it is over. It is like cutting off a dog's tail—it can't be done again," said Henry Clews.

His observation proved correct. The New York bankers supplied funds, with J. P. Morgan & Co. offering one million dollars at 6 per cent, and the prosperous economy rode out the storm.

July 17, 1899

Saturday's market gave very little evidence of much tendency either way. It was narrow and controlled by the bank statement. It is important to notice, however, that however much the traders attempt to play upon the fears of others in regard to a falling reserve in the banks the effect is only temporary. It is beginning to be better understood that falling reserves and a higher money rate are the inevitable accompaniments of growing confidence and reviving business. The more active business becomes, the more likely the resources of the banks will be drawn upon, and the lower the reserves will consequently be. It is thought to be very likely that within a few weeks the 25 per cent limit will be passed by the banks and that they will run below it.[1]

The swing of prices is very plainly upward, and if it were to be checked by the condition of the money market, that check would have been given before this time. It is plain, therefore, that the business men of the country are looking rather at the growing crops and the revival of business than upon the immediate rate for money as the controlling bull factors in the situation.[2] It was so in previous bull markets and can safely be counted upon to be repeated at the present time. Bull markets grow largely out of increasing confidence of the people in the stability of the institutions and prosperity of the country. There probably has never been a time in the history of the country when the outlook has been brighter than it is today and when the whole world in fact has been as busy with as much promise of increasing prosperity as today.

Money abroad has worked to a higher basis for that reason, and it is natural that similar conditions should prevail here as harvest time approaches and the farming communities demand the currency to pay labor.

It is certain that the monied interests in the Street are thoroughly alive to this situation. They express no uneasiness because the money rate rises for the reason that they find the country is taking securities and this is freeing a certain amount of money all the time for the current uses of Wall Street speculation.

The investment demand for securities may be slow, but it is nevertheless steady and apparently comes from all parts of the country. People are spending more money also for luxuries, as is shown in the tremendous passenger receipts in transportation lines and companies of all kinds and in the growth of those trades which deal in luxuries. With such prosperity it is not considered likely that the passing influence of falling reserves will exercise immediate effect upon the minds of the people generally.

Any haste, therefore, on the part of traders to sell stocks may be counted upon to mean certain loss for the time being.

In order to make clear again the position occupied by many of the leading monied interests of the Street, it may be stated that the controlling factors are the increasing railroad earnings and promising outlook for dividends resulting from the growing prosperity of the country. The crop situation is, of course, the basis of them all. Spring wheat and corn are about as satisfactory as could well be hoped for, while abroad we have conditions which in a measure will tend to give a market for a large part of our surplus products.

Our export business in other directions is steadily increasing, while from many other different evidences, the people are becoming more contented with the business and the institutions of the country.

There is a growing stability in business, which is becoming marked and effective and leading the monied interests of the country to adopt measures to make more stable the transportation industries of the country, which in itself ensures greater value and higher prices for railroad securities. The great combinations which have been projected and are in fair way of being accomplished soon have not yet begun to be felt as they are expected to be felt in the speculative markets when completed.

The swing of the market is plainly still upward. The advance which has been made since the first of June shows it is a bull market, and because it is a bull market, on the law of averages this swing should carry prices upward and beyond the limit reached at the time of the culmination of the spring movement of 1883. This means an advance still before the middle of August of anywhere from four to six points on the average. It is always in order, however, to predict that accidents may change the natural swing of prices for a time.

July 19, 1899

. . . strikes, like a higher money rate at this time, indicate prosperity. The workingmen want better wages because their employers are making more money, while money works tighter because it is in more active general use to fulfill the demands of improving trade.

. . . .

July 22, 1899

In this editorial, which is quoted in part, Dow employs a concept of liquidity preference.

Money has finally eased enough to take away anxiety from the speculative community, and with the relief comes more desire to invest money in securities. Securities are really wanted more than money is wanted at present, and as long as this condition exists in the minds of people with money, it is certain that the price of securities will rise.[3] The more probable also is this likely to be the case when general conditions are as favorable as at present.

July 24, 1899

The market is still sensitive to bank statements, as shown by the course of prices on Saturday. This statement showed that the banks were losing cash in spite of severe contraction in loans. The suspicion that withdrawals of cash would continue and that a higher money rate must inevitably follow aroused fears of trouble again among the trading element. The sensitiveness, however, plainly affects surface movements of the market rather than the undertone, which is decidedly strong because of the character of the broad facts in the situation.

The trade reports for another week and the clearings as well as the railroad earnings bear ample testimony to the decided progress of industrial activity throughout the country. Such activity is certain to draw upon the circulating medium of the country to a great extent, much more, in fact, than has ever before been seen probably in this country. It is a natural sequence of prosperity, and higher rates for money may be considered an index to prosperity at this time.

The country is full of money, as shown by the statements of trust companies not only in this city but also throughout the country and also by the lower interest rates in different centers outside of New York, where heretofore the rates have been high when business has been dull. It is common to hear western men refer to the buying of commercial paper by country banks and to the large surplus reserves held in different cities and to the possibility that the West this year may be able to move the crops without large borrowing from the East.

A natural question might be as to why, therefore, the money rate should work much higher in the East if the West is so full of money. In answer the statement is made that the general prosperity is felt even more in the manufacturing centers of the East, and this is calling for more money.

It is also a fact that the new extensions of business not only by industrial corporations but also by the railroads are calling for new money. At any rate the large surplus earnings which some of the railroad companies have been using for loanable funds in Wall Street are slowly being withdrawn to build new branch lines and to get more equipment.

It is noticeable that there is a falling off in the demand for low-rate first-class bonds. This is producing a somewhat sagging tendency to bond prices although not bringing out many bonds. This course is natural in view of the possibilities which holders of money have in employing it and investing it to better advantage on a rising interest basis.

The movement in this direction is still slow because it is difficult for the rising generation to get used to higher money rates. Interest has been so low for so long a time that to many people a rising rate produces a sort of alarm, and it is natural to expect a considerable lapse of time before this will disappear under the new conditions.

Prosperity, a higher interest rate and a boom in the stock market have seemed to be impossibilities, and yet there is a slow but sure changing of belief in this respect among many, and not a few hold the conviction that this condition is a near possibility.

August 1, 1899

. . . .

. . . All the industrial companies are crowded with business, just as are the railroads; even the coal stocks can legitimately claim logical reasons for strength. Usually there are some black spots in the picture, but at present there are none, granted that the money situation is all right. Consequently, the big interests can with propriety advance all their specialties and give good excuse for doing so.

The month of August is a natural bull month, for it brings the crops to maturity or at all events decides their fate. Unless the crops are an absolute failure, relief from uncertainty almost always stimulates an advance in stocks. . . .

. . . .

August 7, 1899

Dow again returns to his liquidity preference concept.

. . . .

A higher money rate brings with it a readjustment of values, which in turn is apt to unsettle margin accounts in stocks and cause disturbance of loans generally.

Money really is getting to be wanted more than securities where the prices are higher than the money rate.

No matter how promising the crop conditions may be or how brilliant the prospects for business, the foundations for prosperity rest to a certain and large extent upon the ability to get money at a rate which will be profitable.

. . . .

August 9, 1899

. . . .

. . . It is more to the purpose to educate the public to a right understanding of the cause of higher money rates at this time than to use undue influence to keep the rate down.

The higher money rate is natural and logical, and reflects sound, healthy business prosperity, and simply calls for patience in such readjustment of values as are called for by the new conditions.

. . . .

August 12, 1899

The editorial is quoted in part.

The forces at work in the market are changing their character somewhat in view of the change in money conditions.

There must be a readjustment of values to the money basis.

This is affecting the bond market particularly, because banks and institutions which were unable to lend their money profitably some time ago, purchased low-interest-bearing bonds of first-class quality and held them until this time.

Now there is a demand for their money at profitable rates. The rate is in fact more profitable than that which the banks get from the bonds they have held. Therefore, they will sell the bonds and lend the money.

A declining bond market is thus acting sympathetically to a certain extent upon the stock market, especially upon the high-priced stocks, which, like bonds, do not return to the holder as much money as he can get by lending his money.

At the same time this decline in the price of high-classed securities is tempting investors who have been letting their money lie idle in trust companies for just such a period as this.

Consequently, this investment money is being converted into securities, while the more speculative capital is getting out.

Speculative capital moves more quickly and in larger volume and can therefore be counted upon as likely to produce a more immediate effect in declining prices.

The effort will be to get the best possible prices as soon as possible, because so many people move at such times under a similar impulse, and the first one out gets the advantage.

Each day, therefore, from now on ought to bring more speculative liquidation along the lines indicated.

August 29, 1899

An interesting point is contained in this editorial.

. . . .

The gross earnings of the railroads are still an encouraging feature, although the net earnings are beginning to be affected by the increased cost of materials entering into operations of the roads.[4] . . . .

. . . .

September 11, 1899

An interesting observation is contained in this editorial with respect to liquidity. The editorial is quoted in part.

The supply of available money is being drawn upon more rapidly than some operators had expected it to be, and a fear that it may lead to higher money rates has started a little more preparation for such a contingency. It is natural under the circumstances that there should be a certain amount of liquidation by those who will need money for the legitimate channels of trade.[5] The stock and bond market is the most convenient source of releasing funds through liquidation. It is also the most ready market.

The times are such, however, that people who are making large profits in their business are ready either to lend money or buy good securities. This tendency is to give an even tenor to speculation and to the money market.

September 12, 1899

. . . .

The higher money rate has been in a measure prepared for, but no matter how good the preparation, it is nevertheless a fact that when the high rate prevails there is a class of holders of stocks who sell to get the money for other purposes. When money is tight, it is harder to get loans because of the discrimination shown by money lenders through fear of adverse possibilities growing out of the situation under such circumstances.

. . . .

October 2, 1899

This editorial shows the influence of William Stanley Jevons. The use of the seasonal variation was a familiar theme in Dow's writings. Dow was familiar with the work of Jevons, whose books were available in American editions. The editorial is quoted in part.

The tightness of money has brought a halt to bull speculation; but in no more marked degree than has been the case at this season of the year heretofore.

In 1894, for instance, September showed a decline in twenty active stocks from the 1st to the 29th of 2.14; this decline continued in October, the low point, 2.56, being reached on the 30th. Prices then rallied 2.96 to November 10th, followed by a decline of 3.21 to November 30th.

In 1895, there was a decline almost continuous during September, October, and November, September averaging 3.64, October, 2.95, and November, 2.15.

In 1896, prices in September advanced 4.08 to the 30th, and in October declined 2.41 to the 12th, when they rallied 4.17 to the 31st. The advance at that time continued in November to the 9th of 4.15 farther, and then declined 3.17 to the 30th.

In 1897, the bull market culminated September 17, with an advance of 3.74 from the 1st, then declined 4.62 to the 30th. The decline continued in October, 2.51, the low point being on the 28th, with a further decline to the 8th of November of 3.75.

In 1898, the decline for September was 3.36, to the 30th, while in October fluctuations were small, but nevertheless prices showed a decline of .12 to the 24th, then a rally of 1.19 to the close of the month. The bull market in November of that year raised prices 4.30.

This year, 1899, there has been an average decline for the month of September of 2.47.

The question now is as to the probable course of prices during October. From the record given above it is plain that October has not been heretofore a desirable month to bull stocks. The market has generally been a narrow one with a sagging tendency. It is noticeable, however, that the autumn decline has frequently culminated in October and good rise in November occurred half the time.

There is no doubt that a similar general cause has operated to produce this effect, which is certainly in evidence also this year. This cause unquestionably is the movement of the money market.

October 4, 1899

. . . .

. . . Money is clearly getting dearer all over the world, and as speculation rests on the money which is not wanted for other purposes, its share of the whole may remain for a time smaller than usual.

This disadvantage, of course, is offset by the ability of the speculator to pay a higher rate for money temporarily than the investor is willing or able to pay permanently, which restores the equilibrium and enables the operator in stocks to obtain money for all undertakings which promise more than usual profits.

As a result of this, the money market should drop back to about 5 per cent as the usual rate, running up to high rates whenever a temporary derangement of demand and supply unduly increased one or decreased the other. The effect of this may be unfavorable on the high-priced dividend stocks, but perhaps favorable to the best industrial preferred stocks, which would then receive attention as paying 7 or 8 per cent on a normal cost of carrying [on margin] at 5 or 6 per cent. In buying such stocks the question of stability ought to be carefully considered.

. . . .

October 16, 1899

. . . .

. . . It seems clear that the surplus in the New York banks will be smaller for some time to come than it has been in the past. Active business all over the country means the active employment of credits, and increased credits mean increased holdings of cash as protection for deposits. This means that the money which goes west and south will be held to a somewhat greater extent than usual on the basis for the business that is being done.

This does not mean that Wall Street is not going to have a reasonable supply. A speculative market, while dependent ordinarily upon the surplus fund of the country, is nevertheless in a position to pay more for the use of money than can be paid by what are called legitimate lines of business. The market of 1879 advanced strongly, with money at a premium. In a market which has a clearly advancing tendency, operators can afford to disregard rates for money, because 6 or 12 per cent forms a very small part of the expense of trading in stocks, provided that the movement in the market is one which permits quick and considerable profits on purchases. It is a dull market which cannot stand dear money.

. . . .

October 18, 1899

. . . .

The bear [unfavorable] facts in the situation are the gradual exhaustion of the surplus investment fund and the creation of securities on a large scale. Actual dear money may be a factor in speculation at any time, although the drift of opinion seems rather the other way. The cutting off of the gold supply of the Transvaal should have the effect of checking expansion, but does not necessarily operate against the basis already existing.[6]

The real point, therefore, is whether there has been a dangerous overcreation of securities. The answer turns upon the extent to which these securities are being carried on borrowed money. The mere turning of the ownership of a business from an intangible partnership to a corporate stock form does not of itself make any additional demands upon the money in the country. It is only when these certificates pass into loans and appear in speculative accounts that the burden is liable to appear.[7]

There can be no certainty as to the extent to which industrials [stocks of industrial companies] have entered loans. In this market some of the new stocks have been accepted in a moderate way as collateral, while others have little or no borrowing power. The question of the commitment of underwriting syndicates is more important, because these underwriters have provided the money which has been paid to the original owners for their property. The actual danger in this matter depends upon the ratio of underwriting commitments to the resources of the underwriters. Commitments large in aggregate might prove to be safe on account of the strength of the underwriters.

. . . .

November 2, 1899

. . . .

This market may be termed a "rich man's market." It is much easier for the big interests to borrow money than for commission houses. The rich man has ways of getting money which commission houses have not. Big trust companies, insurance companies and large capitalists are more inclined to lend for large operations than for small ones. The request of large interests for large sums are usually met and their demands supplied before the smaller trader can hope to provide for his needs. The result is that when money is a dominant feature, the small trader is compelled either to stay out of the market or pay rates which are sometimes hazardous.[8]

. . . .

November 9, 1899

. . . .

The keynote of the market is undoubtedly the money situation. British success in the Transvaal is regarded as a certainty sooner or later. With the fall elections out of the way, there is no political factor at home likely to be disturbing for some months, so that there remains only the money supply as a menace. It is, however, a very different thing to have money dear because the country is prosperous and is using money freely, from what it would be to have money dear because of lack of confidence in the stability of the currency or in the mercantile situation.

The dear money which comes from prosperity is only relatively dear. It is much better to pay 6 or 8 per cent for money and have a condition of prosperity reflected by large railway earnings, large industrial profits and a speculation averaging 700,000 shares a day than it is to have the reverse of these conditions and money 1½ per cent. Interest is a very small item in speculation when stocks are active. It is burdensome only when they are dull. Consequently, money for speculative purposes will not be lacking at a price as long as speculators, on account of their profits, can afford to pay the price.

. . . .

December 12, 1899

Of course, a good many people have had to take severe losses in the stock market, and they feel disheartened, to say the least.[9] On the other hand, the liquidation which has taken place is looked upon with a good deal of satisfaction by conservative and powerful interests in the Street.

The liquidation has already cleared the atmosphere considerably, and brings to the Street a vast amount of money [new investment buying] and produces an extensive decrease in loans [as margin speculators are sold out].

It is one thing to see a market decline under the pressure of sales produced by failure of crops or some other great calamity and quite another thing to see liquidation produced by a high money rate as a result of high tension of business activity.

The former condition brings failures and widespread ruin. The latter reduces the wealth of a few but easily brings a cure by liquidation of a disturbing element and makes recovery from depression a comparatively easy matter.

Everyone experienced in Wall Street has seen a market similar to the present one time and time again. The shake-up is severe but not fraught with permanent blight to the business of the country.

Therefore, a recovery from this depression can safely be counted upon to be among the near probabilities.

December 19, 1899

Yesterday will be long memorable in Wall Street as the occasion of one of the wildest and most unreasonable panics in its history. Even at a distance it is impossible to give a sufficing reason for any panic, and close to it, it is sometimes a little difficult to see the wood for the trees.

In the ordinary theatre panic one idiot cries "Fire" and a thousand other idiots kill each other, all trying to get to the door at once. In a money panic such as yesterday's the parallel is curiously similar. The real demand for money on the account was actually smaller than it has been for some time, and at 12 o'clock it looked as if the market were in a thoroughly healthy condition.

Then without rhyme or reason the rush commenced. It might have been the fear of further failures. It might have been some bank, acting on the principle of the gentleman who called "Fire" in the theatre, calling in its loans, but anyway the stampede started.

It sounds almost absurd to quote the price that money touched; 200 per cent was actually paid at one time. At such a moment the action of sane people is disregarded. The real value of the whole thing is shown by the operation of so conservative a firm as J. P. Morgan & Co., who in the height of the scare went into the market and lent $1,000,000 at the rate of 6 per cent, which had been ruling in the morning.

The City Bank also lent timely assistance to the market, although not at so moderate interest, and at the close the bankers' clearing house took effectual steps to prevent the recurrence of such an event.

The bank presidents at a meeting in the afternoon canvassed the financial situation thoroughly, in all its aspects; and it was decided in the event of any pressure being brought to bear of a monetary nature on any of the institutions or prominent individuals, the banks would unite to support them.

It may be taken from this that the situation has been thoroughly examined by those in a position to gauge exactly where any weakness lies, and their action places further financial danger utterly out of the question.

The failure of the Produce Exchange Trust Co. seems to point in what direction the weakness lies, but with the guarantee of the whole financial strength of New York behind, any further fears are as baseless as the absurd panic of yesterday.

The official statement of the assets and liabilities of the trust company which closed its doors yesterday shows a surplus of over $3,000,000.

The position of the British and the action they have taken facing the situation in South Africa when markets are restored to sanity must have its beneficial effect. A British army of 180,000 men with power to raise at least another 20,000 in Cape Colony for protection of communications is quite big enough to take on even the awkward contract the British have undertaken in South Africa.

Advices from London show that the unsound bull account opened there has been practically liquidated and the horizon seems to be clearing generally.

December 20, 1899

The editorial is quoted in part.

The course of markets yesterday conveys a very important lesson. If the Stock Exchange is occasionally at the mercy of unreasoning panic, it is equally obvious that combined action is equally powerful to save it.

The action of the banks in combining to support the markets and protect weak interests, which otherwise would be a danger to the commercial community, seemed to have cleared away the last remnants of fear.

In taking such action the banks did not bind themselves to do more than they ordinarily do in the usual course of business, and while admitting the service rendered, the position seems to show that by means of more constant co-operation such dangerous crises as the money panic of Monday might be obviated altogether.

Very few firms can stand the pressure of a sudden calling in of all loans in a falling market, and the whole system of lending upon stocks is one mutually profitable to the lender and the borrower and makes a fluent and easy market, where its absence would paralyze the conditions of trade altogether.

However, all is well that ends well, and although the drop of Monday did some damage, it is probably one of the best testimonials to the market that it did so little.

December 23, 1899

The market confirmed the idea that the inadequate rally of the middle of the week reflected a condition tending toward prices lower than those made on Monday. Several stocks made new low records, and the buying, while good in some cases, was on cautious scales, apparently framed with considerable uncertainty in the minds of the buyers as to how far down prices would go. Rumors exerted an influence, and there was a growing uneasiness on this account.

At such a time, the essential thing is to see clearly the causes which are at work; the prosperity of the country, the establishment of the gold standard, large railroad earnings and other factors of the highest importance for the long run may be set on one side. The market has responded to these conditions and will respond to them again, but there is an immediate acute condition which outweighs the[se] factors, which are important, but less pressing.

The afternoon rally was on information that leading interests in the Street had combined for the protection of the market and with a view to the purchase of lines of stock. The rumor probably had foundation and may lead to at least a temporary recovery in prices.

The immediate factor in speculation is the relation of money to speculative accounts. There has come a demand for the readjustment of investment values and a general conviction that the basis of speculative operations must be temporarily rearranged. Stocks which were considered cheap on a 4 per cent money basis, are not attractive, either for speculation or for investment, when money at interest is worth a third more than the return on the investment. People who have underwritten enterprises under the belief that the sale of the securities would afford a large profit have discovered that these securities must be taken by the underwriters and carried indefinitely, without being available as collateral. It is undoubtedly true that institutions which some time ago anticipated large profits from the employment of their capital are finding themselves, in many cases, tied up to an extent which is vexatious if not disturbing.

The practical question, of course, is whether there will soon be a change in the situation with reference to the supply of money. It is certain that such a change will come and that money will again be a drug in the market, but it is not at all clear that this time is near. It may be quite remote.

Undoubtedly the main factor in the dearer rate for money has been the advance in prices, including not only securities all over the world, but commodities. There is scarcely an article which has not advanced, which means an immensely larger sum required for carrying the ten thousand commodities which make up the business of the country. The iron trade furnishes a striking illustration of this change. The table following shows the prices of specified products compared with the price prevailing only one year ago with the percentage of increase in price.

Commodity	*Dec. 20, 1899*	*Dec. 20, 1898*	*Adv. Per Cent*
Foundry pig No. 2, Philadelphia	23.25	11.25	106
Southern pig No. 2, Cincinnati	20.50	9.25	122
Steel billets, Pittsburg	34.00	15.00	126
Steel rails, Philadelphia	20.00	8.50	117
Refined iron bars, Philadelphia	2.05	1.10	86
Tank plate, Pittsburg	2.25	1.00	125
Wire nails, Pittsburg	2.95	1.10	125

Prices of iron products throughout the entire list have much more than doubled within one year. Increase has not been confined to this country, but has been general, and its extent is suggested by the estimate that the world's production of iron ore this year will be 85 million tons, of which the United States will produce about 13 millions.

An advance of 100 per cent or even 50 per cent in commodity prices shows what has become of the surplus money in the country and in the world. Money will come back to speculative centers when prices and especially commodity prices decline, and they will decline when produciton begins to exceed the current demand. Paradoxical as it may appear, decline in the prices of commodities may prove temporarily helpful to the stock market. There have been some declines in iron products in the past two weeks; also in metals and a few other articles, but in the main prices remain near the high level.

NOTES

[1] Under the National Banking Act banks in central reserve cities, which included New York City, were required to hold reserves of 25 per cent of their deposits.

[2] Cf. Mitchell, pp. 574–575: "But it is impossible to keep selling prices rising for an indefinite time. In default of other checks, the inadequacy of cash reserves would ultimately compel the banks to refuse a further expansion of loans upon any terms. But before this stage has been reached, the rise of prices is stopped by the consequences of its own inevitable inequalities."

[3] See John Maynard Keynes, *The General Theory of Employment, Interest, and Money* (New York, 1936), ch. 15. The expressions "Securities are really wanted more than money . . ." and "Money really is getting to be wanted more than securities . . ." (editorial of August 7, 1899) show that Dow holds a liquidity preference concept which bears a relationship to changing interest rates.

[4] Cf. Mitchell, pp. 422–427.

[5] See Keynes, ch. 15. Dow realizes that there is a demand for money for the business motive as well as the speculative motive.

[6] In 1898 the Transvaal mines produced $75,000,000 in gold which represented more than one-fourth of the world production for the year. With the outbreak of war in October, 1899, output virtually ceased.

[7] Cf. Veblen, *Theory*, pp. 140–143.

[8] See Mitchell, p. 589: ". . . the great banks, insurance companies, and investment houses which dominate the financial markets of New York, London, Paris, and Berlin have developed intimate relations with each other, and can be controlled by a few small coteries of financiers."

[9] This refers to losses experienced in a drop in stock market prices on December 11, 1899.

CHAPTER THREE

January 3, 1900—June 29, 1900

THE year 1900 brought, in the words of Wesley C. Mitchell, "a brief pause in a period of exceptional prosperity." Although the volume of general business remained enormous, there were sufficient signs to indicate that all segments of the business economy were not participating equally.

In March the Congress passed the Currency Act of 1900, better known as the Gold Standard Act. This legislation declared the gold dollar consisting of 25.8 grains $9/10$ fine to be "the standard unit of value." This expression was not only new to American and English law but was unknown in the monetary laws of other countries as well. The term "unit of account" had appeared in currency laws, but the term "standard unit of value" was a new one.

Under the terms of the law the Secretary of the Treasury was instructed to maintain all forms of money "at a parity" with gold. The principal effect, however, was psychological. It merely proclaimed that the United States was on a gold standard.

In April, according to many stories, John W. Gates announced at a party at the Waldorf that the steel mills of the American Steel & Wire Co., which he directed, would be closed on the following day. Asked the reason, he said, "We're short of stock." The mills were duly closed, and the stock duly declined in price.

In May the brokerage firm of Price, McCormick & Co. failed. It was one of the largest and most expensively conducted firms in Wall Street at the time. It was estimated that it cost $1,000 a day to open the doors of its offices. It employed almost two hundred men, and had a number of branch offices. The firm traded in grain and cotton as well as securities and was represented on the New York Stock Exchange, the New York Cotton Exchange, the New York Produce Exchange, the Chicago Board of Trade, and the New Orleans and Liverpool Cotton Exchanges. The cause of the failure was an ill-fated attempt to effect a corner in cotton.

In June the Boxer Rebellion in China claimed the attention of investors the world over, and although prices on the New York Stock Exchange remained steady, the attempt to drive the "foreign devils" from Chinese soil was the news of the day.

During the first six months of 1900 Dow wrote many articles on business cycles. In some of these he clearly used the methodology later employed by Wesley C. Mitchell. There is no doubt that these editorials, published at the turn of the century, should secure Dow a place in the history of economic thought as one of the early members of the American school of economics designated as "Institutionalism." Much of Dow's thought is similar to that of Thorstein Veblen, but it is closer to that set forth a decade later in 1913 by Wesley C. Mitchell in his monumental quarto volume, *Business Cycles*. The likeness in scope, methodology, and findings is remarkable.

In the spring of 1900 the Industrial Commission made a number of preliminary reports. The Commission was established by an act of Congress on June 18, 1898, which authorized "the appointment of a non-partisan commission to collate information and to consider and recommend legislation to meet the problems presented by labor, agriculture, and capital."

The act also provided "that it shall be the duty of this commission to investigate questions pertaining tc immigration, to labor, to agriculture, to manufacturing and to business, and to report to Congress and to suggest such laws as may be made a basis for uniform legislation by the various states of the Union, in order to harmonize conflicting interests and to be equitable to the laborer, the employer, the producer, and the consumer."

During 1898 and 1899 a great deal of testimony was taken and much use was made of experts in many fields. Professor J. W. Jenks, of Cornell University, played a leading role in this respect.

It is interesting to note that Dow, in his editorial of March 3, 1900, recognized the importance of the preliminary report on "Trusts" which was guided by Professor Jenks. It has been said that Veblen devoted a great deal of time to the study of the reports of the Industrial Commission.

January 3, 1900

. . . .

The dry-goods trade is a gauge of the industrial conditions of the country because all men and women follow the advice of Polonius in one respect at least—"costly thy habit as thy purse can buy." For a series of years beginning with 1893 the effort of the majority of wage earners was to find out how much in the way of new clothing of all kinds they could do without. During that time the dry-goods trade languished. Prices touched the lowest point ever known.

. . . .

January 10, 1900

. . . .

The real problem, however, is as to what factors will influence [stock] prices during the spring. It is safe to say that the factor coming closest to prices will be railroad earnings on the part of railroad stocks and industrial profits for the industrial shares. Both will be influenced by general business, but this tendency in general business may come to the surface in railway earnings as soon as at any other point.

Railroad earnings have been increasing for the last two years. They have been larger in the last year than ever before. The gain has been the result primarily of the great gain in general business and secondarily on the account of the large movement of products from the interior to the seaboard. What are the chances for the continuance or increase of this movement?

The first important fact in answer is that the shortage of the wheat crop last year is likely to affect the earnings of Granger roads unfavorably in the next few months. This is already shown by the large falling off in grain tonnage into Chicago during December and the first week of the present year. . . .

In support of this idea is the fact that the percentage of increase in earnings has been dropping off. A few months ago the average weekly gain by sixty roads was about 12 per cent. This has run down until forty-five roads reporting for the fourth week in December show a gain of only 1.42 per cent. The Granger group showed for December an increase of only about 4 per cent compared with gains of 12 to 14 per cent by the trunk lines and central western roads. The evidence on this point, as far as it goes, is in favor of further falling off in earnings in the next few months.

The evidence bearing on industrial prosperity is not so clear. It is quite probable that many products may be lower in the next few weeks, but this may not mean smaller profits for the industrial corporations. Indeed, it is quite probable that the best profits in companies like Federal Steel and Steel & Wire may come after the boom in business has received an unmistakable check, because these companies will then be delivering goods under contracts made at prices higher than those which will then be quoted.[1] Sentiment, however, is a great thing, and declining prices may carry a weight in speculation greater than they fairly deserve. . . .

The situation seems somewhat contradictory. It looks as though the earnings of western roads might decrease while the earnings of eastern roads increased. It is possible that a check in general business may be followed by increased profits by industrial corporations. . . .

. . . .

January 11, 1900

A correspondent writes: "You seem to always advise buying high-priced stocks. Why do you not recommend low-priced stocks, which cost less, can fall less and may become high priced?"

This looks plausible, but is unsound. The terms low-priced and high-priced are misleading. A high-priced stock may be very cheap on value, just as a low-priced stock may be very dear on value. Whether cheap or dear depends on value and to a considerable extent upon the time of decision.

A bull market is not the inflation of a balloon. It is more like a rising tide. Prices are an effect, not a cause. Therefore, when beginning at a low point in values, business begins to improve and profits begin to increase, prices gradually respond. A solvent railroad must be able to pay charges at the lowest point of earnings or it will cease to be solvent. When improvement comes, the first price effect is upon the bonds, which may, for instance, be selling at 80. As larger earnings increase the margin of safety for the bonds, they work up to 90 and then to par.

As improvement goes on, the preferred stock, which may have been selling at 60, begins to feel the effect of earnings which may be applicable to dividends on the preferred stock, and its price slowly advances. Further growth of earnings adds value to the second preferred and, in the course of time, the common stock responds to an exhibit of dividends earned, even if there is little prospect of dividends being paid.

Advice in regard to buying these securities, to be intelligent, should be based upon the progress which has been made by earnings and upon the advance which has occurred in each of the securities. At the beginning it would certainly be wise to buy the bonds, and it would be very foolish to buy the common stock perhaps two years before there was any chance for earnings on the common stock, unless, indeed, the buyer had so much confidence in the future as to be willing to wait two or three years before expecting improvement.

Ordinarily, it would be better to hold the bonds for a time; then change to one of the preferred stocks, and still later to the common stock. The course of Erie in the current bull period furnishes an excellent illustration of this growth. The bull market had been under way over four years before Erie common showed the slightest response. The same was true to almost the same extent in regard to Reading. Examination of the list will show this to have been true to a greater or less extent in most of the active stocks. Speculation responded to improvement in values with large regularity except where special causes temporarily produced special results.

Exactly the same reasoning holds good in considering a bear market. The first falling off in earnings will take value from common stocks. Therefore, they will be the first to sag off and not recover. The higher-grade securities of the same property will drop off, perhaps more even than the cheaper stocks, because of greater speculative activity, but they will recover more because their value is still unimpaired. The common stocks will recover less or not at all because value is impaired, especially where the margin [of earnings] for the common stock is small. If earnings continue to decrease, other stocks [the preferred issues of the same corporation] will suffer in their turn the same way.

This is why we seldom at present advise buying low-priced stocks. If a stock remains low priced after more than five years of bull market, the presumption is that capitalization is too large for present earnings, and that there will have been some years of development before the common stock can have much value or much price. Hence, buying it at this time would result in the probability of carrying it for some years at a loss, because it is too late in the bull period to expect very great increases in values.

At the beginning of a bull market, a low-priced stock could be carried at least with hope of improvement. Near the end of a bull market, it would be carried with almost certainty of loss. Whoever believes the bull period to be far advanced must of necessity believe in buying only stocks which have a margin of safety for dividends large enough to prevent any reasonable doubt of the maintenance of dividends, consequently having assurance of recoveries from such declines as may occur.

In an established bear market it is seldom worthwhile to buy anything except to cover shorts; but many people dislike the short side. Even when they admit that a bear market is in progress, they try to work against the main tendency. Such people should buy only on quite large declines, should not expect recoveries to be much more than half the amount of the fall, and they should stick to stocks which they believe will continue to pay dividends without difficulty should earnings show as large decreases as they have shown in bear periods in the past.

January 12, 1900

. . . .

It is quite safe to conclude that consumers of iron products and, for that matter, of most other products, are not buying for speculation. The buying is for immediate requirements, and the fact that so large a demand exists shows the volume of current business. Its being current business means it continuance until there comes a check to general trade large enough to sensibly diminish requirements.

January 18, 1900

. . . .

There is one factor bearing upon operations for the year which is likely to come into very definite prominence. This is the labor situation. The advance in the price of commodities during the past year has been general and in many cases large. The cost of living is perceptibly higher than it was a year ago. There have been some advances in wages, but they have not been general, so that in cases the good times have worked to the disadvantage of labor. Of course, the added employment has relieved the distress of the unemployed, and the aggregate distribution in wages has been much larger than heretofore, but this has not helped individuals who have earned no more but who have to pay more for supplies.

This situation will certainly crystallize into demands for increased wages in many lines of employment. In others, existing contracts will make it worthwhile to pay an advance rather than to risk strikes, but in many others there will be a feeling that good times will not last and that the temporary excess of profits is only a fair return for the years when establishments were run without profit or at a loss, largely for the purpose of keeping employees together and giving them something to do. It will be difficult to make employees accept this reasoning, and a period of strikes and labor disturbance is probable during the year.[2]

. . . .

January 26, 1900

. . . .

. . . Nobody looking at the situation today can say that the industrial tide has turned or that business conditions are working against security values. . . .

It can be said that the prices of commodities are so high they are likely to decline before they have much farther advance. Nevertheless, in practically all lines the demand for goods, even at current prices, is fully up to the supply. It can be said that railroad earnings will fall off because they must compare with the large earnings last year. They have not fallen off yet. It can be said that money will be again dear. Possibly and probably, but the condition of the bank reserves suggests a fair working surplus for at least six weeks to come, and maybe for a longer time.

It can be said that the public will not buy again and that institutions and individuals are loaded with stocks which they will sell as soon as they can do so without loss. This can only be known to be a certainty by the event. The wealth of the country has enormously increased in the last three years. The firmness of 4 per cent bonds last month and the activity and advance in bonds this month shows that there is money for investment, and where there is money for investment, there is always money for speculation if people believe that buying affords a fair chance for profits. People who now declare that they would sell and stay out of the market if they could get out of the stocks they have are the identical traders who will be likely to increase their lines when the market advances, because they will think it wise to go with the current.

The whole effect of this is to prove that while the unfavorable side is surely coming, it cannot fairly be said to be here. Nobody can say precisely when it will come. The momentum of the volume of prosperity has become very great.[3] It will sweep over obstacles that would have checked the progress of a smaller boom. Some of the most competent judges of business conditions believe that the present period of prosperity will last years rather than months. If this view is correct, the market may have stronger advances than any which have yet occurred. We regard this as unlikely, but it seems almost as probable as to assume that a period of important declines is just at hand. Wall Street will undoubtedly discount the turn in the industrial situation, but the people who discount it too long ahead may have to extend their notes.

. . . .

March 3, 1900

The report of the Industrial Commission brings before Congress a matter which from every point of view deserves attention. There is reason for thinking that the importance of the subject is appreciated at Washington and that both on political and economic grounds there will be an effort to work the conclusions of the commission into legislation. The essential conclusion reached is that the preferred stocks of industrial corporations may be supposed to represent approximate values, but the common stocks and in some cases part of the preferred may be regarded as water; furthermore, that in order to protect investors, industrial combinations should be required to give a reasonable amount of publicity to the results of their operations.

It is as certain as anything in the future that industrial securities will form the principal medium for speculation in this country. The field for the formation of industrial corporations is vast, and varying degrees of skill in management, coupled with the succession of good times and bad times, will make constant changes in values which will be discounted by movements in the price of stocks.[4]

. . . .

March 12, 1900

. . . .

Indications of a check in business accumulate. The increase in iron stocks, the delay of orders for shoes, cancellations in orders for woolen goods, the scarcity and dearness of coke, the Chicago strike [a lengthy strike of 50,000 men in the building trades], the expectation of dearer money are all factors which militate for the time being against continuance of the boom in business. The checks are not very great, and are in most cases explainable, but they are beginning to exert a *cumulative influence.* [Italics supplied.]

March 20, 1900

. . . .

There appears to be some belief that the stock market never advances much in a presidential year. This is a fallacy which should not last. The market moves in cycles. When [the] presidential year comes in a period of rising market, prices go up. When it comes in a period of falling market, prices go down whoever may be chosen chief magistrate. For instance, rising prices prevailed in the presidential years of 1872, 1880 and 1888. Falling prices were the rule in 1884, 1892, and in 1896 down to the presidential nominations, after which the market turned.[5]

. . . .

April 11, 1900

. . . .

There will be no more anxiety about dear money until August. The bank reserves, while low, meet present requirements, and money will flow to this center [New York City] before it again flows from it. Last year, the surplus rose from 15 millions the second week in April to 44 millions the first week in June, then falling, however, rapidly on account of the unusual midsummer demand. In 1898 the surplus rose from 21 millions the second week in March to 62 millions the last week in June.

Circulation has for the first time in the history of the country gone above $26 per capita, and the total money in the country has for the first time reached the sum of two billion dollars. In April, 1890, the total stock of money in the country was $1,437,494,052. It is now $2,021,274,506. The stock of gold and gold certificates has risen in ten years from $508,562,567 to $785,845,549. The relative strength of the Treasury situation has improved. In 1890, 35 per cent of the total money was in gold, while now the percentage has risen to about

39 per cent, with the added advantage that there is no longer any doubt as to the meaning of the word dollar and it will no longer be possible to deplete the gold reserves through the operation of the greenback endless chain.

. . . .

April 17, 1900

. . . .

We think the answer [to the question as to why the public will not buy "at least" the preferred stocks of the iron and steel companies and why insiders are selling steel stocks] must be found in the condition of the iron trade as a whole and in the capitalization of the newer iron and steel companies. It is well understood that the prices of iron and iron products have advanced more than 100 per cent in the last year and a half. . . .

For the last four months the iron trade, as far as new business is concerned, has been comparatively dull. Prices have been held to a large extent, and the companies have been busy with old orders, but buyers have held off through a very natural feeling that with the increase in production attending such an advance in prices there would presently come concessions.

A year ago there were 205 furnaces in blast; now, 289 furnaces. The production of iron from January 1 to April 14, 1899, was 3,530,760 tons. For the same time this year it has been 5,054,111 tons. Since the first of January furnace stocks have slowly increased, rising from 127,346 tons to 197,532 tons. This bespeaks the popular sentiment, namely that iron is relatively high and that it is time for buyers of all classes to wait rather than to load up. This is probably more keenly realized by insiders in iron companies than by anybody else and is perhaps the strongest reason for anticipating smaller profits in the iron trade.

It may be said in reply that consumption of iron has increased greatly; that the business in sight is still large and that even a moderate decline would bring in a large amount of waiting business. We do not know what is wrong with this statement, but evidently there is something wrong in view of the sale of the iron and steel stocks.

Everybody knows that many of these properties are overcapitalized. Common stocks represent in most cases little more than good will, and depression in the iron trade would mean inevitably the abandonment of dividends on common stocks. . . .

. . . .

April 18, 1900

. . . .

It has been shown many times in the history of trade that a moderate advance in prices has exerted a far-reaching influence upon consumption. The products of the Steel & Wire Co. go direct to the consumer to a large extent. It would naturally be one of the first to experience a falling off in demand resulting from a feeling that building or fencing or some other work requiring the use of wire or nails could wait until prices had dropped to a lower level.

. . . .

April 19, 1900

. . . .

It must be remembered also that the iron and steel situation has one element of weakness entirely apart from the action of any individual companies. This is that prices under the stress of extraordinary demand have gone to figures so high as to check industrial development and to materially restrict buying. If the managers of iron and steel companies are wise, they will take the opportunity afforded by the Steel & Wire incident to lower prices moderately in order to bring in the buying which has been delayed and to encourage undertakings which are now held in abeyance on account of the abnormal cost of iron and steel products.[6] A fair profit and steady business is vastly better for any iron company than abnormal profit and restricted business with violent fluctuations in prices or profits.

April 20, 1900

A flood of inquiry has been turned upon the iron and steel trade as a result of the developments in Steel & Wire. From confidence that the steel trade was abnormally prosperous, sentiment has veered around to doubt whether even a normal degree of prosperity exists. Rumors of deep cuts in prices and of cancelled contracts on a large scale have been current and have been accepted as true.

It is desirable at such a time to get at the facts. It is true that there has been a decided check in the demand for iron and steel since the first of January. The mills have been well supplied with orders running through the first half of the year, and the discussion about prices has been to a large extent over orders for the second half of the year. Buyers have held off, with the result that in one case after another prices have been reduced. These declines have not been very great. . . .

The effect of these declines has been to give buyers more and sellers less confidence. During the last week the market at Pittsburg has been especially dull for pig iron, Bessemer pig, and steel. The association has not ventured to fix the price for Bessemer for delivery after July. . . .

The situation in Philadelphia is described as resembling that of the Quaker farmers who say that their butter and chickens are so much, but if the customer seems inclined to slip away, they tell him that they have something from a neighboring farm which they can sell at a lower price. . . .

It will be seen from the foregoing that while the iron trade has not by any means gone to pieces, buyers have obtained a distinct advantage and are evidently disposed to hold it. This means that somewhat lower prices may be seen, but the situation, as far as the trade is concerned, carries its own remedy. Whenever decline in prices brings general buying, the difficulty will be over and there will probably be quick recovery, because when buyers become convinced that prices will go as low as they will go, all will want to buy at once.

. . . .

April 21, 1900

. . . .

. . . If purchases of nails and wire have fallen off on account of high prices, it stands to reason that purchases of other iron products have been reduced or will be reduced for the same reason. It is absolutely certain that an advance of 100 per cent in the price of any staple commodity must have a very important influence on the demand.

There is a great deal of business that cannot be delayed. There are buyers who can afford to pay high prices because they get high prices for what they have to sell, but in the end the high prices come down to the actual consumer who uses and does not sell the goods bought.[7] In this country the largest consumer is of necessity the farmer, and the products which the farmer has to sell have not advanced enough to encourage him in liberal purchases of commodities which have gone up in one year from 50 to 100 per cent.

. . . Indications are that the iron trade has received a check which will result in lower prices, especially for finished goods, and in a temporary further curtailment of the demand. As the iron trade is regarded as the best barometer of general conditions, decline in iron prices will have a sentimental effect all over the country.

. . . .

April 24, 1900

The reduction in prices announced by the Steel & Wire Co. amounted to from 25 to 30 per cent and measured as closely as the executive committee was able to do the drop needed to re-establish business. Whether other companies will be compelled to make similar reductions remains to be seen.

It is evident that falling off in business as a result of high prices must strike the manufacturer of finished goods first. The man who buys to sell again had as soon have one price as another provided his margin of profit is the same, but every line of goods ultimately reaches the consumer, who does not sell again and to whom the price is vital.[8]

It is vital in a sense to the whole iron trade that finished goods should move freely into the hands of consumers. If this does not occur, the manufacturer of finished goods must buy less of partly finished products, and that must lead to smaller purchases of raw material, which in turn must reduce the employment of labor and thereby curtail the public power of buying food products and goods of every description. Trade continually works to such a circle, and the steps in this progression constitute the difference between rising and falling markets.

Great interest will be felt in knowing whether reduction in steel and wire goods restores the jobbing demand and gives retailers normal trade. If it does, the crisis in the iron trade will have been only temporary; trade will resume its normal condition and the Steel & Wire incident will soon be forgotten. If, on the other hand, the public is not able or willing to buy at the new prices, it is only a question of time when the difficulty will break out in the same or in some new spot.

The chances are that the reductions will stimulate demand; that reductions will be made by other producers, and that a large volume of business in various lines of iron products will be done in the next few weeks. If there is a moderate amount of buying at the start, the chances for increased business will be favorable, as the tendency of buyers is to want goods at the same time.

The same principles hold good in industries apart from the iron trade. It behooves all manufacturers to know that their products are going freely into consumption. If they are not and are prevented therefrom by high prices, it will be found better to make moderate reductions to meet the views of buyers than to be obliged to make large reductions in order to tempt semi-speculative buying. It must not be forgotten that the buying capacity of the consumer is found in the price of products, the yield of crops, the output of mines and the wages of labor. There has been improvement in all of these, but in comparatively few has there been any such measure of advance as has been seen in certain lines of manufactured goods.

Stated in percentages and comparing January, 1899, with April, 1900, leather has risen from 92 to 106.38, boots and shoes from 85.91 to 95.70, pig iron from 51.2 to 108.5, iron products from 48 to 94.88, woolen goods from 58.8 to 74.4, and cotton goods from 49.9 to 67.8.

Stated in prices and comparing January, 1899, with April, 1900, petroleum has risen from 7.50 to 9.90, tin from 19.70 to 31.50, copper from 13.25 to 17, lead from 2.92½ to 4.70, tin plate from 2.85 to 4.80, and silk from 3.76 to 5.07.

These advances mean increased cost of living and explain in part the disposition on the part of labor to strike for higher wages as a means of sharing in the prosperity believed to be afforded to employers as the result of advanced prices.

The action of the market suggests that bulls gave support on the unfavorable iron and steel news probably in order to strengthen confidence and check sales of long stock. It would be very natural for the market to be rallied somewhat in the next few days, especially if there are no unfavorable trade developments. Quite a proportion of the active stocks have had a fair average decline. It is not likely, however, that there can be a sustained advance until some new thought becomes dominant in the speculative mind. People today are wondering if the market will rally enough to let them get out at a profit, and this means realizing on advances, which is not what a bull manipulator wants. This, however, does not prevent temporary improvement.

April 25, 1900

The announcement of the closing of one of the Federal Steel Mills on account of the agreement to temporarily suspend deliveries to the Steel & Wire Co. was to have been expected. When the sale of the finished product in any line of goods falls off, the demand for partly finished products must fall off in consequence. The closing of the Federal Steel Mill will check demand somewhere else, and so the shrinking process will go on until the leeway of demand that lies between the various points of contact takes up the loss. When falling off in demand is general through the country, shrinkage is also general through the country. When, as in this case, the falling off in demand is limited to a single industry, or perhaps to a part of a single industry, the general effect will be much less.

The effect, however, of the large reduction in Steel & Wire prices must be to check the demand for iron and steel goods where reductions in prices have not been made. Every buyer that can do so will delay purchases in the hope of decline in prices. Buyers who may have been, two weeks ago, on the point of making contracts will now be disposed to wait until the last minute.[9]

This is going to be particularly true in regard to certain classes of railway purchases. The railroad is a consumer.[10] It does not buy rails and bolts and locomotives to sell again; consequently, the price is of the utmost importance. It has been recognized for months that the net earnings of railroads this year must be seriously affected by the increased cost of material. The extent of this increase is hardly realized outside the railway circles, but among officials of roads the feeling has become strong that good policy requires the suspension of all work requiring much material until supplies can be obtained at a lower figure.

Of course, in an industry like that of railroads in the United States there must be an immense amount of buying for pressing needs and without regard to prices, but the amount that can be deferred is also very large. It is extremely probable that there will be, before long, enforced curtailment of production in some departments of the manufacture of railway supplies.

In other words, the Street is confronted with a new situation. We have had a period of advancing prices and increasing prosperity. There has come a check. There will now be a period of readjustment of values. It may come quickly, with some sharp breaks in prices, or it may come slowly, as the result of sagging declines, but in one way or the other buyers and sellers are going to do business on a somewhat lower level of prices and perhaps with some shrinkage of production and possible curtailment of profits. The example set in the iron and steel trade is likely to be followed in other trades.

The effect of this upon the [stock] market will not be bullish immediately. There may be temporary advances, but the probabilities are that there will break out here and there trade disturbances which will have the effect of reducing the demand for stocks and increasing the supply on advances. This will probably last until a feeling prevails that values have been established and until confidence at those values has been restored. It does not follow that the market is going down every day while this process is going on. It probably does mean a narrow market with sagging tendencies.

Another factor in the situation may come into prominence. It is certain that there will be competition between political parties this year in their denunciation of trusts; political orators will not discriminate very closely between legitimate combinations of capital and the combinations which have been prohibited. For political purposes every large industrial corporation will be a trust.

The Republicans will go as far in denunciation as the Democrats, and they have one important advantage. They are in power in Congress and can initiate, if not perfect, legislation against combinations. There is reason for thinking that measures are under serious consideration in Congress looking to interference with certain corporate privileges. Before the end of the summer the industrial situation may be menaced by amendments to the Sherman Anti-Trust Law, and the speculative effect may be considerable.

The policy of some of the industrial combinations in making materially lower prices for their products abroad than they have made at home furnishes an argument not likely to be neglected by Congress in looking for a method of combining sound legislation with good political results in a presidential year.

April 27, 1900

The vital question is whether prices of commodities generally will be lowered rapidly or slowly. The answer to this question is probably also the answer as to the next move in the stock market.

The Steel & Wire cut in prices has had the inevitable effect. Demand in all directions has been checked, and buyers are awaiting developments. The policy of sellers is varied. Some are claiming that there has been no essential change in the situation; that demand is satisfactory and that prices are being maintained. Others admit the necessity of lower quotations and are making them more or less openly.

Other trades are being affected. Lumber prices have become irregular and in some instances materially lower. The coke market is beginning to be sensitive to rumors of reduced output. Small producers of iron are endeavoring to make contracts at prices which will show a profit, and salesmen who were laid off duty last year have been re-engaged with instructions to use every effort to secure contracts.

The great railway interests are helping the demoralization in prices to a certain extent. An advance of 100 per cent in iron is a very serious matter when applied to railroad supplies. In the last two months roads have been feeling the effects of the high prices as not before, and the result is not agreeable. In some cases the increase in gross earnings has been more than offset by the increase in expenses resulting from the high cost of material. Net earnings in the next few months will be unfavorably affected by this situation.

If commodity prices are lowered and buying is resumed in normal amounts, the speculative situation will improve at once. If sellers resist decline and buyers hold off, the stock market is likely to be dull and unsettled, because the large operators are watching the general situation closely and will not buy or undertake [a] bull campaign until they see such an improvement as will in their opinion justify expectation that stocks can be sold on an advance.

. . . .

May 3, 1900

. . . .

Now for the other [unfavorable] side of the picture. Prices have been going up since 1896. Stocks which were selling at the time of the last presidential election below 20 are selling above 50. Stocks on which assessments were then being paid are now paying dividends. *The wheel has turned round, but the wheel never stops, and after the circumference reaches the highest point, it begins to go down.* [Italics supplied.] The great railway and financial magnates, the shrewdest operators and the most experienced brokers have in the past been deluded into buying great quantities of securities at what proved to be practically the highest prices. The fact, therefore, that powerful interests are buying stocks and are negotiating new combinations is not conclusive evidence that the great cycle has not begun to turn down.

There has come an unmistakable check in business. Iron prices are irregular and uncertain. Prices of other commodities are off, and sellers are in search of buyers. This is always a danger signal after a boom. *The momentum of the country is great and probably sufficient to carry the business* [of the country] *over a reasonable number of hard spots, but if hard spots accumulate, the increasing friction can have only one result.* [Italics supplied.]

. . . .

May 5, 1900

A correspondent takes us to task for assuming that a period of depreciation in business and of decline in prices must follow the recent period of prosperity. He says in effect that there is no such thing as cycles in trade and that one time is as good as another as far as the operation of general law is concerned.

We differ with the opinion above given. Students of prices and of commercial changes came to the conclusion long ago that rise and fall in business conditions was certain and so regular as to be subject to intelligent forecast. Records in this matter go back many years, and while there is variety in fluctuations due to the interruption of special factors, principally wars, the outcome adheres closely to the theory.

The facts can be brought out more clearly in regard to the stock market than in other ways because prices are the index of these movements and Stock Exchange prices are kept. We have given occasionally the figures of recent movements, but it will do no harm to give them again. Stock Exchange prices rose from about 1868 until 1872, declined until 1877, rose until 1881, declined until 1885, rose until 1890, relapsed and recovered, making about the same point in 1892 as in 1890, apparently as a result of the Baring failure; declined until 1896 and have since had the advance which perhaps reached its high point last year and perhaps has some distance yet to go.

The prices of commodities have moved to a certain extent with the price of stocks. It is more difficult to show this because the movement has been more irregular, and being denoted chiefly by index numbers representing a large number of commodities, the changes have at times been slow and at other times comparatively small. Nevertheless, the general results have been essentially the same.

It is inevitable that this should have been so, because the stock market is not a cause, but an effect. Prices of stocks rise because values increase. They decline because values decrease. The manipulation conspicuous on the surface conceals the deeper flow; but it is there, and values inevitably determine prices in the long run.

When business is good, tonnage of all sorts increases and earnings increase. When the public begins to buy goods freely, it stimulates every department of industry. There is more demand for raw materials and for finished products, labor is better employed, and better prices are obtained for food products. The transportation of everything that enters into a nation's life means earnings and values. The change from a period of depression to a period of prosperity is very pronounced, and so is the reverse.

Business moves in cycles because everybody in business tries to make money when they can and to save it when saving is the only thing that can be done. For instance, in a period of depression, the keeper of a country store buys no more goods than enough to meet current requirements. When some day he finds that the demand for consumption in his locality has increased, perhaps on account of better sale for agricultural products, he increases his orders on the nearest wholesaler. Presently he finds himself unable to get as good prices from the wholesaler as before because other retailers are increasing their demands. This happens three or four times, and each time the retailer regrets that he did not buy more when prices were lower. Under the influence of this feeling, he buys for future requirements as well as for present needs, with cumulative effect upon the prices of the goods which he requires. This goes on all over the country. Experience shows that it takes three or four years to create general confidence in values and a general willingness to buy for future requirements.[11]

But there comes a time when the large jobber finds that he has bought too much and could have obtained goods cheaper if he had waited. After an effort to maintain prices he lowers them, and the local distributors find that they too have overbought. They also hold prices as long as they can and then lower them, convincing the retailer that he has been oversanguine. The coil then contracts. The retailer buys less, the wholesaler buys less, and so it goes on until the demand upon the producers of manufactured goods has fallen so materially as to compel a reduction of wages or the closing of mills, which, in turn, strikes at the buying power of the general public in all departments and gives another turn to the wrench which is working consumption and prices down. This goes on until production is closely adapted to actual requirements.

As the country never stands still, it can be said accurately that times are always becoming a little better or a little worse. [Italics supplied.] It seems to take about ten years at present for a complete revolution of the industrial and speculative wheel. The going-up process is more rapid, more vigorous and necessarily much more agreeable than the decline.

The decline is slower because everybody except those who are able to be short decline as strongly as possible. It is not impossible that with better knowledge, greater wealth and wiser methods the extent of the advance and of the decline may be smaller, but until human nature changes materially, there is not likely to be abandonment of the law of expansion and contraction in business or discontinuance of its effects on prices of stocks.

May 8, 1900

. . . .

. . . It is customary in thinking of the value of industrial stocks to consider the earning capacity of the company and to take it for granted that there has been overcapitalization. This is wrong. It is capitalization and not earning capacity which should be considered, because it is capitalization which forms the basis of competition.[12] Any plant which is overcapitalized and which pays dividends on overcapitalization invites competition by announcing that a competitor capitalizing his plant at true value can earn dividends.

If there is overcapitalization, there is certain to be competition, and such competition is certain in the end to pull down or destroy the dividends paid on excessive capital. This of course takes time. Because a company is overcapitalized today, it does not follow that it will suspend dividends tomorrow. Special conditions, including patents, ownership of raw materials and advantages of one kind and another have also to be considered; but in the end the result is the same.

It is an economic law that profits in any line of business will not continue to exceed a fair return on the capital properly invested in the plant. Dividends on excessive capital mean abnormal profits. Abnormal profits insure competition, and competition compels reduction in dividends to a sum which represents a fair return on fair capital, no matter what the capital of record may be.

May 10, 1900

. . . .

The question therefore is, "Has there been a change which alters the entire speculative situation?" There has been a change in the condition of the iron trade. It is probably true that the boom in iron is over. There has been a check in demand in other great lines of trade. Clearings have fallen off; gold is beginning to go abroad. These are unfavorable features, but are they sufficiently fundamental to change the business situation?

It has often been said that as iron goes, so goes the country. It seems almost impossible, however, that the momentum of the enormous business of the United States could be checked in a few weeks or even in a few months. It is more reasonable to think that the check is on the surface, and that underneath conditions are and must remain for a considerable time essentially sound. The great manufacturing and mercantile interests of the country are not going in a single month from great prosperity to depression.

The stock market discounts tendencies.[13] Stocks went up before the improvement of business became pronounced. Stocks will discount depression before depression actually exists, but this discounting quality in stocks makes them run to extremes. They discount shadows as well as substances and often anticipate that which does not occur.

. . . .

May 19, 1900

. . . .

It seems to us that general considerations are clear in one respect. There has been a halt in industrial progress. There has been a violent reaction in the iron trade, and a smaller reaction in practically all lines of business. Now over all the country people are watching to see whether this check will be followed by renewed confidence and the revival of business at a lower level of prices, or whether demand will be found lacking and business will run into the position where prices have to be lowered again in the hope of tempting a buyer who is already overstocked. In the former case the stock market will gain in strength. In the latter case prices will certainly decline.

May 23, 1900

The methodological treatment used in the following editorial, which is quoted in its entirety, is similar to that later employed by Wesley C. Mitchell. Note that Dow discusses "lags," or in his words, "Commodity prices were having their delayed movement in 1896 . . ." and "The English market for commodities started late compared with our stock market and has also been late in turning." Mitchell treated the subject of commodity and stock prices a decade later in his "Prices of American Stocks 1890–1909," which appeared in the Journal of Political Economy, *Vol. 18, No. 5 (May 1910), on pages 372–376.*

Dow's reference to the "mining boom in England and the Rand gold output" as a stimulus to prices in Great Britain is an interesting one. The Rand, located in the southern Transvaal, was famous for its gold mines. Production began in 1887, and by 1899 this region yielded about 20 per cent of the world's production. In 1895 there developed a period of wild speculation in gold-mining shares in London and in Johannesburg.

We referred some time ago to the fact that commodity prices work in a general way in accordance with stock prices. Correspondents have asked for more details on this subject. A number of compilations are kept for the purpose of showing the movement of commodity prices. The Sauerbeck tables have been kept for many years with this end in view. The London *Economist* has maintained an index number, governing twenty-two commodities for a considerable number of years. Bradstreet's maintains an index number representing 100 commodities. Each has some advantages and some disadvantages for the purpose of comparison.

We have taken in the tables following the London *Economist* index number, partly because the commodities taken seem to us fairly representative in character, and partly because the fact that the movement of commodity prices in Great Britain corresponds approximately to the movement of American railway stocks in New York is more impressive than if commodities of this market were employed. Some of the commodities in the *Econòmist* list have an international market.

We have divided the tables into four groups. The first covers the period from July, 1885, to July, 1890. This was a time of rising prices for stocks. The average of twelve stocks rose in that time from 61.95 to 96.88. The advance was fairly uniform, and it will be observed that there was a slow but steady rise in the index number of commodities during the same time.

Jul., 1885	22 commodities 2053	12 stocks 61.95
Jan., 1886	22 commodities 2023	12 stocks 80.47
Jan., 1887	22 commodities 2059	12 stocks 89.85
Jul., 1888	22 commodities 2121	12 stocks 84.37
Jul., 1889	22 commodities 2236	12 stocks 89.06
Jul., 1890	22 commodities 2259	12 stocks 96.88

The period from 1890 to 1896 was an interrupted bear market. In other words, prices of stocks were at about the same level in the spring of 1892 as they were in 1890, so that the decline really began in the spring of 1892 and became pronounced in 1893 and afterwards. We have condensed the record in this case so as to give the main movement. Twelve stocks fell from 96.88 to 66.90 Commodity prices declined until 1895, when the commodity decline was arrested by the great bull speculation in South African mines and the increased gold output. The movement follows:

July, 1890	22 commodities 2259	12 stocks 96.88
Jan., 1894	22 commodities 2082	12 stocks 75.06
Jan., 1895	22 commodities 1923	12 stocks 72.53
July, 1895	22 commodities 1931	12 stocks 77.86
Jan., 1896	22 commodities 1999	12 stocks 74.82
July, 1896	22 commodities 1947	12 stocks 66.90

A bull market was in progress from July, 1896, until April, 1899. Twenty stocks rose in that time from 45.93 to 87.04. Commodity prices were having their delayed movement in 1896, and the index number did not reach its low point until July, 1897, or some ten months after the lowest point in American stocks. Here again was an effect of the mining boom in England and the Rand gold output. It delayed but did not prevent the commodity decline. Furthermore, while the advance in stocks started from about 45.93 the average gained only six points in six months and only about eight points in a year, so that the stock move did not get under strong headway until about the time that the commodity movement was ready to begin. Since 1887 [1897] commodities have been moving upward. The figures are of interest:

July, 1896	22 commodities 1947	20 stocks 45.93
Jan., 1897	22 commodities 1950	20 stocks 51.71
July, 1897	22 commodities 1885	20 stocks 54.30
Jan., 1898	22 commodities 1890	20 stocks 61.86
July, 1898	22 commodities 1915	20 stocks 65.56
Dec., 1898	22 commodities 1918	20 stocks 71.41
Apr., 1899	22 commodities 1973	20 stocks 87.04

The high point in American railway stocks was reached in April, 1899, although the high point in April this year was only a little lower. English commodity prices have steadily risen, reaching the high point in April of the present year.

Apr., 1899	22 commodities 1973	20 stocks 87.04
Aug., 1899	22 commodities 2028	20 stocks 84.35
Nov., 1899	22 commodities 2128	20 stocks 84.49
Jan., 1900	22 commodities 2145	20 stocks 78.80
Apr., 1900	22 commodities 2210	20 stocks 82.91

Turning now to American commodity prices, there will be seen a quick response to the decline in the stock market during the past six months. The figures employed are from Dun's *Review* and are stated in percentages with reference to prices at distant dates.

	Nov., 1899	*Feb., 1900*	*May, 1900*
Hides averages	160.26	151.14	144.62
Leather averages	109.61	107.56	106.26
Pig iron averages	112.80	110.90	103.50
Iron products averages	99.60	97.60	84.52
Coal	4.15	4.20	3.90
Copper	.18	.16	.17
Lead	4.60	4.70	4.30
Glass	2.89	2.17	2.38
Silk	5.16½	5.25	5.00
Rubber	1.07	1.04	.98

The English market for commodities started late compared with our stock market and has also been late in turning. But the turn has come, as will be shown by the index number of May. No further demonstration is needed as far as the market for home commodities is concerned.

It all goes to show what we so often try to point out; namely, that the movement of stocks is an effect and not a cause. It appears sometimes to be a cause because of discounting, but it is not. The condition of general business is the key to the stock market, as a whole, just as the investor is the person who determines the value of each stock in the long run.

May 25, 1900

The market derived its chief feature from the announcement of the failure of Price, McCormick & Co., one of the most active commission houses in the Street. A large amount of securities were closed out under the rule for the account of this firm. No details were given as to the cause of the failure, but it was understood that wide-spread operations in stocks and large commitments in cotton were important factors in the unfortunate event.

The chief significance of the failure marketwise is the effect which it will have on sentiment. People will say justly that when one of the most active and best-known houses in the Street fails in a comparatively quiet speculative period, it implies a variety of losses and bespeaks the existence of conditions which must have had an unfavorable effect upon other financial concerns.

This is exactly where an important danger has been recognized by all close students of the situation. A bull market extending over three or four years is like a rising tide. It floats up everything that will float, and the flotation is always found to include a great deal that lacks value and consequently lacks salability when the tide begins to recede.

In other words, the tendency on the part of commission houses in a bull market is to lock up capital in unsalable stocks originally bought for customers, but which, through the exhaustion of margins, or the inability of customers to carry, finds a resting place in brokers' boxes. What is true of the ordinary commission house is true on a larger scale with reference to financial institutions, which through underwriting and loans find their capital changed from liquid into fixed forms, and fixed into forms from which there is no escape except through the medium of heavy loss.

This situation exists to a greater or less degree all over the country.

It exists rather more than usual because of the great creation of industrial stocks in the last two years. Many houses and many institutions have, no doubt, steered clear of this danger, but the securities have been created, and such of them as have gone out of the hands of promoters are somewhere and, to a large extent, are somewhere where they are not wanted.

The result of this situation will be seen whenever the market goes into a period of decline in failures here and there, subsequently explained on the ground that the concern was loaded with securities on which it could not realize. This fact will have a tendency to increase caution on the long side, and, while this will be an advantage as a whole, it will be a disadvantage to individual concerns, because those who do not have such stocks will be reluctant to buy them and this will increase the difficulty on the part of those who have them and who wish to sell. It will operate somewhat against the public interest in stocks because solvent customers will be required more and more to take up such securities, even at the expense of reducing their activity in the market and their power to acquire stocks of a better class.

We do not wish to be understood as saying that one failure in the Stock Exchange is going to make any radical change in the situation as seen on the surface. We only wish to bring out the facts which are under the surface so that their influence on the market can be foreseen. This influence will, in any event, be exerted slowly. Declines, when they come, will be intermittent and accompanied by frequent and vigorous rallies. The practical bearing of the case is that operators should, if they are convinced as to the character of the general market, sell stocks of the poorer class on rallies and buy only the best stocks on declines.

Burlington and St. Paul will decline in a flurry just as much in any one day as stocks of much less intrinsic value are likely to fall; but everybody who knows the facts about Burlington and St. Paul will look at them when down in the light of possible investments and will think about them, not from the standpoint of whether they will rally, but with reference to what they will yield for permanent holding. Burlington at 120, therefore, becomes not so much a speculation as a 5 per cent investment, and the investment buying will check decline. Exactly the reverse of this will be true in regard to stocks which have no such investment value. When they decline, the lack of value will prevent buying, and they will, therefore, go down more continuously and rally less than better stocks.

May 26, 1900

The following editorial illustrates the method later employed by Wesley C. Mitchell. Note that Dow is aware that stock speculation reflects in the figures for New York clearings. Also note Dow's statement: "These comparisons could be indefinitely increased without changing the essential conclusion, which is that business of all kinds moves in periods of alternate expansion and contraction." The definition of business cycles by Burns and Mitchell includes the words, "a cycle consists of expansions occurring at about the same time in many economic activities, followed by similarly general recessions, contractions, and revivals which merge into the expansion phase of the next cycle. . . ." [14]

In suggesting, some days ago, a course to be pursued by a small operator in stocks, we said that it was in a high degree essential that the operator should make up his mind whether he was trading in a bull period or a bear period, and that this was to be determined by a study of general conditions.

A correspondent observing this says: "The ordinary reader may not be in a position to judge this matter, and it would be interesting to have you give reasons why, for instance, that we can expect any important period of depression to follow the present period of prosperity. Can you expect a town to become again a village?"

That depends. There are a good many former towns in western Kansas which have become even less than villages. Many dividend-paying investment stocks have, in the course of time, been reorganized out of existence. Present value does not mean future value unless present conditions are maintained. All this, of course, will be agreed to, and we assume the real question to be whether there is reason for believing in trade cycles and that every boom carries with it the potentiality of a serious relapse. There is no way to judge the future but by the past. Therefore, we have compiled a few tables showing what has occurred in the past.

First, let us take the clearings at New York City and compare their rise and fall with the movements in the average price of stocks. We have given in clearings the high and the low points in the several swings without any reference to the years in which stocks show high and low points. It will be observed, however, that the correspondence is exceedingly close.

Clearings (in Millions) at N.Y.C. and Average of Stocks

1873	35,461	1872	Average 60 stocks	76.57
1876	21,597	1877	Average 60 stocks	36.33
1881	48,565	1881	Average 60 stocks	99.80
1885	25,250	1885	Average 60 stocks	41.28
1890	37,660	1890	Average 20 stocks	78.03
1894	24,230	1896	Average 20 stocks	41.82
1899	57,638	1899	Average 20 stocks	87.04

It may be said, however, that clearings at New York reflect to some extent stock speculation and are not a good guide. Let us, therefore, take the customs revenue of the United States which bears upon general trade and particularly upon the ability of people to consume more or less liberally duty-paying goods. Here again we find a second correspondence. The high point in customs revenue was in 1872 the same as the high point in stocks. The next low point was 1887 in stocks and 1878 in customs. In the ensuing high point, customs revenues were a year behind stocks. In 1894 customs revenue reached its low point before the lowest in stocks; in other years turning points were the same.

Customs Revenue and Stock Averages

1872	$216,370,286	1872	Average 60 stocks	76.57
1878	130,170,680	1877	Average 60 stocks	36.33
1882	220,410,730	1881	Average 60 stocks	99.80
1885	181,471,939	1885	Average 60 stocks	41.28
1890	229,668,584	1890	Average 20 stocks	78.03
1894	131,818,530	1896	Average 20 stocks	41.82
1899	206,128,481	1899	Average 20 stocks	87.04

Here again the point may be raised that customs revenue might be affected by changes in tariff laws which stimulated imports at one time and checked them at another. In order to overcome this point we will make the comparison with internal revenue receipts which bear upon a great variety of articles of home production and consumption. Again the correspondence appears in the expansion and contraction. Internal revenue turning points were a year behind the turning points in stocks in three instances and varied from it radically only in the year 1893, when internal revenue collections were large at a time when stocks were going down. It may be said here, however, that the year 1892 would have answered for the turning point in stocks almost as well as the year 1890 and if this date had been employed, there would have been no essential divergence.

Internal Revenue			*Average of Stocks*	
1870	$184,899,756	1872	Average of 60 stocks	76.57
1878	110,581,624	1877	Average of 60 stocks	36.33
1882	146,497,595	1881	Average of 60 stocks	99.80
1886	116,805,936	1885	Average of 60 stocks	41.28
1893	161,027,623	1890	Average of 20 stocks	78.03
1895	143,421,672	1896	Average of 20 stocks	41.82
1899	273,437,161	1899	Average of 20 stocks	87.04

Some critic may say that we have not yet taken a comparison which fairly represented the whole business of the country. In order to get the widest possible application, therefore, let us compare stock prices with the net earnings of all the national banks in the United States. This, it will be seen in the table following, simply adds confirmation to what has already been shown. The turning points were almost precisely the same in every year except 1894, when the earnings of national banks recovered from the panic of 1893 more rapidly than recovery came in the prices of railway stocks, probably because in the latter case there was a long period of liquidation and railway reorganization which did not occur in bank earnings.

Net Earnings of All National Banks and Average of Stocks

Sept., 1874	$30,036,811	1872	Average 60 stocks	76.57
Sept., 1878	13,658,893	1877	Average 60 stocks	36.33
Sept., 1881	29,170,816	1881	Average 60 stocks	99.80
Mar., 1885	21,601,202	1885	Average 60 stocks	41.28
Mar., 1891	40,145,974	1890	Average 20 stocks	78.03
Mar., 1894	19,762,826	1896	Average 20 stocks	41.82
Sept., 1899	29,830,772	1899	Average 20 stocks	87.04

Iron is admitted to be the one commodity which represents natural conditions more closely than any other. It is practically impossible to control either iron production or iron prices for any great length of time by manipulation. Nothing reflects actual conditions better. We give, therefore, the high and low points of pig iron and bar iron since 1872, and here again we find that the turning points occur with one exception either in the same year or the year succeeding the turning point in stocks. The one exception of moment occurs in 1887, when pig iron rose to 20.92, which was higher than the high point in 1890. It may be remembered, however, that the stock market had an important advance in 1886 and 1887, followed by a rather large decline in the spring of 1888, so that the seeming variation was really a very close sympathetic movement between iron and stocks in that period.

Average No. 1 Pig Iron	
1872	48.88
1878	17.63
1882	25.75
1885	18.[00]
1890	18.40
1898	11.66
1899	19.36

Average Best Bar Iron Per Ton	
1872	97.63
1877	45.55
1882	61.41
1885	40.32
1890	45.92
1897	29.40
1899	46.29

Coal prices are probably not as good as iron prices in indicating business tendencies; nevertheless they have a certain value, and we insert them to show that here again the low point and the high point for coal coincide very closely with the turning points in iron, and in stocks [and] in the other indications of the rise and fall in business that have been given.

Bituminous Coal Per Ton	
1873	4.84
1878	2.86
1881	3.75
1886	2.10
1890	2.60
1897	1.80
1899	2.00

Anthracite Coal Per Ton	
1871	4.46
1877	2.59
1882	4.63
1886	4.00
1892	3.97
1896	3.50
1899	3.75

Railroad earnings next to the iron market are the closest reflection of general business, and we find here again the same number of upswings and down-swings that have occurred in every other test made. Gross earnings reached the high point in 1873, a year later than stocks; in 1883, two years later, and 1893 and 1897, one year later. If we assume the high point in stocks to have been practically the same in 1890 and 1892, the dividends paid show turning points the same in number as stocks, but with the dates later, which is naturally accounted for by the fact that the payment of dividends is often delayed until some time after they have been earned. First, because increases in earnings are used on the property at the outset, and then because conservative directors like to feel certain that improved business will last for a time before materially increasing distribution in dividends. The essential fact, however, is that a record of twenty-five years shows a rise and fall in dividends and in earnings closely corresponding to the rise and fall in stocks.

Gross Earnings All Roads		*Dividends Paid All Roads*	
1873	$ 526,419,935	1875	$ 74,294,208
1877	472,909,272	1878	53,629,368
1883	817,376,576	1883	101,662,548
1885	765,310,519	1885	76,112,105
1893	1,207,106,026	1893	94,295,815
1897	1,032,966,485	1896	81,364,854
1899	1,284,994,191	1899 *	109,000,000

* Approximate.

These comparisons could be indefinitely increased without changing the essential conclusion, which is that business of all kinds moves in periods of alternate expansion and contraction. Since the Civil War the tendency has been for the period of expansion to culminate in the first year or two of each decade and for the period of contraction to culminate near the middle of the decade. As the country increases in wealth and in the magnitude of its business, it is probable that these periods will become somewhat longer in time and somewhat smaller in volume, as the resistance to change will be greater. It is doubtful, however, if as long as human nature remains unchanged, there will be abandonment of the tendency on the part of individuals to be too optimistic at some times and too pessimistic at others. While this lasts, the stock market is likely to feel the effects.

We believe that the stock market, as a whole, should be regarded always as an effect of general conditions, and that the way to study the stock market, as a whole, is to study general business conditions. Having considered the market as a whole from this point of view, it is then necessary to consider each particular stock with reference to the special conditions pertaining to it, remembering that while good and bad stocks rise and fall together with general conditions, each stock has its own independent movement and, as the outcome of a series of advances and declines, will invariably reach an approximation to its true value from the standpoint of an investor or permanent holder.

May 29, 1900

. . . .

One feature of the case is new in the experience of the Street. In years past merchants and manufacturers have worked in harmony with the banks with which they did business. Statements of assets and liabilities have been presented, and the banks have loaned money on the credit of individuals and on the security afforded by materials in process of manufacture or distribution. The industrial capitalization of the last three years has changed this materially.

Today the banks are lending, not on individual credits and goods, but on stocks representing the former property of many individuals. In one sense probably the banks are better secured than before, because they hold an asset theoretically marketable and one where the loan, as a whole, must if possible be kept properly margined.

On the other hand, however, banks are likely to find themselves in some cases the owners of this collateral through inability on the part of borrowers to furnish more margin and through their own inability to sell the collateral in hand without great loss. There is no longer the close personal knowledge of conditions and the personal character of makers of notes as bank security. Should there come any serious flurry in the money market or a panicky feeling in stocks, this condition might prove temporarily serious in its effect on quotations. Those who are carrying industrial stocks on margin ought to bear this in mind as suggesting the necessity of being able to protect such stocks to a greater extent than would be required in ordinary railroad stocks.

. . . .

May 31, 1900

. . . .

It is entirely possible that when we come to look back at the forces operating in the present bull period it may appear evident that the rapid creation of industrial securities caused a temporary collapse in industrial speculation at just the time when the South African war cut off the Rand supply of gold, and the combination of the two caused a halt in speculation lasting, perhaps, until after the close of the South

African war and the result of the presidential election in this country, after which, with peace abroad, the effects of the new currency bill began to be felt at home and led to another period of prosperity, during which the bull market of the period finished its interrupted course.

Nobody can say that this will be so, but it is a stubborn fact that bull periods heretofore have not been as short as three years, and if the bull period is over, it occupied something less than [three] full years, notwithstanding conditions that might fairly seem to have justified its continuance the average length of time.[15]

. . . .

June 1, 1900

. . . .

It is probable that railroad earnings will be less favorable from the bull standpoint. Net earnings are showing very small gains as a result of increased expenses. Decreases in net will soon be in order, and decreases in gross are probable when comparison comes to be made with the large gains of 1899 over 1898. Losses in earnings, while not more important actually than falling off in business, will have more effect speculatively because the relation between earnings and dividends is closer than that between general business and railway dividends.

. . . .

June 5, 1900

. . . .

We have frequently called attention to the fact that the extent of the rise would depend, after the first covering [of short sales], upon the amount of public buying that ensued. The amount thus far has not been very large and shows no signs of any material increase. One reason for this is that the class of people who buy stocks see in their own lines of business and in lines [with] which they are familiar decided evidences of a check to prosperity. The man who as a woolen manufacturer sees the demand for his goods suddenly disappear, or who as an iron dealer finds prices uncertain and bills receivable becoming somewhat doubtful in quality, is not quickened thereby to trade on the long side of stocks. He is much more likely to sell stocks that he may have and generally to set about strengthening his own financial position.

. . . Furthermore, the check to business means reduced profits for many of the great corporations. A director of the Steel & Wire Co. has been quoted as saying that his company went in sixty days from the position of earning $1,500,000 net per month to the position of earning practically nothing net per month, and it is to be feared that this experience has not been altogether unique among manufacturing concerns.

There is no escape from the economic law that abnormal prices check consumption. This brings about overproduction, which in turn brings a decline in prices until checked by the demand which springs from inadequate production. The operation of this law is sometimes quick and sometimes slow, but it is never suspended.

June 6, 1900

. . . .

The law which makes money flow to the spot where it finds the most profitable employment creates a great tidal movement in the reserves of New York banks.

. . . money flows to New York in December, January, February and early March, also in May, June and July. As the local demand for money over the country improves, generally in connection with the movement of crops, surplus funds are called back, resulting first in a demand on the interior centers and gradually affecting New York. In response, money flows from New York in the last half of March and April and with a much stronger flow in August, September, October and sometimes November. The bank reserve is always comparatively low in the fall and sometimes is low in the spring.

June 8, 1900

. . . .

In other words, the public exactly reflects the sudden but serious change in general business. Men who find paper profits in various industries disappearing, who discover their shelves stocked with goods which they cannot sell at a profit, who are annoyed by contracts likely to be unprofitable, who see overproduction and no satisfactory way of checking it, are in no frame of mind to buy stocks. Such people are in many cases looking to the short side of the stock market as a means of escape from the long side of business commitments.

. . . .

June 9, 1900

. . . .

The business situation shows additions here and there to the general story of a check in trade and loss of profits. When a period of contraction sets in, there are always collapses at one point after another as the pressure breaks through weak spots. The fabric representing general business is so intertwined that serious disturbance in one great industry cannot fail to affect others, just as the failure of one important house is very apt to result in other failures, sometimes at distant points.[16]

The change in the situation has not greatly affected railroad earnings, but effects are sure to come. When people stop buying goods, sellers stop transporting freight to an equivalent extent. When buyers find themselves unable to take goods for which they have contracted, the goods are not shipped, and in cases where shipment continues, pressure begins to be exerted for lower rates and for rebates in one form or another. This is going on now, and the results will gradually come to the surface in the form of decreased earnings.

. . . .

June 14, 1900

. . . .

. . . There is no change in the *great industries*. [Italics supplied.] The policy of readjustment continues. In iron, in lumber, in woolen goods and in great trades supplies are large, consumption has been checked, and contraction is under way. Nobody can say how long this will last.

The aggregate consumption is enormous, and if it once were in a position to gain on production, recovery in the business situation would be rapid. But unfortunately there is no clear evidence that production has gone below the normal demand. It is probable that more time must elapse before the right relations between producer and consumer can be re-established. While this is going on, the facts will be apparent to many people, and this will militate against any large public buying of stocks.

. . . .

June 15, 1900

. . . .

It is absolutely certain when furnace stocks [inventories] increase about threefold in five months that prices must give way under the anxiety of makers to sell, and it is only a question of time when falling prices will compel the furnaces operating at most disadvantage [the antiquated and less efficient furnaces] to reduce output.[17] That this has not been done shows that the situation is not yet accepted and that hope of sufficient improvement to restore prices still exists.

The shading of iron products goes on. . . . The coke output decreases, and over 2,500 ovens are now idle. All this shows that the progress of readjustment is going on with no definite signs of culmination. It begins to be believed in the trade that decline in iron will not stop until prices get near the cost of production. When bedrock is reached, there will be recovery and probably a considerable period of good business at steady prices. The quicker iron gets to a resting place, the quicker general business will be relieved from the uncertainty which is now a serious factor in trade.

June 16, 1900

The fundamental fact in speculation is that the market is always adjusting itself to new conditions. It reflects the efforts of thousands of the richest and ablest men in the world to anticipate something which they foresee. On this account, successful speculation consists chiefly in anticipating the market that is to be.

As this is inevitably the result of general conditions in a broad sense and of conditions pertaining to each stock in the narrow sense, the one way to forecast the market is to comprehend the tendency of events both as applied to general business and as they bear upon any stock in which dealings are contemplated.

We showed, some time ago, that the stock market, in its turning points, kept close company with all the other great indicators of the rise and fall in business. The turning point in stocks coincided time after time in a matter as remote from speculation as the customs revenue, and the same was true of clearings, of profits of national banks, of deposits in savings banks and of the prices of commodities as afforded by index numbers and the prices of great staples reckoned in averages. [Italics supplied.]

All pointed to one conclusion; namely, that the stock market was an effect of railroad profits and of industrial profits, which in turn were produced by general business throughout the country and probably with equal truth throughout the civilized world.

In order to apply this matter to speculation, it is necessary to watch continually the progress of events, and to realize that decreasing clearings mean decreasing business; that decreasing foreign trade is against a rising market for stocks; that shrinkage in railway tonnage, that decline in iron production or in coal output on a large scale denotes a general shrinkage, which, ramifying through a thousand channels, comes to the surface in the form of prospective reduction in dividends and consequent shrinkage in the intrinsic value of some industrial or railroad stock.

We have had, during the last two months, a violent reaction from the boom which was under way during 1897, 1898 and 1899. Prices of leading commodities have declined materially, and, while production has not been greatly curtailed, it is as certain as anything need be that this curtailment will come in the not very remote future.

The momentum of the business of a country is tremendous and is checked only by falling prices, which by reducing or destroying profits compels curtailment of output because there is no use in producing goods to be sold at a loss. It seems, therefore, reasonable to believe that the fall in the price of iron and iron products, for instance, will continue until it forces curtailment of output and enables demand to overtake production and use up some of the now rapidly accumulating stocks.

The same thing is true in its application to cotton goods, woolen goods and many other industrial lines. Therefore, as far as the immediate future goes, contraction seems to be inevitable.

It will not do, however, to anticipate that shrinkage will continue indefinitely. Whenever bedrock prices are clearly reached, there will be a basis for improvement in general business which may run for a very considerable time. If it should become clear during the next six months that consumption was overtaking production in iron and that it was necessary for buyers to pay attention to getting supplies, there would follow a somewhat rapid recovery in iron prices and then a period of steady business on a basis generally profitable to both the maker and the user of iron and its products.

There is a great amount of business awaiting this condition. There are thousands of buildings to be erected, thousands of tons of rails to be laid and thousands of tons of supplies of all descriptions to be acquired and utilized whenever it is felt that the time has come to again take hold of construction work. This time, when it comes, will be reflected in the stock market just as certainly as has been the period of current depression. Should such a time come in the last half of this year, it would probably lay the foundation for a rising market of considerable proportions toward the close of this year or in the first half of 1901.

Meantime, there is nothing in the situation to show that the turn is near except in the form of temporary rallies. The increase in iron output during the month of May with the number of furnaces in blast at the top is no indication of immediate improvement in the iron situation, and, when coupled with overproduction elsewhere and crop damage of a rather serious character, the combination [points] to the existence of conditions calculated to force stock prices lower. There will be rallies, but if the reasoning of this article is sound, the market will be found a sale on rallies until the fundamental facts under the market show a change for the better.

June 22, 1900

. . . .

There is beginning to be improvement in the iron trade. The makers of pig iron show their appreciation of the situation by an effort to reduce production as much as 25 per cent. Rolling mills propose to shut down for two weeks, and perhaps longer. The reduction of $7 per ton for beams and $9 per ton in angles brings those branches of the trade down to the level of the market. It is too early to say that iron prices have become stable, but recognition of difficulties and the lowering of prices is in the right direction and points to a better trade position before long. The first thing in the way of remedying an economic difficulty is to recognize clearly the difficulty that exists. This is being done in the iron trades.

In other trades readjustment is, perhaps, further away, but necessity is bringing restriction of production, and this in time will cure existing evils. . . .

. . . .

June 27, 1900

We have received an inquiry as to whether the record shows the market is more likely to advance at one time in the year than at another. This question can be readily answered.

The market is more likely to advance in midsummer than at any other time. The stock market has in the past been essentially a railway market, controlled in summer by the outlook for crops. July makes the wheat crop a certainty, while July and the first half of August determine in most years the results in corn.

Large operators spend money freely in June and July in order to get correct information as to the crop outlook. If their reports indicate good average crops, they buy stocks quietly with the idea that other buying will follow and that a rising market can be maintained up to about the first of September, when they propose to take their profits and leave their following to adjust prices to suit themselves.

Years ago, when St. Paul was emphatically a one-crop road, it used to be the regular custom for speculative insiders to make an important turn in St. Paul on the crops during the summer and early fall. It was in those years near a certainty that, with favorable crop conditions, St. Paul was good for at least ten points rise in July and August if the general market were in any degree favorable.

Another factor operating in favor of a midsummer rise is that corporations have chosen to make the interest on bonds payable in very many cases in January and July. Consequently, January and July disbursements are the largest of any two months in the year. July investments have therefore usually displaced money which has become available for speculative purposes.

The return flow of currency from the interior reaches its maximum in July, furnishing usually an abundant supply of money for a July–

August speculative campaign. There are, therefore, sound reasons why this period should be the one most frequently selected by bull operators for an advance, starting with manipulation but obtaining sufficient following to carry prices up and permit realizing on a large scale at the advance.

We have compiled in the paragraphs following a brief statement of the midsummer advances which have occurred since 1885, showing the duration and extent of each movement. The figures show the average price of a number of stocks, twelve in the earlier years and twenty in the later years:

1885.—Advance began July 2, average 61.95; rose to Aug. 17, average then 72.10.

1886.—July 9, average was 83.82; rose without much reaction to 94.25 Dec. 3.

1887.—Rise began July 30 at 82.51; Aug. 16 reached 85.63.

1888.—June 13 average 77.12; rose without much setback to 88.10 Oct. 1.

1889.—Began July 28 at 86.28; rose to 93.67 Sept. 11.

1890.—The market declined in July and until Aug. 21. It then rose from 91.78 to 94.70 Sept. 3.

1891.—Average July 31 was 81.00; rose to 92.95 Sept. 21.

1892.—Advance began July 7 at 89.60; reached July 29, 92.48; relapsed in August.

1893.—Rise began July 29, 63.72; rose until Oct. 28, when average was 78.63.

1894.—Rise began July 1, 71.60; ended August 27 at 78.93.

1895.—There was a slow advance from Feb. 28, 68.88, until Sept. 4, 84.23.

1896.—The market declined from June 17, average 55.26, to Aug. 8, average 41.82; then rose to 50.21, Sept. 30.

1897.—Rise was uninterrupted from April 17, 48.12, until Sept. 16, 67.23.

1898.—Rose from July 19, 64.30 to Aug. 26, 70.16.

1899.—Rose from June 1, 77.38, until Sept. 5, 85.55.

The foregoing shows the movement of the market during a portion of July and August for fifteen years past. In nine of the fifteen years, an advance started during the month of July, generally after the 9th of the month. In four years, an advance, previously under way, continued through July and August, while in two years the market went down in July and did not begin to recover until in 1890, August 21, and in 1896, August 8.

In seven of the fifteen years the rise culminated in September. Four times it came to an end in August, twice about the middle and twice at the end of the month. In three years the advance continued through September, and in one year it came to an end on the 29th of July.

This produces the following conclusions: In eight years of the fifteen a rise was under way during a considerable portion of July and August. In six years of the fifteen there was no rise of importance in July, but there was an advance during a portion or the whole of August. In one year there was an advance in July, but not in August. From this it appears that in fourteen out of the fifteen years last past there was an advance in the market during the whole or a part of the month of August.

June 28, 1900

. . . .

The decline in the price of materials, while unfavorable from the standpoint of those who have heavy stocks or burdensome contracts, will work to the advantage of the railroads by reducing the cost of supplies. The advance in coal and in iron products has become a serious factor in railroad expenses. It has been figured roughly that the cost of iron products used by railroads has doubled, coal has increased in cost over 30 per cent, and wages over 10 per cent. Had this continued at a time when gross earnings decreased, the effect on net earnings would have been very serious. It will probably be serious enough as it is, but railroads can replace supplies now at very much better figures than those prevailing three months ago, and this will help make good the loss in gross earnings that may be expected to come from a smaller volume of general business.

It should be remembered in forecasting the future that while business will continue to move in cycles, and down-swings will prevail, the general level rises. The low point in a growing country in one decade is not as low as it was in the previous decade. [Italics supplied.] In other words, business becomes better distributed, and a great deal of it becomes comparatively stable, so that the earnings of roads which have a diversified business gradually increase in stability, and the minimum, in due time, gets to a point which removes all apprehension in regard to the maintenance of dividends on reasonable capitalization.

. . . .

June 29, 1900

. . . .

It is possible that improvement in trade may be near enough to become a market force. Iron prices for the week are lower. Attempts to control prices by associations have in some cases been abandoned, and makers are free to accept what terms they will. This on the surface is unfavorable, but it is the quickest and best way of reaching bedrock. The sooner production is curtailed; the sooner antiquated furnaces go out of blast; the sooner prices get to a level where buyers are satisfied to take hold, the better it will be for both buyers and sellers.

The large industrial companies know this as well as anybody, and the fact that there is beginning to be accumulation of iron and steel stocks shows that insiders think the decline in iron not many weeks away. This, of course, applies to conditions for some months ahead, and not to permanent conditions. In the end, iron will go much below the present level, but there will be a halt in the decline and a temporary recovery first.

. . . .

NOTES

[1] On the importance of business contracts as mentioned above see Veblen, *Theory,* p. 196: "The reason for this retardation, whereby the close of an era of prosperity is always delayed, other things equal, beyond the lapse of the cause from which it has arisen, is (1) the habit of buoyancy, or speculative recklessness, which grows up in any business community under such circumstances, (2) the continued life of a considerable body of contracts for future performance, which acts to keep up the demand for such things as are required in order to fill these contracts and thereby keeps up prices in so far." Veblen does not mention the profit picture in this respect, as Dow does.

[2] Cf. Veblen, *Theory,* pp. 211–212: "To the workmen engaged in industry, particularly, substantial benefits accrue from an era of prosperity. These benefits come, not in the way of larger returns for a given amount of work, but more work, fuller employment, at about the earlier rate of pay. To the workmen it often means a very substantial gain if they can get a fuller livelihood by working harder or longer, and an era of prosperity gives them a chance of this kind. Gradually, however, as prosperity—that is to say, the advancing price level—rises and spreads, the increased cost of living neutralizes the gain due to fuller employment, and after the era of prosperity has been under way for some time the gain in the amount of work obtainable is likely to be fairly offset by the increased cost of living. As noted above, much of the business advantage gained in an era of prosperity is due to the fact that wages advance more tardily than the prices of goods. An era of prosperity does not commonly bring an increase in wages until the era is about to close. The advance in wages in such a case is not only a symptom indicating that the season of prosperity is passing, but it is a business factor which must by its own proper effect close the season of prosperity as soon as the advance in wages becomes somewhat general. Increasing wages cut away the securest of that differential price advantage on which an era of prosperity runs." Also cf. Mitchell, pp. 464–465; Mitchell claims that the reason wages rise less than wholesale prices is the result of the "unlike organization of the labor and commodity markets."

[3] On "the momentum of the volume of prosperity," see Mitchell, p. 473: "Of course prosperity confers no immunity against disasters which interfere with the course of business; but over many such rocks the accumulated momentum of good times may run without serious mishap."

[4] Note Dow's expression "the succession of good times and bad times," which illustrates his belief that business moved in cycles. Professor E. S. Meade, of the University of Pennsylvania, quoted from this paragraph of the editorial in reference to the speculative value of industrial shares. See *Trust Finance* (New York, 1913), pp. 150–151.

[5] On the relationship of industrial depressions and presidential elections see George H. Hull, "Industrial Depressions and The Pig-Iron Reserve," *The Engineering Magazine,* XIX (August 1900), p. 646. Hull claims that many Americans believe industrial depressions occur in presidential election years. He lists the years of industrial depressions as 1814, 1818, 1826, 1837, 1847, 1857, 1867, 1873 and 1882 and illustrates that these years do not conform to the years of presidential elections.

[6] The "Steel & Wire incident" refers to the closing of several mills by the American Steel & Wire Co. on April 16, 1900.

[7] See Mitchell, p. 460.

[8] Cf. Mitchell, loc. cit.: "Since the successive sets of business men who handle a given commodity are generally successful in their endeavor to pass on the increase of prices from one to another, the onus of the advance finally falls upon the ultimate consumers. For present purposes, these people belong to one of two classes—individuals who buy consumers' goods for personal use, or investors who buy equipment for business use." Also see Mitchell, p. 502.

[9] Professor F. W. Taussig later was to use the terminology "the penumbra theory" with respect to this delaying action on the part of buyers in placing orders.

[10] Note that Dow classifies the railroads as consumers, i.e., "investors who buy equipment for business use."

[11] Cf. Mitchell, p. 454: "While retail shopkeepers are the first beneficiaries of the increasing consumers' demand, they are compelled to place fresh orders promptly with wholesale merchants, because they have let their stocks run low during the dull times. Since the wholesale merchants have pursued the same policy, they are likewise prompt in placing fresh orders with the manufacturers. Thus the whole chain of trades engaged in furnishing consumers' goods soon feels the stimulating effect of a revival of business, no matter in what locality or industry it starts. And each enterprise which finds its own trade increasing becomes an agency in extending activity to still other enterprises—those from which it buys producers' goods, and those which supply consumers' goods to its own personnel."

[12] Dow's concept that capitalization forms the basis of competition is an interesting one. Adam Smith in *The Wealth of Nations,* Bk. I, ch. ix, says: "When the stocks of many rich merchants are turned into the same trade, their mutual competition naturally tends to lower its profit; and when there is a like increase of stock in all the different trades carried on in the same society, the same competition must produce the same effect in them all."

Dow follows this to the inevitable conclusion that competition results in "a fair return on fair capital."

[13] Dow firmly believed the stock market discounted general business. See George W. Bishop, Jr., *Charles H. Dow and the Dow Theory* (New York, 1960), pp. 106–108. The concept of the stock market as a leading economic series is not of recent origin.

[14] A. F. Burns and W. C. Mitchell, *Measuring Business Cycles* (New York, 1946), p. 3.

[15] The reasoning herein seems to conform to Mitchell's thought: "Every business cycle, strictly speaking, is a unique series of events and has a unique explanation, because it is the outgrowth of a preceding series of events, likewise unique." See Mitchell, p. 450.

[16] Cf. Walter Bagehot, *Lombard Street* (New York, 1883), pp. 125–126: "And there is a partnership in industries. No single large industry can be depressed without injury to other industries; still less can any great group of industries."

[17] See Mitchell, p. 476.

CHAPTER FOUR

July 3, 1900 — December 29, 1900

THE month of July, 1900, witnessed the nominations of President McKinley and William Jennings Bryan as well as the assassination of King Humbert of Italy. The New York Stock Exchange was relatively quiet during the summer months, declining somewhat on balance. The iron and steel industry was closely watched by investors and financial journalists.

In September stock prices dipped as the anthracite coal miners went on strike. However, the strike was of short duration and was settled in October.

The election of McKinley in November caused a great burst of speculative activity on the New York Stock Exchange. Stocks opened after the election with "gaps" on the up side of two and three points. The advance assumed "boom" proportions and continued throughout the close of the year.

July 3, 1900

. . . .

The iron trade, while improving from one point of view, is in a position where the surface is unfavorable. When it is decided to reach bedrock prices by allowing everybody to make prices to suit himself, it means the survival of the fittest. The process of crushing out the least fit will be unpleasant for the victims and will make the situation appear worse than the facts really are. . . .

. . . .

July 6, 1900

. . . .

The industrial situation is rather likely to be bearish in its tendency first and bullish afterwards. The reduction in iron prices goes on, and it is reasonably certain that declines will continue until bedrock prices have been reached. *When, however, this is accomplished, the best-equipped producers will be in a strong position and will probably have a period of prosperity* [italics supplied]. There are indications already of buying in the iron stocks, apparently with the intention of accumulating a line at low prices.

. . . .

July 13, 1900

. . . .

Iron trade reports were unfavorable. The reduction in output during June was less than had been expected. Only nine furnaces were out of blast. . . .

The good feature in the iron trade is that declines in prices are clearing up difficulties and creating a situation with which the companies can deal within a few weeks. A number of propositions looking to curtailment of production have been made. As long as prices held up there was not much use in making plans, but with prices down the companies will be compelled in self-defense to restrict output, and this in the end will bring stability.

. . . .

July 19, 1900

. . . .

There is beginning to be talk of an international iron combination. It grows out of a feeling that the iron industry has become international in its character. Great changes in prices of iron in one country are reflected in other countries. Iron has a universal quality and a tendency to move toward the point where it is of most value. Hence a question has been raised whether it might not be practicable to bring about an international agreement to regulate in a broad way both the price and the production of iron and steel in order by maintaining uniform stocks to prevent the undesirable advances in quotations at one period and the equally undesirable periods which follow. The matter will be talked over in London this summer, and while results are uncertain, some good may accrue.

. . . .

July 20, 1900

. . . .

. . . The iron trade shows improvement in a sense of a better demand at the low prices. In many cases, prices are believed to be about as low as they will go. When advance in raw materials is taken into account, prices of iron products show a margin of profit not materially greater than that existing two years ago.

. . . .

July 21, 1900

. . . .

The strength in the iron and copper stocks furnishes additional evidence that, in the opinion of insiders, the decline in iron prices is drawing near a close. Every day brings reports of new business and additional confidence. Some inequality in prices still exists. Steel rails notably have to come down, but, as a whole, quotations are getting to a point where profits are only reasonable unless [if] there can be brought about a lower cost of production.

It is as certain as anything need be that the volume of delayed orders, when they come to be given, will make the appearance of another boom in iron. Prices will not go back where they were, but they will advance, and there will be many reports of companies which have orders for a year or more on hand at satisfactory prices. This will be considered healthful business, and will be made the basis for many calculations as to the earnings and value of iron and steel stocks.

It will be said that while the 1899 boom was fictitious, the large business of the last half of 1900 is real, and means lasting prosperity. This will not be all true, but it will be true enough to exert a very decided influence upon the price of stocks which have fallen from 40 to 60 points in the last seven months. There will probably be an active speculation in iron and steel stocks within the next few months.

July 27, 1900

The forenoon market was dull and featureless except for some strength in the traction stocks, particularly Brooklyn Rapid Transit. During the afternoon prices declined moderately, with Baltimore & Ohio and Sugar showing rather special weakness. London did very little. Commission houses had no business, and the trading was entirely professional.

A correspondent asks us why earning power is not the true test of adequate capitalization. The point of the inquiry is whether the interest of the investor is not altogether in the return and not in the amount of capital on which this return is paid.

This is a very common but a very erroneous view. If anything were needed to demonstrate its unsoundness, it would be the present price of many industrial stocks. It is easy to buy preferred stocks of industrials to pay 7 to 8 per cent on the investment at a time when some 5 per cent railroad stocks sell much above par. This difference may be regarded as due to uncertainty in regard to the maintenance of present dividends on industrial preferred stocks. No doubt this is a factor in the case, but it is not the factor of primary importance.

The difficulty with industrial combinations is that they have been capitalized greatly in excess of value, and the reason why earnings are insecure is that capitalists, whenever they think the time opportune, will have no difficulty in duplicating industrial plants for much less than the capital of present concerns. The newcomers will then be able to earn dividends on the amount legitimately invested at prices for goods and with profits which will not permit dividends on existing stocks.

Stability in industrial stocks will not come until there have been reorganizations and a reduction in the volume of capital to figures representing something like actual value. When this time comes, people will buy industrials with confidence because they will feel that nobody can establish new plants and get return on their money to any better advantage than can the companies in existence.

It has been said that this reasoning, while true with regard to the industrials, does not apply to railway properties. This again is untrue, although a railway company can stand excessive capital better than an industrial corporation. It is comparatively easy to build mills; it is difficult to build railroads on account of the difficulty of getting into villages and cities and of securing terminal facilities to advantage. It would be impossible to duplicate any of the great systems of roads for their present capitalization.

This is the foundation of the confidence which exists in a railway property once established. Its securities command a relatively high price, not so much on account of the earnings as they do on the conviction that the property is stable and cannot be torn up or set aside. The necessities of a railroad continually increase the value of the plant and continually tend to correct the errors of overcapitalization.

It is, in railway properties as well as in industrial securities, of the first importance to judge whether the capitalization of a property is excessive or not. If it is, competition will certainly bring down the return. If it is not and the management is good, the securities are likely to grow in confidence and advance in price. The true test of overcapitalization is whether the property can be duplicated for less money. If the evidence is reasonably clear that it cannot be, the situation from the standpoint of the investor is infinitely better, even if returns on the securities are small, than it is where returns are large but where there is the constant danger of the destruction of the principal through competition.

July 31, 1900

The market had a general decline under the leadership of Sugar, Brooklyn Rapid Transit and Tobacco. Bear traders led the way in making low quotations, but there was enough realizing to keep them supplied with stock and to prevent rallies of importance. Sentiment at the close was that the market looked like going lower but that in view of its narrowness rallies might come at any time.

The recent check to business had raised a question whether the prosperity of the last few years has been substantial. Some people have tried to show that, while prices have advanced and production has been stimulated, the development has been artificial and that conditions have not greatly improved. The recent decline in prices is cited as evidence on this point.

An examination of the facts shows that prosperity during the last few years has been extraordinary. Four years ago the country was in a fever of apprehension in regard to the stability of values. There was general fear that people possessing property would have the value of their possessions cut in half by the adoption of a silver standard. The argument of the silver party which carried most weight was that the supply of gold was insufficient to adequately measure the stock of commodities. Believers in the quantitative theory of money enlarged on this point and made some converts.

Starting from this, it will be admitted that a large increase in the stock of gold in this country would be the best possible form of gain in the general situation. In 1896 the official statement of gold in the Treasury and in circulation was $599,597,964. The gold in the Treasury and in circulation in 1899 was $963,498,364, an increase in three years of $363,900,420. This was a gain of nearly 60 per cent, and the value of the gain whether regarded from a qualitative or a quantitative point of view is unquestionable.

The portion of this increase which is counted as in circulation may be open to question in the sense that it cannot all be definitely located. There is no doubt, however, in regard to the location of the Treasury holdings of gold coin and bullion which increased from 144½ millions in 1896 to 283½ millions in 1899, a gain of 139 millions or almost 100 per cent. This as a basis for maintaining silver and United States notes at a parity with gold was of the very largest importance. Nor has this country been alone in increasing its holdings of gold. The world's output rose from $202,251,000 in 1896 to $315,000,000 in 1899, a gain of $122,749,000.

The great additions to national wealth come out of the ground in the form of crops and of mineral products. The value of the wheat crop of this country for the three years ended June 30, 1896, was $774,443,561. The value for the three years ended 1899 was $1,141,862,690. The addition, therefore, to the national wealth from the wheat crop in the last three years was $367,419,129 greater than for the three years preceding.

The value of the corn crop for the three years ended 1896 was $1,590,711,663 and for the three years ended 1899, $1,682,306,490, showing the value for the last three years to have been $91,594,827 greater than for the three years preceding. The value of the cotton crop for three years ended 1896 was $795,399,000 and for the three years ended 1899, $842,719,000, a gain for the past three years of $47,320,000. The anthracite coal output for the year 1896 was about

43 million tons and for 1899 47½ millions. The pig iron output in 1896 was about 9 million tons, worth an average of $10.39 per ton for grey forge, compared with output of 13½ million tons in 1899 with an average for grey forge of $16.71 per ton.

There is no mistaking the substantial character of these additions to the national wealth. The additions reflected by the various exponents of trade are equally significant. Clearings in the United States in 1896 were a little less than 51½ billions, while in 1899 they were 93¾ billions. Deposits in national banks in October, 1896, were $1,798 millions. In October, 1899, they were $3,037 millions. The holdings of lawful money by the national banks increased in the same time from $343 millions to $466 millions.

Exports of merchandise for the three years ended June 30, 1896, were $2,582,285,675. For the three years ended June, 1899, they were $3,509,499,188. The excess of exports of merchandise for the three years ended June, 1896, were $415,596,414 and for the three years ended June, 1899, $1,435,570,633, or more than three times as great as in the three years preceding. Merchandise exports for 1900 were $1,394,186,371, an increase over 1899 of $317,749,250. As indicating the employment of labor, exports of manufactured goods in 1890 were over 432 millions, compared with 253 millions in 1896.

As showing the bearing of all this prosperity upon railway security [securities], the item of railway gross earnings is of the first importance. In 1896 the gross earnings of all roads reporting were $1,125,632,025, and in 1899, $1,408,523,883, an increase of $382,891,858. In the face of such an exhibit it is idle to question the genuineness of the improvement in recent years or to believe that such enormous gains in wealth will not have more than a temporary influence upon the country.

August 2, 1900

It seems to be a law of cycles that a great commercial depression comes once in about twenty years and a sensible, although smaller depression about once in ten years. The great panics and commercial crises of more recent times have been those of 1837, 1857, 1873 and 1893. Each intervening ten-year period has, however, been characterized by a well-defined area of depression, noticeable in 1846, 1867 and 1884. Assuming the rule to hold good, the depression of the present decade will be of the smaller type and will not be a general commercial panic.

There are several reasons why this should be so, and one of the most important is the extraordinary development of foreign trade. One of the causes of the depression felt so heavily from 1873 to 1896 was the inability of manufacturers to find a market for their goods. It became evident that the ability to produce in this country had outrun the ability of the country to consume, and that there must be either markets found outside of the United States or a temporary lessening of the output of manufactured goods.

Competition brought prices to a point which permitted the development of markets abroad, and when the requirements of these markets were discovered, pains were taken to develop them, resulting in a growth of foreign business which is likely to provide employment for mills and for labor in this country during the next few years to more than the ordinary extent.

The country will not go back to the volume of production shown in 1896. The home demand will represent the growth in wealth since that time, while the foreign demand will afford a large addition thereto. *Events have shown that this country with its high-priced labor can successfully compete in many lines of goods with the low-priced labor of Europe. What is lost in wages is made up in better machinery and larger individual output.* [Italics supplied.]

The figures which support these conclusions are most impressive.

Exports of merchandise for the year ended June 30 last were $1,370,476,158, an increase of $317,749,250 over those of any preceding year. There was an increase, compared with 1899, of 50 per cent in exports to Europe, 95 per cent to other parts of North America, 237 per cent to Asia and 324 per cent to Africa. In other words, the growth of exports has been largest relatively to those countries regarded as the best new markets for manufacturing nations.

The ability of the United States to hold its own in this competition is shown by the fact that exports from Great Britain increased from 1890 to 1899 from 1,317 millions to 1,320 millions. Exports from Germany increased from 811 millions to 950 millions, while exports from the United States increased from 858 millions to 1,252 millions, rising in 1890 to 1,370 millions. Great Britain had comparatively little gain, Germany a moderate gain, and the United States a very rapid gain in ten years.

An important part of this gain was in manufactured goods. The total exports of manufactures in 1900 were $432,284,366, an increase for the year of $92,608,808. Manufactures formed about 31.50 per cent of the total exports in 1900, compared with 23.14 per cent in 1895, 20.25 per cent in 1885 and 15 per cent in 1870. While total exports of 1890 were four times as great as those of 1860, those of manufactures were ten times as great.

In 1870 exports of manufactures by Great Britain were about 900 millions, and those of the United States 68 millions. In 1890 exports of manufactures by Great Britain were 1,080 millions; those of the United States had risen to 151 millions. In 1898, the latest figures on hand, exports of manufactures by Great Britain were 936 millions, probably considerably more than 1,000 millions in 1900, while those of the United States in 1900 had reached 432 millions.

All this points clearly in the direction of a rapid advance by the United States toward a liberal share of the markets of the world. The policy of expansion has been important in the last five years. Comparing 1896 with 1900, exports to Cuba rose from 74 millions to 264 millions; to Porto Rico from 2 millions to 44 millions: to Hawaii from 4 millions to 13½ millions and to the Philippines from $162,466 to $2,640,449.

There is one feature connected with this growth which is unfortunate. Of the total volume of exports, there were carried in American steam vessels goods valued at $66,186,540 and in American sailing vessels $21,632,984, a total of about 88 millions out of about 1,200 millions carried by water.

Foreign steam vessels carried $1,113,645,666 of the amount, British vessels getting about two-thirds of the whole. Foreign sailing vessels carried about as much of this tonnage as was taken by all steam vessels sailing under the American flag. It scarcely needs to be said that in the outlook for new business that of developing an American merchant marine should not be overlooked in view of the magnitude of the interests involved.

August 3, 1900

The iron trade is in a somewhat peculiar condition. There have been lately very large sales of steel bars by the principal manufacturers. The Carnegie Company, the Steel Hoop Company, the Republic Steel Company and others have made sales estimated in the aggregate at several hundred thousand tons at prices in the neighborhood of a cent per pound, or less than half the price which prevailed a few months ago. Large consumers of bars were ready to buy, and sellers determined to make quotations which would secure the business. The buyers include implement-makers, railway companies and car-builders.

These purchases have, it is thought, supplied the requirements of the large consumers for the remainder of this year and, in some cases, for a portion of next year. It is considered doubtful whether the sellers can make a profit unless they are able to reduce the cost of production below current figures.

The practical bearing of these large sales is that sellers have secured business for several months at cost or perhaps at a small profit. Manufacturers which have not been able to get this business will not find buyers scarce and will be compelled either to make still lower quotations in the hope of developing business or reduce their own output. Quotations as low as nine-tenths of a cent have been made in the last day or two, apparently with a view of finding orders.

The low prices at which the buyers have obtained material will permit comparatively low prices for finished goods and in this respect will be an advantage to railway and other interests. A cent per pound for steel bars means further decline in other iron products in order to establish a parity in quotations. It is, for instance, an anomaly for steel bars to be quoted at a cent a pound at Pittsburg and common iron bars at one and a half cents. The price of steel becomes especially important in connection with the price to be made for steel rails. The lower the price for steel, the lower the price for rails next year. On the present basis of steel, it does not seem probable that the price of rails can be fixed above $25, and it is possible that a lower price may be made.

The large volume of business is significant in one respect. It has been thought that when orders came they would lead to recovery in prices. The orders have resulted in very low prices, buyers apparently making pretty much their own terms. This is clear evidence that the iron situation, as seen from the inside, shows overproduction and a probability that buyers in round lots will continue to control prices for some time.

September 1, 1900

It is with the market as it is with the weather. When it is hot, it never was so hot before, and when the market is dull, it is declared to be the dullest market ever known. The present inactive period, while depressing, is not more quiet than many periods in the past. It is a natural reaction after the great speculative activity in recent years. The fact that the market was more active in 1898 and 1899 than ever before is perhaps a reason for thinking that the dull period may be a little more pronounced than usual, but it will pass away, and the longer the market stands still, the stronger the movement will be when it comes.

Fluctuations in the market are partly manipulation, but more the adjustment of prices to values, which are changed by changing conditions. The process of adding to or taking from values never stops. It goes on while the market stands still, and if prices remain quiet for a long time, they have to go further in order to reach the position occupied by values. Should the various forces which are now holding the market in check give way, so as to bring about advancing quotations, it could be said with truth that the increases in earnings in the last six months called for a very decided advance in prices to represent that tangible gain in values.

As a whole, the stock market must be more active in years to come than it has been in years past. This is inevitable, because of the enormous increase in the wealth of the country and the tendency to put the ownership of property into the form of securities. Thousands of people are interested in the prices of stocks and bonds today where there were only hundreds so interested a few years ago.

The tendency in all countries is for great commercial or financial interests to center in one place. It seems to be established in this country that the great grain market shall be in Chicago, and that the great financial market shall be in New York. The fact that whoever wishes to buy or sell St. Paul either as an investor or as a speculator and whether he lives in Maine or in California must, generally speaking, send his order for execution to a particular spot in the New York Stock Exchange, means the concentration in the Stock Exchange of an amount of interest which insures a business of large average magnitude.

There were weeks and weeks in 1876 when business in the Stock Exchange was at a minimum. In the dull period of the next decade, the average amount of business was greater than in 1876, and the dull periods of the present decade will see a still larger average volume of transactions than those of 1887. It is as certain as anything need be that the time will come when the business of a dull day in stocks will be larger than was the business of an active day in a former time.

The practical bearing is that people who trade in stocks should not be discouraged by dullness and by an accumulation of interest charges without the opportunity for profits. The outside operator can feel confident that if he can select a stock which is below its value and buy it, there will be other persons who will discover the same thing and whose purchases will gradually advance the price, assuring a profit for those who were early in discovering the fact. A dull period like the present is always a time to study values, because some of the ablest men in the country are doing the same thing. They have leisure to do it in dull times, and their conclusions are almost certain to be followed by changes in quotations.

September 13, 1900

We have frequently demonstrated that the stock market, while full of short fluctuations, has a continuing main movement, which often runs in one direction for three or four years at a time. We have also shown that this movement in stocks is accompanied by, or perhaps may be called the result of, similar tendencies on the part of commodities, which when grouped so as to be represented by index numbers show the same persistent rise or fall.

The Bureau of Economic Research has recently compiled a large number of index compilations intended to show the movement of commodities since 1878. [The Bureau of Economic Research mentioned herein is not to be confused with the National Bureau of Economic Research, which was not founded until 1920. The Bureau of Economic Research was located at 35 Lafayette Place, New York City, and was under the direction of Professor John R. Commons. The index numbers to which Dow refers were included in a quarterly bulletin issued in July, 1900. The work was done by Professor Commons with the assistance of N. I. Stone.] The method adopted has been to ascertain the average price of an article for ten years, 1879 to 1889, and give that price the value of 100. All other quotations of the same article are expressed in percentages calculated from the base. The percentage obtained is the index number. For instance, the average price of No. 2 wheat at Chicago for 1879–89 was 94 cents. Giving this the value of 100, the average price of wheat for the year 1898–99, 71 cents was 76 per cent of the average of 1879–89, making 76 the index number for the year 1898–99.

The Economic Bureau has treated 66 commodities in this way, taking an average for each month and for each year from 1879 to 1900. The resulting diagram closely follows the movement in stocks during the same period. The commodity movement has shown five distinct tendencies.

First.—There was a rise from the index number of 90 in 1878 to

120 in 1881, a gain of about 33 per cent. This agreed precisely with the stock market move of that period.

Second.—There was a fall from 120 to 90 or about 25 per cent between 1881–82 and 1885–86. This also agreed precisely with the bear period in stocks.

There followed an irregular movement in commodity averages, the index rising to 94 in 1887, falling back to 90 in 1889–90, and recovering to 95 in 1891–92.

The movement in stocks was relatively greater than the movement in commodities, but stocks rose in 1885–86, fell back in 1887–88, recovered in the spring of 1890, declined in the Baring panic of that year, and recovered again in the spring of 1892.

The next decline in commodities began some months earlier than the decline in stocks, starting during 1891 with the index at 95 and falling to 70 in 1896–97 reaching the low point about the same time as the low point in stocks, which fell from May, 1892, to August, 1896.

Since 1896–97, the commodity index has risen from 70 to 94, touching the highest in April, 1900. The rise was about 31 per cent. Sauerbeck's index numbers gave the rise during the same time as 27 per cent, while the index numbers compiled by the Bank of Japan agree with the results shown by the Bureau in a gain of 34 per cent. The movement in stocks during this time was a continued advance from August, 1896, to April, 1899, since which time there has been decline with partial recovery.

A continuation of the averages up to the present time would show quite an important decline since April, bringing the commodity movement into close harmony with the fall in stocks. The index number would undoubtedly stand now a shade below 90 or a little below the level of the years 1885 to 1892. The average, however, is more than 15 points above the lowest and comes pretty near being an average for ten years.

It is difficult to draw a practical conclusion as regards stock probabilities. It could have been pronounced a certainty last winter that commodity prices would go down or stock prices would go up. Now that harmony in direction has been restored, it remains to be seen whether stocks or commodities will give the next lead. *Comparing turning points closely in the past, it will be seen that stocks have generally started first, due to the discounting by speculators of future events* [italics supplied]. This being the case, the chances perhaps are that stocks will move first, and that the movement will be the discounting of such general conditions as can be foreseen in the year to come.

Assuming the election to bring no essential changes in policies, the outlook for the coming year cannot be considered unfavorable.

November 8, 1900

. . . .

In a broad way, the probability of a large advance in prices [in railroad stocks] is much smaller than it was four years ago. Prices were then low because values were low as the result of general depression. Four years have brought great advance in values with accompanying rise in prices. In order to have a corresponding rise in prices in the next few years, there must be an equivalent increase in values. It does not seem probable that conditions will bring an addition to the value of railroad stocks in the next four years bearing large proportion to the increase in values of the last four years.

It is more probable that the period of steadily rising values and prices is well along in its course. It is, however, not unreasonable to believe that we may have some years of stability in earnings and profits at a high level. This, if it occurs, will have a tendency to maintain prices of securities at a high level, and to create a period in which prudent men can make good profits in their respective lines of trade and in which the stock market will afford by stable values many good opportunities for acquiring moderate profits with comparatively small risk.

November 14, 1900

. . . .

It is worth remembering that the market has not had its full main swing. The rise was from August, 1896, to April, 1899, followed by more than a year of decline or stationary prices. There is no case of recent record where a pronounced bull market has stopped with less than three years between the high and low points. There have been, however, cases where a bull market has had a year or more of interruption after which has come the secondary move establishing the high price of the period.

A striking illustration of this kind occurred in 1888, when after about two years' advance prices had a material decline, followed, however, in 1889 and 1890 by full recovery and high point of the period. The theory of swings would call for the market to establish its high point in 1901, and conditions now seem favorable to that result. The average of twenty stocks is a little more than two points below the highest of 1889, so that a new record this year is easily within the possibilities.

. . . .

November 24, 1900

The forenoon reaction was rapid and general. The mid-day rally did not carry prices back to the best figures, and selling predominated during the afternoon. It is the almost universal feeling that the market should have further decline.

The principle of action and reaction applies in the market almost as certainly as it does in mechanics. The secondary movement as a rule bears some relation to the primary movement. The larger the original advance, the larger the reaction. This is qualified, however, by the fact that when an advance represents an adjustment of prices to new conditions, a relatively large part of that advance is retained.

The ordinary rule of reaction in a rising market is that it will be from three-eighths to five-eighths of the amount of the advance. In large movements, for well-defined causes, this rule does not hold. It is rare, however, that reaction, even against large movements, does not amount to one-quarter of the primary move. It is probable that when the normal reaction comes, it will amount to more than three points in the average of twenty stocks.

Reactions come in two ways. Sometimes they take the form of a sudden slump in which prices drop from three to ten points within two or three days. The more general course is a sagging movement in which prices work off for from fifteen to thirty days. The former case usually applies when there is alarm and a sudden liquidation; the latter when the liquidation represents a gradual preponderance of selling over buying orders.

No one can ever tell with certainty when the market is at the top. It is the opinion, however, of many experienced brokers and traders that the market is very near the top for this year. Their argument is that the rise has been large; it is known that many stocks have been sold, and it is believed that, in some cases at least, stocks are regarded even by insiders as too high. When this state of mind exists on the part of influential people, it usually spreads through the Street and promotes realizing.

Again, December is generally a month of closing of accounts and of realizing rather than of new commitments. It is one of the maxims of the Street that stocks go off in September and in December, as it is a general rule that they go up in the last half of July or during August. There is therefore a general basis for thinking that prices may work off slowly from about this time until sometime in December.

It is fair to say that some of the large operators do not share this view. They lay stress on the admitted fact that the Street is not loaded with stocks. They think this will make realizing sales comparatively slow and will produce dullness in speculation rather than much decline.

Whichever theory proves right, it will not be disputed that the market has had a large rise and in the last few days has begun to have frequent relapses. When one stock has been bid up, others have not followed. Bull manipulation has failed to bring a good response. This is always to be heeded, and has already found expression in a lower level of prices.

Those who believe that the situation justifies the present level of quotations should buy good stocks on small declines, perhaps taking small profits when they come. Those who believe that the situation calls for a declining market for a time should sell the weaker stocks on bulges, perhaps taking them in on breaks with the idea of selling again on the next rally.

December 29, 1900

Periods of great speculative activity in recent decades have had well-defined causes. The bull period which ran from 1867 to 1872 represented the energies of something like two millions of men released from the pursuits of war and turned to the development of the country. The war took men, particularly of the North, out of their local surroundings and gave them views which, on the return of peace, led them into the industrial development of the West upon a scale up to that time unknown.

The bull period extending from 1877 to 1881 was the epoch of railway building. Roads which in 1878 were local lines of a few hundred miles became substantial systems by 1881. The systems of St. Paul, Northwest, Burlington, Rock Island and many others were either created or greatly enlarged in that period. From a financial point of view, it was the day of railway building for the purpose of making money out of the construction of roads. The best business of the period was the manufacture and sale of railway securities.

Growth in railway earnings sent stocks from normal prices to par, and the interests of promoters and speculative managers led, in many cases, to the payment of dividends far beyond the limits of conservatism. The country paid for this expansion in the bear period which followed. Indeed, it has taken from ten to fifteen years for the country to grow up to the railway mileage created in about four years. The growth of the country has finally justified the policy of expansion, and today the great systems of the West are better off than they would have been had a more conservative policy been pursued.

The feature of the bull period which began in 1896 and which has not yet culminated has been twofold. It was, first, the period of industrial expansion and, second, the period of railway combinations.

The policy in industrials was to take all the concerns engaged in a given line of business and combine them into one with an issue of stock greatly in excess of the true value of the property combined. It was a period of industrial expansion on an enormous scale.

The railway policy of the period, on the contrary, has been one of contraction, not in railway mileage, but in the control of railway properties. It has been the expansion of systems, but the contraction of responsibility. It has seen New York Central absorb road after road, until it stands at the head of railway mileage in the United States. It has seen Pennsylvania pursue a similar policy. It has seen Southern Railway cover the South; and Canadian Pacific, Southern Pacific, Atchison, Union Pacific and Northern Pacific concentrate railway mileage in their territory until they exert a controlling influence over an immense territory.

Today 28 railway systems control more than 117,000 miles of road or more than 60 per cent of the railway mileage in the country. Fifteen corporations exert a controlling influence in railway affairs over a large proportion of the country. Eight men stand at the center of railway influence. They are J. J. Hill, W. K. Vanderbilt, George Gould, A. J. Cassatt, J. H. Schiff, J. P. Morgan, J. H. Speyer and E. H. Harriman. They stand for New York Central, Erie and the anthracite coal roads, for Pennsylvania, Baltimore & Ohio, Chesapeake & Ohio and Norfolk & Western: for Southern Railway, Chicago & Alton, Illinois Central, St. Paul and Northwest: for Great Northern and Northern, Union, Southern Texas and Missouri Pacific. In fact, they represent all the great systems except Burlington, Atchison, Denver and Louisville & Nashville, and the end of concentration of railway power is not yet.

The effect of industrial overcapitalization has been seen in an overcapitalization collapse. The remedy will come with reduced capitalization and establishment of the properties on a conservative basis.

The effects of the railway policy cannot fail to be far-reaching. They will include a check to the long-continued fall in rates. It is not likely that rates will be unduly advanced. Many influences stand against that, but when railway earnings run from three to ten mills per ton per mile there is no great danger of average rates being too high. With decline in rates checked, railway profits will become more stable. This will make the securities of controlled roads safer as investments, while changes in business, by producing variations in the profits of controlling roads, will cause price fluctuations, which will be important and desirable from a speculative standpoint.

There will be drawn a clear distinction between investment stocks and speculative stocks, and this will be to the advantage of investors. Those who, twenty years hence, look back at the present period will see in the combinations made and being made the foundations of a period of steady prosperity for railroads and for careful investors in railway securities.

CHAPTER FIVE

January 31, 1901—June 29, 1901

THE first half of the year 1901 witnessed two striking events that claimed the attention of Charles H. Dow as well as that of all other financial journalists. The first was the launching of the United States Steel Corporation in February, and the second occurred on May 9th in the form of the famous Northern Pacific corner.

Reviewing the railway stock average that appeared at the time in *The Wall Street Journal* shows that the rail market generally advanced from January until the Northern Pacific panic in May. From that time until the end of the year the average remained in a rather narrow range. On the other hand, the movement of industrial stocks was generally upward until the middle of June.

At the beginning of 1901 the boom that followed the second election of President McKinley in the previous November continued, with considerable speculative activity and high volume on the New York Stock Exchange.

J. P. Morgan purchased the Central Railroad of New Jersey for the Reading in January, and in the following month the United States Steel Corporation was incorporated in New Jersey. The huge capitalization (for the times) of $1,404,000,000 caught the imagination of the investing public and caused a great deal of discussion in the financial press about the nature of the trust as well as the financial stability of the enterprise. In the same month Union Pacific purchased a controlling interest in Southern Pacific.

The high tide of speculative activity on the New York Stock Exchange occurred in April, when total volume of 41,719,086 shares were reported for the month, the largest previous total having been 30,285,286 shares in the previous January. On April 30th volume reached 3,281,286 shares, the largest daily volume reported to that date.

The Northern Pacific panic was truly an unusual catastrophe. Enormous losses were incurred despite sound financial and business conditions because of a fight for control of a particular stock. The corner was a financial accident. Dow's editorials at the time of the corner and panic are included herein as a contribution to financial and business history.

After the panic the market recovered, but in June the suspension of the Seventh National Bank in New York City and the failure of the firm of H. Marquand & Co. weakened the stock market situation. Bank failures in Germany were also reported in the American press in the same month.

January 31, 1901

A person watching the tide coming in, and who wishes to know the spot which marks the high tide, sets a stick in the sand at the points reached by the incoming waves until the stick reaches a position where the waves do not come up to it, and finally recede enough to show that the tide has turned.

This method holds good in watching and determining the flood tide of the stock market. The average of twenty stocks is the peg which marks the height of the waves. The price-waves, like those of the sea, do not recede all at once from the top. The force which moves them checks the inflow gradually, and time elapses before it can be told with certainty whether high tide has been seen or not.

Take the market in the last few weeks, as shown by the table following:

20 railway stocks Saturday, Jan. 12	97.85
20 railway stocks Saturday, Jan. 19	93.56
20 railway stocks Wednesday, Jan. 23	95.00
20 railway stocks Thursday, Jan. 24	93.90
20 railway stocks Wednesday, Jan. 30	96.08

Here are the waves as they have come in: the high point January 12, the recession on the 19th, the next wave on the 23rd, another recession on the 24th, and now another high point, crossing that on the 23rd, but lacking more than a point of reaching the high level on the 12th.

Nobody can say with any certainty whether high tide has been seen or not. If the average rises above the level on the 12th, it will increase the probability of a new high level in the near future. If this does not occur, the chances will favor a receding tide and a level lower than that on the 19th.

The market shows great strength in view of the unquestioned fact that quite a proportion of the strong interests are not participating in the advance, and, as far as their influence goes, are turning from rather than toward higher prices. The advance in St. Paul has destroyed the probability of an early deal in that stock. The advance in other stocks has led cliques to realize and induced prominent and successful houses to advise caution instead of confidence.

It has, on the other hand, led some operators to extend themselves with the idea of taking advantage of favorable conditions. If these operators obtain public support, they will succeed, yet commission houses are not very bullish, and the public has not shown a great disposition to follow leads given by strong stocks.

There are indications that somebody long of the market is making advances in one stock after another for the purpose of drawing attention to them while he sells elsewhere. This is the generally accepted explanation of some of the recent moves in St. Paul and of the advance which occurred yesterday in Rock Island. It takes a large operator a good while to turn round. It is necessary sometimes to do a good deal of manipulation in order to market a moderate amount of stock, and something of this kind may be going on.

Six months ago we occasionally pointed out that leading roads had increased earnings very materially in the course of six or eight months, while prices had actually declined. This was abnormal, and certain to result either in large loss of railway earnings or advance in stock prices. Whoever will look over the record of net earnings during the last six months will see only moderate gains except in special cases. Nevertheless, prices have gone up from 20 to 40 points. This has been partly a response to improved conditions early in the year, but it is a question whether the advance in prices has not discounted in most cases the improvement which has occurred.

There remains the advantage to be derived in the future from community of ownership. This is a fact of real importance and will have weight, but the rise in the market has interfered with these plans to such an extent that it is a question whether all that is involved in community of ownership will not be promoted more by receding prices than by advancing.

The market may be going up a great deal more, but there is no escape from the fact that it has risen a great deal in the last few months, and is at a level where prices occupy no such relation to values as they did six months ago.

February 21, 1901

We have received the following inquiry: "When, in your opinion, will the present bull period end, and what will be the evidence of its culmination?"

The bull period will end when the forces which have been lifting prices up become weaker than those which tend to press prices down. The evidence of this increasing weight will appear in various ways, but chiefly in the form of expansion in business, in prices, commitments, responsibilities and undertakings.

The prices of stocks are always an effect and not a cause. High prices are produced by large earnings and increase in dividend funds, whether applied to rails or industrials. Large profits are the consequence of active trade and general prosperity. Therefore, the stock market and the commodity market move substantially together. The stock market is usually a little ahead of the commodity market because of the tendency of speculators to discount the future.

For the past twenty-five years the commodity market and the stock market have moved almost exactly together. The index number representing many commodities rose from 88 in 1878 to 120 in 1881. It dropped back to 90 in 1885, rose to 95 in 1891, dropped back to 73 in 1896, and recovered to 90 in 1900. Furthermore, index numbers kept in Europe and applied to quite different commodities had almost exactly the same movements in the same time. It is not necessary to say to anyone familiar with the course of the stock market that this has been exactly the course of stocks in the same period.

If, therefore, the past is any guide to the future, we are nearing a time when the advance in commodities and in stocks will halt and then turn down for a somewhat prolonged decline. Also, judging the future by the past, it is probable that the decline in the next few years will be less pronounced than the decline from 1890 to 1896, but will be more like the down-swing from 1881 to 1885. One reason for this is that the growing wealth of the country establishes increasing stability in values. Another is that the establishment of the currency on a firm basis removes one of the great sources of danger. Another is that the railway combinations which are being made will have a tendency to give railway stocks the benefit of more stable earnings than heretofore.

But after allowing for all these things, it is fair to assume that the trait in human nature which makes cycles in trade has not changed and that it will work out the same overtrading and overcommitments which have been the cause of declines heretofore.

A period of prosperity always encourages trading. As long as people make money, their tendency is to enlarge commitments. This is true of everybody from banking syndicates to the keeper of a cross-roads general store. When, on the other hand, ventures cease to be profitable, contraction invariably follows, increasing with the shrinkage which contraction promotes.

Nobody will deny that this has been a period of great expansion. Clearings in the United States in 1895 were about 53½ billions. In 1900 they were 86 billions. Clearings in New York City the first week in August, 1896, were 444¾millions. For the first week in February they were 1,631 millions. Philadelphia clearings rose in the same time from 49 millions to 94 millions; Boston from 75 millions to 128 millions, and Chicago from 87 millions to 125 millions. Nothing could show more impressively the expansion of general trade.

Pig iron production in the last half of 1896 amounted to 3,646,891 tons. In the last half of 1900 the production was 6,146,673 tons, or almost double. The average price of No. 1 foundry iron in 1896 was $12.95; in 1900, $19.98. Bessemer iron averaged in 1896, $10.39; in 1900, $16.90. Steel billets in 1896 averaged $18.83; in 1900, $25.06.

The loans of the New York banks the first week in August, 1896, were $469,535,900; last week, $911,623,000. Deposits in 1896 were $485,019,000; last week, $1,011,329,000. Cash holdings of the banks in 1896 were $138,982,100; last week, $265,684,700. Here again appears the enormous volume of commitments incident to a period of great activity. Such an increase in four years shows the margin for decrease when business activities may be curtailed.

Look at the effects of all this upon the prices of a few active stocks. Comparing August, 1896, with the present time, Burlington has risen from 53 to 144, St. Paul from 60½ to 148, Rock Island from 49¼ to 124, Missouri Pacific from 15 to 88, Northern Pacific from 3⅝ to 83, and Union Pacific from 4⅛ to 93. It is true that increasing value has accompanied this advance in quotations, but the advance in value has been the result of the improvement in general trade and rests upon the maintenance of the activity and the profits which have increased railway earnings.

The earnings of 131 roads with 97,351 miles in July, 1896, were

$41,677,094. The earnings of 107 roads with 101,882 miles in January, 1901, were $58,137,266. Increases in earnings have fallen off somewhat of late, and this, if continued, will probably be one of the earlier signs of the turn. Falling off in clearings will be another indication, and it is not improbable that weakness in stock prices reflecting the foresight of those best able to judge the future will be among the early evidences of the turn in the tide.

It is impossible to say when this turn will come, but it is clear from the figures given that the expansion of the period is far along and that it is a time for much greater caution in commitments on the long side than has been necessary in the last few years.

March 12, 1901

The question is frequently asked whether the present era of prosperity can be considered as any more permanent in its character than have been prosperous times in the past.

Everything has to be considered relatively. Good times resting on a substantial basis can be overdone as surely as good times resting on a weaker basis. There is sure to be overproduction, and that is always what brings commercial reaction. Nevertheless, the country may be a good deal longer in reaching the point of overproduction at one time than at another. The real question is whether the forces which have been lifting this country into prosperity at home and prominence abroad are strong enough to justify expectation that they will continue over more than the ordinary length of time.

. . . .

March 14, 1901

We pointed out, a few days ago, that the present period of prosperity had been stimulated in no small degree by the remarkable increase in the excess of exports over imports of merchandise in the last few years. National profits do not differ from individual profits in the sense that to sell more than is bought results in a surplus for the seller. The periods of great prosperity in this country have been closely connected with periods of large profits in national trade.

The great speculative period twenty years ago was characterized by this feature. From 1863 to 1876 this country had an excess of imports of merchandise in every year but one. The tide then turned, and there was an excess of exports of merchandise as follows: 1876, 79 millions; 1877, 151 millions; 1878, 257 millions; 1879, 264 millions; 1880, 168 millions; 1881, 259 millions, and 1882, 26 millions.

From 1882 to 1895 there were fluctuating balances. An excess of imports was shown in three years, and a comparatively small excess of exports in six years. In 1896 the trade conditions, which have been so important in their bearing upon this country, began to be felt, with results following: excess of exports of merchandise 1896, 102 millions; 1897, 286 millions; 1898, 615 millions; 1899, 529 millions; 1900, 544 millions; a total gain to this country in its merchandise balances in five years of about $2,000,000,000.

This great sum has either been paid to the people of the United States in the last five years or is still due in some form. People of other countries have had this money to pay either in cash or the liquidation of obligations. A great deal has been paid in the form of securities formerly held abroad but which have been returned to the United States. Much has been paid in the form of carrying charges. This form of payment will undoubtedly continue to be easy to people abroad as long as the United States has no merchant marine. But it is not so certain that other forms of payments will be as easily arranged.

It is true that consumers of goods will buy them where they can be bought cheapest, and that if the manufacturers of this country can undersell the manufacturers of other countries, we shall continue to have a large foreign demand for manufactured goods. But if this competition by crippling industries abroad reduces the employment of labor, it will reduce purchasing power to an extent which will be felt in all markets. It is impossible to suppose that this country can maintain a high degree of prosperity in its manufactures with other countries like England and Germany under severe depression.

The principle of barter is at the bottom of all trade. If people cannot sell, a time soon comes when they cannot buy. This country must meet the problem whether it will materially increase its imports or see a material decrease in its exports. To go on at the rate of the last few years would drain the civilized world of its gold in payment for our products. Both natural and artificial laws of trade will combine to prevent any such result carried to serious consequences.

Either horn of the dilemma presented to this country will lessen the present extraordinary prosperity in manufacturing lines. If the line of least resistance in trade proves to be buying more goods abroad, there will be necessarily curtailment in some manufacturing lines at home.

If foreign ability to buy is cut off and our exports decrease, the same result will be seen. Manufacturing will fall off because of the smaller demand for goods.

There is one important modification possible. That is the discovery of new markets. If China or South America or Africa can take the manufactured goods in quantity of any of the great manufacturing nations, it will benefit the trade of all, and particularly the trade of that nation which is able to manufacture the goods of most general consumption at the lowest cost.

Probably new markets for the products of this country will be found. In the general scramble for trade this country will hold a good position on account of its possession of cheap iron and coal. Trade changes generally come slowly, and even when the period of contraction clearly comes, there will probably be time for manufacturers and merchants to adjust their business to new conditions.

Combinations like the community of ownership in railroads, like the United Steel combination, and this principle carried further, with the object of steadying output and prices, will exert a strong influence in the right direction. Experience will teach each nation what it can do to best advantage; what it can make cheaper than its neighbors. But after allowance has been made for all this, the great law of supply and demand, applied nationally and internationally, will surely bring reaction from the bull period of 1896 to 1901, and this ought to be taken into account by all who are calculating upon trade conditions as the foundation for continued rise in railway or industrial securities.[1]

March 30, 1901

The bull market which culminated in 1872 was represented by about ten active stocks, and transactions in active days were only about 200,000 shares. The bull market which ended in 1881 was represented by about twenty active stocks, and transactions reached 700,000 shares. The present bull period has seen transactions approach 2,000,000 shares a day, and the active list includes over sixty active stocks. There were transactions Thursday in 169 stocks, of which sixty-five were industrials. At least sixty of these industrials were not in existence until within a few years.

This brings into clear view the great change that has taken place in recent years and shows how closely the stock market has been brought into relations with capital all over the country. Wall Street manipulates stocks and in a narrow sense makes prices. In a vastly larger sense, the public furnishes the money to pay for stocks and determines the price by setting investment values.

When speculation was limited to a small number of railway properties, the country as a whole had but little interest in stocks. There were but few stocks to be owned. Twenty years later there was a great expansion in public interest because of a greatly enlarged public ownership. The last twenty years, and especially the last ten years, have seen this interest multiplied fivefold by the conversion of partnerships into stock companies and the combination of the small companies thus created into great corporations.

The consequence has been that tens of thousands of investors who formerly received dividends from John Brown & Son, manufacturers of saws or locomotives, or woolen goods, and whose ownership was represented by an entry upon the books of a firm, now hold shares in the stock of some company and take an interest in the quotations recorded daily on the Stock Exchange.

The effect of this has been twofold. It has greatly changed the character of loans. The small concerns that formerly borrowed money from local banks on their notes have gone out of existence, and such borrowing as is required to carry on that business is done at some financial center and on collateral security. The tendency has been to increase loans at great centers and to change the character of loans at smaller centers.

The second effect has been to increase speculative interest in stocks. As long as ownership was intangible and could not change hands, there was no fluctuation in value. When ownership was transferred to a certificate, the price of which changed every day, it was inevitable that owners of these certificates should endeavor to make money by buying and selling the stocks which they knew most about. This has made no inconsiderable part of the industrial market, and the importance of this class of trading will increase rather than diminish.

As community of ownership does its work, trading in railroad stocks will decrease and the industrial market will become the great market in Wall Street. There will come the sharp discrimination in industrial stocks that has existed in railway stocks. Ever since the railroad companies began to print monthly statements of gross and net earnings and gave in annual reports details which enabled experts to figure out for other people the integrity of net earnings and the essential facts bearing upon the values of stocks, the public has been accumulating the best stocks and fighting shy of the others.

Exactly the same thing will occur in industrials. Far-sighted managers will see that the best results in the long run will be obtained by dealing fairly with the public. Information will be prompt and adequate. The right of stockholders to know the facts will be recognized by companies which have nothing to conceal, and this will create a class of industrial corporations which will stand high with investors. Corporations which are run as money-making schemes for insiders will gradually fall into disrepute because the public will find that it loses money in these stocks, and the lack of actual value will establish a low investment basis.

The probable activity and possible investment value of U.S. Steel will attract new attention to industrial properties. We think the rule for such people to follow is to limit their operations to the stocks which they can learn most about. If a man is familiar with the iron trade or the woolen trade or any other business, he is likely to be better able to judge an industrial company in that line of business than in any other. His next step should be to endeavor to get into personal relations with the people who manage that particular property.

This can be done sometimes personally and sometimes by correspondence. Many companies which give very little information to the public feel under obligation to give information to stockholders of record. If a man owns even one share in an industrial company, he has certain legal rights and frequently some moral rights which the officers of the company respect, and which will enable him to learn enough to form some general opinion of the investment value of that stock.

Then, by watching fluctuations and buying when the stock is below demonstrated value, the opportunity for speculative profit as well as fairly safe investment will be very materially increased. Blind speculation in industrials is folly, but there is such a thing as intelligent speculation in industrial stocks.

May 8, 1901

The leaders in every department of business have become impressed with the magnitude of the forces which underly the present situation. It is a day of great things and the dawn of a period in which changes may be of the most impressive and far-reaching character.

Mr. Morgan, who stands as near the center of business as any one man, says: "The United States can solve every commercial problem if given time, and it can supply all the markets of the world." Mr. Carnegie utters the same thought in saying: "Hitherto the business of the world has been carried on by little divisions. America is now coming to the front and will have a predominating voice in the industries of the world. Nothing can arrest the progress of the American Republic."

What does this mean? Primarily, that the United States is free from a large part of the burdens which bear so heavily upon European nations as a result of large standing armies and the taxation necessary to carry on their systems of government. Nations which have an aristocracy support an upper class in idleness and also a lower class which lacks the ability to support itself, leaving only the middle class as the creators of national wealth.

Furthermore, customs have wedded peoples of Europe to methods whereby labor is comparatively cheap but production is small and inventive skill is not greatly encouraged. Some of these countries lack food-producing areas; others lack coal and iron, and in others still, the supply of these essentials to modern progress is being reduced at a rate which threatens soon to have a serious effect upon the cost of production.

The United States has inexhaustible resources of iron and coal, an immense food-producing area, and a singularly ingenious, resolute and aggressive people. It has been a new country with a vast amount of preliminary work. It has had the enormous physical labor involved in settling the country, in establishing means of communication, discovering its natural resources and finding the best means of employing them. Legislation has produced its own set of difficulties, while unwisdom in financial matters has delayed progress and impaired confidence. Enormous debts incurred for the development of the country have had to be paid.

At last, however, the time has come when the United States may be fairly regarded as a world power, not only in the domain of international politics, but in its population, wealth, skill and throughout the great departments of trade and commerce. It has been said that the country which can make the cheapest steel must command the markets of the world.

The great captains of industry see that the time has come when plans must be made not for domestic trade alone but for world trade. The great combinations between railroads and between industries have as one of their purposes power of concentrating management, cheapening cost and providing transportation whereby the natural advantages of the United States can be utilized to the fullest extent. It is of no use that the mountains of West Virginia are full of coal or that the Carnegie works can make steel cheaper than it can be made elsewhere, if provision is not also made for transporting coal and iron to the points where finished goods are required by the consumer.

The great leaders who say openly that this country is entering upon a period of unprecedented prosperity rest their opinion on a belief that this country will, for a time at least, have such an advantage in the markets of the world as will make good times for practically every well-managed business in the United States.

How manufacturers and producers abroad who lose trade as a result of this will recoup themselves remains to be seen. Efforts in that direction will certainly be made, and government help may be given, but governments will be slow to legislate too greatly in favor of the producer as against the consumer, and, in the end, the law of the survival of the fittest will prevail, in business as well as in the evolution of species.

The stock market may advance or may decline. Individual fortunes may wax or wane, but to the United States as a whole the new century opens with the horizon widening out and with magnificent possibilities in view.

May 9, 1901

Northern Pacific has again brought menace to the speculative situation. It is singular that this stock should have played an important part in railway affairs at three periods so widely separated as 1873, 1884 and 1901. Twice Northern Pacific has brought ruin to those who were long of the stock, and now it has brought very heavy losses to those who were short. Northern Pacific pulled down the house of Jay Cooke & Co. and defeated the ambitions of Mr. Villard and his associates.[2] Where the burden of loss will finally rest this time remains to be seen.

The story of what has occurred in the last two weeks shows the terrific power possessed by great financial interests when they come in conflict. The beginning was with the purchase of Burlington. That operation changed the balance of power and set at work the forces which have since been so influential in making prices.

The Burlington purchase and the establishment of the Hill-Morgan transcontinental line developed personal antagonisms, long existing, but which flamed up under new possibilities in railway control. We do not know what particular match may have fired the flame, but the explosion took the form of large buying of Union Pacific with the avowed purpose of wresting control from the Harriman syndicate. Immense counter-buying followed, with a semi-official announcement at its close that the Harriman interest remained in control of Union Pacific.

Then the war was carried into Africa. The Harriman syndicate bought Northern Pacific quietly but diligently until, about the middle of last week, it had nearly, if not quite, control of that stock. Selling was partly by insiders who knew that the stock was too high and partly by foreign interests either to realize or for short account. Intimations were then given to the Northern Pacific management that certain measures were desirable, failing which they might be enforced. It was not, however, a declaration of war, but an invitation to peace.

Northern Pacific people did not accept the assurances tendered and thought it necessary to secure safety by largely increased ownership of Northern Pacific stock. Enormous buying orders went into the market and continued up to Tuesday afternoon, when it became apparent that the two great buyers had purchased more stock than there was in existence, and that a close corner had been created without such an intention on the part of either interest.

The situation was extraordinary. Where a corner is undertaken deliberately, the purpose is to compel covering. The owners of the stock wish to sell, and settlement is merely a matter of price. In this case the purpose was entirely different. The object was the accumulation of certificates possessing voting power, and not at all profits on transactions. Hence, the holders of the stock were practically unable to accept private settlements or to release contracts. To do so was to relinquish the very purpose for which the stock had been bought.

The position of the buyers was this: "We do not want your money or to cause you losses, but you must give us the certificates which you have agreed to deliver." As the stock sold amounted to more than 100,000 shares in excess of the stock in existence, it was obviously impossible for everybody to get stock. In the effort to do so, the price was run above 180, and the Street was full of anxious brokers and traders all day.

One of the large interests involved announced early in the day that it would lead stock to arbitrage houses flat as long as the books remained open, this being intended to give such houses time to receive stock on the way from Europe. The offer gave great relief to houses doing a legitimate foreign business. It was also regarded as a great generosity in the house which did this, as it loaned stock flat when borrowers would have been very willing to pay 1 or 2 per cent a day premium, and would have been compelled to pay any premium that might have been demanded.

Anxiety was felt in regard to the closing of Northern Pacific books, which it was thought might be essential in the contest. The management announced, however, that there would be no sudden closing, and anxiety need not exist on that account.

The outcome can take one of three forms. One party can take control and the other can take profits on long stock, or the other party can retain control with assurances bearing upon other properties which will be satisfactory, or a general compromise can be made covering various interests and permitting a return to normal conditions. The effect, even if the contest ends in a compromise, will be unfortunate in its bearings on the general market.

May 10, 1901

The Northern Pacific corner brought a panic in the general list. While Northern Pacific soared from $200 to $1,000 per share for cash stock, other stocks fell from 10 to 60 points, carrying disaster to margin accounts and loss to operators of all classes.[3] The fact that Northern Pacific was unobtainable created the gravest apprehension as to what houses might or might not prove to be solvent, and this caused sacrifice sales without regard to price. Delaware & Hudson, Atchison, Manhattan and Union Pacific furnished striking illustrations.

The panic was at its height when, about noon, Kuhn, Loeb & Co. authorized an announcement that Northern Pacific would not be bought in under the rule during the day. This was followed immediately by a similar announcement from J. P. Morgan & Co. The relief was immediate, and stocks rallied from 5 to 50 points in the next hour.

A sagging market prevailed during the afternoon on an idea that the corner might be found in force again today. Just at 3 o'clock, however, an official announcement was made that, as a result of conferences between representatives of Morgan & Co. and Kuhn, Loeb & Co., arrangements would probably be made by which shorts would be allowed to settle their contracts at very reasonable prices, and the corner would be at an end.

This was not known in time to be reflected in prices at the close, but after hours the relief was very great, and prices considerably above closing figures were bid for leading stocks, under an impression that the arrangement with shorts would be found part of a general settlement which would remove difficulties and bring support into the market, with activity and higher prices today.

This reasoning was based upon the proposition that control of Northern Pacific had been the key of the whole difficulty. There could be no arrangement with shorts without agreement as to how short contracts were to be treated with reference to competitive holdings of stock. No official information was given on this point. It was known, however, that Kuhn, Loeb & Co. had offered to arrange a settlement with shorts and then apply the contracts owned pro rata to certificates actually held, so as to preserve the relative status of the two parties in interest.

It is possible, if not probable, that the settlement has taken a much broader scope. It may be found to include adjustment of questions which have been vexatious since the Burlington deal began to be discussed. If this is the case, it will be all the better for the market, as all interests would then unite in endeavoring to restore the confidence that has been so rudely shaken in the last few days.

The fact that no failures have occurred shows that great leniency must have been extended not only by banks which made arrangements to provide money, but by the holders of Northern Pacific contracts. An effort has clearly been made to preserve the Street as far as possible from the ill effects of a complication which was the result of accident rather than design.

Another point of great importance is the character of the panic itself. It came not through overtrading, not through dear money, although money became dear, and not through calamity, but through the determination of two powerful interests to control a railway property. It was a panic made by determined investment in Northern Pacific rather than by wild speculation.

The absence of failures among brokers proves furthermore that the Street was in a sound position, and that despite the high prices, brokers either had their accounts well protected, or were able to stand the sudden sweeping away of margins without embarrassment.

The panic was a very bad thing for those who lost money or who have been crippled by their commitments. It will be a good thing for those who have been waiting to make investments and who will welcome the level of prices which prevailed at times during the day.

Atchison preferred, Union Pacific common, and Louisville & Nashville around 90, St. Paul below 150, Burlington below 185, Manhattan below 110, and other good stocks at proportionate prices, offer very much better inducements for purchase than have lately prevailed. The country is all right and with special difficulties removed, there will be good recoveries.

May 14, 1901

The Northern Pacific corner was the most remarkable event in American railway affairs. There have been other close corners. Commodore Vanderbilt made one in Harlem for the punishment of faithless legislators. Mr. Gould, when he was only a stock operator and not the far-sighted financier which he became, created a corner in Northwest. Mr. John Duff took tribute from the Street in the Hannibal & St. Joe corner, although he was crushed in the ruins of the structure which he and Mr. Hutchinson built. These and other corners, however, were intentional. They were run for the purpose of taking profits from people who had sold what they were not able to deliver.

The Northern Pacific corner was of another sort. It was neither intended nor desired. It was almost as repulsive to its promoters as it was to its victims. It produced a strange and terrible situation where upright and kindly men found themselves obliged either to prove faithless to trusts which had been reposed in them or to crush innocent people, including some of their own friends. It was for a time an impasse from which there was no going forward nor back.

Let us see what produced this condition of affairs. In the year 1900 a new phrase became current in the railway world. It was called community of ownership. It originated in an agreement between Mr. William K. Vanderbilt and Mr. Cassatt, whereby New York Central and Pennsylvania people were to acquire and hold stocks of other roads for the purpose of avoiding unnecessary railroad building, securing the maintenance of rates, and establishing harmony between the trunk lines from the shore of Lake Ontario to the southern limits of Norfolk & Western.

Excellent results followed, and community of ownership became a potent phrase in its bearing upon railway stocks, because it suggested a method of overcoming serious difficulties and of establishing conditions which seemed to assure peace between railway lines.

It was apparent that if community of ownership were desirable east of the Mississippi, it was equally desirable in its application to the Granger, the Pacific and the southwestern roads. Great plans began to be undertaken. There was an alliance between Great Northern and

Northern Pacific, Mr. Hill becoming the largest stockholder in the line most closely competing with his own. The Vanderbilts absorbed roads in their territory. Steps were taken toward a combination of Gould lines and an extension of the Gould system. Union Pacific grasped the enormous mileage of Southern Pacific, and Reading absorbed Jersey Central.

These various combinations brought in some cases mutterings of discontent, but they were drowned by the acclaim of those who approved the new alliances.

The first real difficulty grew out of the attempt to secure control of St. Paul. Stock was bought in quantity, but the wish of Hill-Morgan interests to acquire St. Paul was defeated partly by the refusal of some of the large holders to sell their preferred stock and partly on account of the opposition of one of the great capitalists, who had other plans in mind.

Then followed the move which has aroused disagreements so radical in their character as to impair personal relations of long standing, to draw new lines between friends and enemies, to compel enormous investments to secure or to retain railway control and to produce all the evils which burst out in the Northern Pacific panic.

The event which led to all this was the purchase of control of Burlington & Quincy by Northern Pacific and Great Northern. Mr. Hill was the inspiring cause. With a breadth of vision which has been unsurpassed in railway affairs, he saw that the growth of business in the Far East made it desirable in the highest degree that the Northern Pacific-Great Northern Pacific system should expand its eastern terminals so as to cover the agricultural regions traversed by lines of the Burlington system. There was probably a wish to derive advantage, also, from the combination of Northern Pacific, Burlington and Erie as a through line, but this was a minor rather than a primary point. The great point was that possession of Burlington put Northern Pacific in a dominating position in the Northwest.

The effect would be to relegate Union Pacific to the second place. This situation came home with great force to the banking house of Kuhn, Loeb & Co., which stood as the representative of Union Pacific interests. It had also been in close relation with Mr. Hill for many years. On one side of the problem lay the possible impairment of established and friendly relations. On the other was the duty of protecting Union Pacific stockholders.

It was pointed out that Burlington paralleled Union Pacific through Kansas and Nebraska: that by means of the western branches of Burlington, Northern Pacific was brought down in Denver: that the western terminus of Burlington approached Salt Lake, with the possibility of a connection with the Clark road to the Pacific, and that Burlington as an independent property had been an aggressive and at times dangerous competitor of Union Pacific. What, then, it was asked, would be its policy and its possibilities under the control of a railway man so able and aggressive as Mr. Hill was known to be?

The first step was to endeavor to reach an agreement. Union Pacific people questioned Mr. Hill as to the reported purchases of Burlington, but received unsatisfactory answers. Within a short time, positive evidence was acquired that Northern Pacific–Great Northern people had been the buyers of Burlington, and a formal conference was held at the house of Mr. G. F. Baker to see if some arrangement could be made. Mr. Hill would not make or accept propositions, and the Union Pacific people then endeavored to reach some agreement with Mr. Morgan.

Two general propositions were made. The first was that Union Pacific interests should be allowed to buy a portion of the Burlington stock which had been acquired by Northern Pacific and Great Northern and participate with Northern Pacific in such traffic relations as might be established. The second proposition was that an agreement should be made with a view to maintaining the integrity of the Union Pacific territory and the maintenance of certain relations with connecting roads. Mr. Morgan had left for Europe before these propositions were fully considered, but the decision of the Hill-Morgan interest was that it was impracticable to change arrangements which had been made or to bring Union Pacific into the combination.

Union Pacific interests then gave formal notice that the acquisition of Burlington would be regarded as an unfriendly act, and that they should be obliged to take such action as seemed necessary for self-protection. Answer was given that while there was no wish to disturb harmonious relations and no intention of treating Union Pacific unfairly, the case would have to stand where it was, let the consequences be what they might.

The Union Pacific syndicate decided that protection could be obtained only by the ownership of such an amount of Northern Pacific stock as would entitle it to a strong representation in the Northern Pacific board. The people who purchased control of Southern Pacific without a whisper of the negotiations being heard in the Street needed no advice as to the best methods of securing Northern Pacific stock. While the Street saw an exhibition of fireworks in Union Pacific and heard stories of buying for control, Kuhn, Loeb & Co. bought in the market and at private sale here and abroad, quietly but rapidly, large amounts of Northern Pacific stock.

On Friday, May 3rd, Union Pacific interests held over $65,000,000 of Northern Pacific stock, and [were] again seeking peace rather than controversy. Mr. Hill was notified of this fact and informed that the stock had been acquired, not with a wish to change the management, but solely for the purpose of protecting Union Pacific. Union Pacific asked for a reasonable representation in the Northern Pacific board, and promised to use its influence and its vote in favor of keeping J. P. Morgan & Co. in control as long as there was no aggression by Northern Pacific in Union Pacific territory. It was supposed that this would be satisfactory to all interests. But it was not.

Northern Pacific people decided that divided ownership was impracticable, and that the advantage of absolute control of Northern Pacific should not be surrendered without a struggle. The ownership of the comparatively small amount of Northern Pacific required to give absolute control became at once a vital necessity to both parties. On Monday and Tuesday last Northern Pacific soared under competitive buying in which the price to be paid was immaterial. As the price advanced, stock continued to be sold, and each party, knowing the skill and resources of the other, kept on buying until, as the world knows, the Kuhn, Loeb interest and the Morgan interest owned every share of Northern Pacific stock in existence and approximately 150,000 shares which had no existence.

It is not too much to say that both interests were appalled by this result. It was apparent that control would be determined by the certificates owned and not by the contracts held. Each, therefore, was obliged to pursue a course which would make short sellers strain every nerve to secure certificates with which to make good their contracts. There was no intention on the part of either to compel speculative losses. Each wished to mitigate the dangers and the cruelties of the corner in every way that did not entail the loss of the precious certificates carrying control.

The high prices obtained for Northern Pacific on Wednesday and Thursday were not obtained by Morgan & Co., nor by Kuhn, Loeb & Co. They were obtained by scattered holders over the country.

As soon as it became evident that a close corner existed, there was great anxiety on the part of the victims, including many wealthy and powerful people. The better the facts and the necessities in the case were understood, the greater the anxiety.

Arbitrage dealers at once made strong representations that they ought not to be punished for the transactions of a legitimate business which made them borrowers of stock while the actual certificates were on the water. Both Morgan & Co. and Kuhn, Loeb & Co. decided at once that they would lend stock flat to arbitrage houses. Anxiety was then felt lest there should be a sudden closing of the Northern Pacific books, but Morgan & Co. quieted this alarm by stating that there would be no sudden closing or other steps calculated to require their opponents to call in loaned stock.

Forbearance was extended in many cases. Kuhn, Loeb & Co. loaned stock freely to those who had sold trust receipts for cash instead of stock. Morgan & Co. expedited the transfer of trust receipts into certificates, although in so doing, they were in many cases changing trust receipts which could have been voted by them into stock liable to be voted by their opponents. Stock was loaned to people on their word of honor that the certificates would be returned the next day no matter what prices then prevailed, and in only one or two cases was this confidence abused.

The honor of Wall Street came to the front impressively. Houses which had sold Northern Pacific on sellers' option and which by a breach of good faith could have made large differences, delivered their stock ahead of time, as one such house said, "to remove temptation." Stock was delivered at a low price when by breaking a promise a high price could have been had. There was strong pressure to induce the great interests to terminate the corner by agreement between themselves. But there was very little effort on the part of shorts to evade their responsibilities. Customers and brokers lost great sums with a smile because their word was pledged.

Conferences were held at intervals all Thursday. Various methods of settlement were suggested, but they involved danger to one side or the other in a contest where the outcome was so evenly balanced. Kuhn, Loeb & Co. offered to settle all purchases of short stock pro rata to holdings of actual certificates so as to end the corner with altering the relative position of the two parties, but the proposition was not accepted.

It was evident, however, that the buying in of stock Thursday under the conditions which then existed would be to break the Street, and it was agreed by both parties that deliveries should not be enforced that day.

Legal proceedings were started with reference to tying up transactions, but they did not affect the actual outcome. Before any knowledge of such proceedings was received, Kuhn, Loeb & Co. decided to settle all short contracts with them on the basis of 150 without any agreement as to the bearing of such settlement on the contest for control. Morgan & Co. decided to adopt the same course, and about 3 o'clock Thursday afternoon the Northern Pacific corner came to an end as far as this market was concerned, with settlements at a price only a shade above the market prices for Northern Pacific on Tuesday.

Neither party wished to make anything out of the corner, and it is probably accurate to say that neither did make any considerable sum or any sum that would not have been gladly forfeited to have avoided the injury done by the corner and by panic which ensued.

The settlement of the corner did not settle the question of control of Northern Pacific. With the short interest located, it was possible for each interest to count its certificates and to know the result. Each interest announced itself in control.

As the houses of Kuhn, Loeb & Co. and Morgan & Co. are composed of men who would not speak lightly in such a matter, it is certain that the statement of each is believed by those who make it. It follows that conditions exist which make the question of control somewhat more involved than appears on the surface.

We understand the point to be this: Kuhn, Loeb & Co. own a majority of the stock, as shown by actual certificates, including common and preferred. Morgan & Co. own a majority of the common stock. It is possible for the preferred stock of Northern Pacific to be retired next January. Should this be done, the majority of Kuhn, Loeb & Co. would be wiped out and Morgan & Co. would be in control. The annual election of Northern Pacific occurs in October. Should it be held at that time, and should present ownership be unchanged, the Kuhn, Loeb interest would win, but should, as the result of legal action, the election be deferred until after the first of January, Morgan & Co. would win.

It seems probable that in a situation so nearly balanced and with men of the largest ability confronting the facts, there will be found some solution of the difficulty. Mr. Hill in his interviews has said some rather hard things. Otherwise, the respective interests speak of each other in terms of mutual respect and good will.

None know better that community of ownership can be made a vital force for good. Instead of a prolonged controversy, liable to injure all interests in the end, there should be the broad view of how the great concentrated ownerships in Northern Pacific, Great Northern, Union Pacific, Southern Pacific and Burlington can be utilized in their bearing upon the Granger and Pacific roads so as to maintain lasting peace and prosperity.

May 21, 1901

We have usually after panics figured out the movement for the purpose of testing in each case the theory that the swing of prices in and after a panic is always the same in character although, of course, not in extent. The figures have almost invariably shown first a severe drop, then a strong recovery, and then a relapse, carrying prices back from one-half to two-thirds the amount of the recovery.

It will be seen from the table following that the decline was very severe and the rally correspondingly strong, amounting in every case to more than half the loss, and in most cases to about two-thirds of the loss.

The succeeding relapse, however, was not up to the average decline in such cases. There were only a few instances where the relapse amounted to half of the recovery, which is decidedly abnormal, and suggests that we may not have had what will be recognized hereafter as the relapse following the recovery.

The moves up to date have been very rapid. We had the drop, the recovery, and the relapse all within a week, when, as a rule, the relapse does not come until from two to four weeks after the first drop. This, therefore, raises the question whether the decline which came on the 11th and 15th was not merely an echo of the panic itself and not the sagging decline which usually occurs in such cases. It may be answered that favorable conditions will prevent the market having its normal movement, or it may be that the normal movement has yet to come.

The table shows the decline from the high point this year, occurring usually either in the last week of April or the first week in May, to the low point on the 9th. The recovery is from the low point on the 9th to the highest on the 13th, while the relapse is to the low prices of the 15th. Since that time, the greater part of this decline has been recovered, showing the market at present relatively high compared with the lowest on the 9th:

Stock	Panic Fall	Recovery	Relapse
Atchison common	17	33	11
Atchison preferred	38	28	8
Baltimore & Ohio common	30	21	10
Bklyn. Rapid Transit	20	9	9
Canadian Pacific	30	23	12
Chesapeake & Ohio	23	18	4
Burlington & Quincy	21	14	3
St. Paul	54	29	18
Rock Island	35	28	13
Delaware & Hudson	80	60	28
Erie common	19	12	6
Louisville & Nashville	35	27	8
Manhattan	48	32	10
Missouri Pacific	44	36	18
New York Central	30	15	10
Union Pacific	57	47	28
Amalgamated Copper	38	32	21
People's Gas	21	13	8
U.S. Steel common	31	22	7

It seems to be a law of panics that the stocks which have the largest preceding advances have also the largest declines. Illustrations of this are afforded by the extent of the decline in Atchison common, St. Paul, Rock Island, Delaware & Hudson, Missouri Pacific and Union Pacific. Brooklyn Rapid Transit afforded a surprise in that it fell only 20 points, a striking contrast to its weakness in 1899, when it suffered from having been overbulled.

The factors entering into different stocks were illustrated by the varying relapses after the first recovery. For instance, Union Pacific, although a good stock, relapsed 28 points, while Burlington & Quincy, sustained by knowledge of the purchase, fell only 3. Delaware & Hudson declined 28 points on account of the absence of any general support and the uneasiness occasioned by the preceding break to 105. Stocks somewhat similarly situated, as, for instance, Atchison, Baltimore & Ohio, Canadian Pacific, Rock Island and Manhattan, declined almost alike.

The great lesson taught by panics always is that in times of great anxiety and fear, values are disregarded, and the best stocks go off as much or more than the worst. Indeed, when people have to have money, they sell the best stocks because there is some market for them, while there is no market at all for others. Furthermore, the best stocks are likely to be in loans, and loans are sold out, while the poorer stocks which have been paid for do not come out because they are not forced out.

The decline emphasizes the inherent weakness of margin trading in times of danger. Of what use was a 10 per cent margin to either broker or customer on the 9th of May? Of course, such periods are exceptions, but they occur and must therefore be included in any calculations that are made. The man who during the past thirty days traded cautiously, paying for stocks outright or having very large reserves, was able to go through the panic practically without loss, because of the large recovery. He, therefore, did not see the profits of months of trading swept away in an hour and before it was possible for him to be notified that his account was in danger.

It shows also from the standpoint of the customer the value of stop orders. There was an hour or more when stop orders were worse than useless. But it is safe to say that anybody who had any amount of stock bought at the highest price prevailing this year, and who had protected that purchase by a stop order at two points would have seen his account closed with a loss very little in excess of the two points. In other words, stop orders generally would have been executed before the market began to break. After the break came, the obvious thing was for a buyer with available money or credit to seize the good stocks which were being slaughtered.

May 25, 1901

Crops will probably be the next essential factor in speculation. We do not mean in the narrow sense of movements in special stocks, but in the large sense of affording a basis on which there will be a broad general move through the active list. Crops are always of the utmost importance in their relation to the prices of stocks. It is an exception when the stock of a railway advances materially in a year when there is serious crop damage on its lines. Northern Pacific and Great Northern have furnished such an exception in the past year, but there were special causes, now well known, which produced this result. Furthermore, the crop damage was only partial, affecting the eastern lines especially, while the cattle trade and the lumber trade on the Central and Pacific divisions made good a considerable part of the loss.

The exceptions in such cases only prove the rule, and the rule is that no great interest would undertake to bull stocks in a large way in the face of serious crop damage. This is all the more important now on account of the high level of prices and the high level of earnings. Serious crop damage would cut down earnings to more than the normal extent because comparison would be made with earnings above the average in amount. Furthermore, the new combinations, which have been brought about by the purchase of stocks at high prices, would be affected very materially by any conditions which indicated that the purchased roads would not be able to pay dividends sufficient to make good the fixed charges entailed by the issue of collateral trust or convertible bonds. In other words, roads like Northern Pacific, Great Northern, Union Pacific and Missouri Pacific will be more sensitive, as far as stock values are concerned, to crops this year than they would have been in some years that are past.

This fact will make the great interests identified with those properties, and with the market generally, indisposed to make large commitments or to take decided positions marketwise until they can foresee, with approximate certainty, what the great crops in the territory traversed by those lines are likely to do. If wheat and corn are up to or above an average, there will be a good deal of confidence that earnings can be maintained near the present level, which means the ability of Burlington and Northern Pacific and Union Pacific to continue dividends at present rates, but, if the great crops should be short, it would have an effect not only in the loss of crop tonnage but in the loss to tonnage indirectly due to crops. Furthermore, operators watching these conditions would consider the market vulnerable in that case and would be likely to undertake somewhat extended operations for a fall.

It is not uncommon to point to the assassination of Mr. Garfield in July, 1881, as the turning point in the bull period which ended that year. As a matter of fact, the high prices of that period were made in the month of May, and the assassination of Garfield, while a depressing incident in the market, would probably have had only a temporary effect on prices but for the drought of that summer, which greatly lessened the corn crop and was the real foundation for the bear campaign which was carried on in the fall of the succeeding winter of that year. Large operators then saw that certain interests were loaded with stocks bought at high prices. They saw that earnings under existing crop conditions could not be maintained and that the time was ripe for a campaign on the short side. Mr. Gould and Mr. Vanderbilt were the great operators then long of stocks and were obliged to fight a defensive campaign for four years before they could fully extricate themselves. Mr. Keene and Mr. Woerishoffer were the bear leaders of that period, working with the situation which was made possible by the high prices and by the corn failure of 1881.

Should there be serious crop damage this year, there will be found those who will take advantage of the resulting loss in business and profits. Hence, every great interest will be disposed to delay operations and postpone commitments until there can be a reasonably correct forecast of crop possibilities this year.

May 29, 1901

We give in tables following the movement of a few active stocks in the panics of 1873, 1884, 1893, 1895 and 1901. The figures include the high prices prevailing shortly before the panic, in some cases those the day previous, and in others several days prior thereto. The low prices are the low points in the panic. The recovery given is to prices established within a week of the low point in the panic, coming in some cases within a few days and others not until nearly a week afterwards.

We are accustomed to think of the panic of 1873 as a very serious event. It was sufficiently serious to compel the closing of the Stock Exchange, but the decline, outside of Lake Shore and Western Union, seems singularly small in view of losses which have been seen since. The panic itself was the culmination of a feverish market which had lasted all the week, the final break coming on Saturday. The average decline in that panic for nine active stocks was 10.32 per cent. Figures follow:

1873 Panic	*High*	*Low*	*Decline*	*Recovery*
N.Y. Central	95	89	6	6
Erie	56⅛	50¾	5⅜	2⅜
Lake Shore	88	68	20	11
Wabash	50	42½	7½	7
Rock Island	95	86	9	10½
St. Paul	37½	30	7½	5½
Lackawanna	92½	86	6½	7⅛
Western Union	76	54½	21¾	19¼

The panic of 1884 reflected a larger average movement of prices, the losses of May 13–16 running from 8 to 15 points. The panic proper covered two days, while the recovery for ten stocks amounted to about five-eighths of the loss. Details follow:

1884 Panic	*High*	*Low*	*Decline*	*Recovery*
Lake Shore	94	81	13	8⅞
Rock Island	116¼	109½	6¾	6¼
St. Paul	77	65	12	7⅝
Burlington	118	114¼	3¾	3¾
Louisville	44	30¼	14¾	5
Missouri Pacific	80	65	15	7¼
Union Pacific	50	41½	8½	3⅞
Western Union	60	51¾	8¼	5⅞

The panic of 1893 was not very severe in the extent of the losses. The average fall in thirteen stocks was 7.34 per cent, and in only a few cases did the loss exceed 10 points. In the leading stocks quoted the losses were from 7 to 9 points, while the recovery was in nearly every case larger than the panic decline.

1893 Panic	*High*	*Low*	*Decline*	*Recovery*
Burlington	74	69¼	4¾	10¾
St. Paul	52	46⅜	5⅝	9
Rock Island	58	53	5	8¼
Louisville	53	47½	7½	10⅛
Missouri Pacific	23	16⅓	6½	6½
Sugar	73	66¾	6¼	8⅜
Chicago Gas	53	43½	9½	8¾
Western Union	75	67½	7½	10⅝

The Venezuela panic of 1895 was about equal in intensity to the panics of 1873 and 1884.[4] The average of fifteen stocks fell 9.72 per cent and a considerable proportion of the losses exceeded 10 points. The recovery was normal, about two-thirds the amount of the decline.

1895 Panic	*High*	*Low*	*Decline*	*Recovery*
Burlington	81⅝	70	11⅝	7½
St. Paul	72⅜	60½	11⅞	7½
Rock Island	72½	59	13½	10
N.Y. Central	98	90½	7½	7¼
Louisville	49⅛	39	10⅛	6¼
Missouri Pacific	27⅝	19½	8⅛	6¼
Jersey Central	105½	93	12½	8¼
Sugar	100½	92	8½	7⅞
Chicago Gas	68½	57½	11	7⅞
Western Union	88¼	82½	5¾	4¼

The following shows the fluctuation in a few stocks in the panic of 1901:

1901 Panic	*High*	*Low*	*Decline*	*Recovery*
Atchison common	90¼	43	47¼	33
Burlington	199⅞	178	21⅞	14½
St. Paul	188	134	54	29½
Rock Island	169⅞	125	44⅞	28
Louisville	111½	76	35½	27¾
Manhattan	131¾	83	48¾	32¾
Missouri Pacific	116¾	72	44¾	36½
N.Y. Central	170	140	30	15
Union Pacific	133	76	57	47½
Amalgamated Copper	128½	90	38½	32
Tobacco	130⅞	99	31⅞	25¾
Peoples Gas	119½	98½	21	13¼
U.S. Steel common	55	24	31	22

The declines are amazing when compared with the losses in other panics. Drops exceeded 40 points each in Atchison, St. Paul, Rock Island, Manhattan, Missouri Pacific and Union Pacific. The figures showing the high point were in some cases a week or more before the low point, but the drop as between the close May 8th and the low point May 9th covered in most cases a large proportion of the total decline.

The recovery was equally noteworthy. Union Pacific fell 57 points and rose 47½ points within one week. Missouri Pacific fell 44¾ points and recovered 36½ points in the same time. Other changes were almost as pronounced, going to show that in the extent of the fluctuations the panic this month was not to be named in the same breath with any panic record in the past.

It came and went so swiftly as to leave onlookers almost dazed. The speed and the extent of the recovery was all that saved the panic from being a financial catastrophe.

A long train of ills followed the smaller declines in panics past. The ills would have been a calamity had the low prices of May 9 continued for twenty-four hours. As it was, it will probably be a long time before the last of the effects of this great drop are felt.

The fluctuations show that while investment stock was not greatly disturbed and while commission houses proved to be strong enough to endure the strain without failure, the large trading which has been the feature of the market this year resulted in a rush to sell which carried prices far below what the decline would have been under normal selling pressure.

In other words, a great market represented by transactions of from two to three million shares a day, carries with it the possibility of movements in prices as much greater than normal as is the volume of trading greater than normal. There is a relation between the volume of business and the movement of prices. Great activity means great movements whenever the normal balance between buyers and sellers is violently disturbed.[5]

June 8, 1901

There is always a disposition in people's minds to think that existing conditions will be permanent. When the market is down and dull, it is hard to make people believe that this is the prelude to a period of activity and advance. When prices are up and the country is prosperous, it is always said that while preceding booms have not lasted, there are circumstances connected with this one which make it unlike its predecessors and give assurance of permanency.

The one fact pertaining to all conditions is that they will change. This change follows modifications of the law of supply and demand. The cycle of trade is well known. Beginning with a period of depression, the small dealer finds himself unable to buy the amount of goods required for hand-to-mouth trading quite as cheaply as when the previous purchase was made. He, therefore, buys a little more. The aggregate of this buying increases the business of the jobber, and this swells the output of the manufacturer, who is enabled to employ more labor, resulting in larger purchases by labor of manufactured goods and agricultural products, which brings the circle round to the producer.

At each step in the proceedings, rising prices bring increased purchases and increased confidence, until the retailer buys without hesitation many times the amount of goods which he would have dared to take at the beginning of the cycle of improving trade. This multiplied by millions makes the demand which at times seems inexhaustible, which supplies the railroads with tonnage, and which in its ramifications creates the investment fund which finally seeks employment in Wall Street.

The declining period is accompanied by steady reversal of these varied transactions. When the retailer and the jobber find that goods cost less than before, they shrink purchases. When purchases in advance of requirements bring loss and not profit, they bring also loss of confidence and curtailment of demand. As the process of shrinkage goes on, it touches all points of trade. It is a kind of flame which creates the fuel which is burned.

Experience has shown that it takes about five years for one of these cycles to complete itself. It takes approximately five years for the country bare of stocks to become the country filled with stocks, and it takes about five years more for the overstocked markets of the country or of the world to become practically bare.

As the stock market is always an effect and never a cause, it must respond to these conditions. As, however, the stock market, while an effect, is also a discounted effect, the decline in prices of stocks usually anticipates decline in commodities, because operators for a fall sell in anticipation of the changes which they foresee in business conditions.

The cause of the next depression in stocks will be a falling off in general trade. It will be distinguished by reduced clearings, decreased railroad earnings, a smaller demand for stable goods, smaller exchanges at the clearing house, an increased amount of idle money and smaller additions to the country's wealth.

There are local causes likely to be influential. One will be the effects of commitments by existing corporations. It will be found in some cases that railroad earnings for the future have been overestimated and that the decrease in net will cut seriously into the dividend fund. The probability of decreased or passed dividends will have a direct bearing on many stocks. Loss in industrial profits will bring decline in some industrial properties. New railroad building will threaten the stability of some railway properties.

The buying up of existing roads has for its primary object the reduction of competition by centralizing management. This will be effective as far as it goes, and in many cases it will go far. The high valuation which has been placed on stocks purchased for control will, however, be a strong incentive to the building of competing lines. It will be argued that if an existing road is worth par for the common stock for control, a new road in the same general section will be worth something more than the actual cost of construction; hence, can be financed with profit to the builder and then perhaps sold with substantial profit to the owners.

This is sure to become a matter of importance. When it is known that parallel lines are being built from one point to another, the knowledge will have a depressing effect on the securities of existing companies, because it will be said that the new road will either get business and live, in which case it will take business from the old company, or it will have to be bought up, entailing a burden on the old company for the support of mileage not required by the business in that section.

The same thing will be true to an even greater extent in the industrial field. The difficulty of paralleling an industrial is trifling, except in a few cases, compared with the difficulty in paralleling a railroad. Yet the opportunity for profit in this will be so great as to insure such building. It will be feasible in many cases in the next few years to sell short a substantial line of an industrial stock, then build a competing plant and operate it so as to take away the profits of the other company, thereby causing a large decline in the stock, which can then be bought at a profit to the short seller. Then, when the down-cycle is complete and the up-cycle begins, the two establishments can combine, issue new stock to the promoters at nominal prices, and by the development of business and the payment of substantial dividends obtain a market for this stock at high prices two or three years later.

We do not know just when the period of decline will begin, nor what properties will most keenly feel its effects, but the general course of events along the lines outlined can be predicted with as much certainty as could have been any of the cycles of the past.[6]

June 27, 1901

The Seventh National Bank incident was briefly this. Customers of the bank drew largely upon its resources, and for a few hours the bank was in delay at the clearing house. Friends of the bank advanced the money, required payments were completed, and outwardly the incident closed, although there were supplemental rumors.

The importance of the matter lies in the fact that a period of prosperity, advancing prices and the development of new enterprises always brings into existence securities which are regarded as promising, but which prove in the end to have been overvalued.

The people who bring out such enterprises are sometimes identified with banks or financial institutions, and, if not, they establish sooner or later relations by means of which they secure loans on this collateral. These loans are sometimes made for personal reasons, sometimes through mistaken judgment as to the value of the property covered, and sometimes through deception on the part of promoters. It ends, however, in the possession by bankers or financial institutions of unmarketable collateral, which at times is sufficient to create financial difficulties.

In a period of declining prices, when bank failures occur and confidence is shaken, it almost invariably transpires that the primary cause of failure was lending money on bad collateral. We do not say that the Seventh National or any of its clients have been doing this. We only mean to say that any bank difficulty, even of an unimportant character, is likely to suggest anew the dangers which exist in such periods.

The great decline in 1899 was due almost wholly to the fact that in the capitalization of industrial corporations bankers and brokers had become tied up in underwriting syndicates to an extent which was a source of embarrassment, danger and loss. Bear operators utilized knowledge of this fact to depress prices, and they will do it again whenever there is evidence that similar conditions exist. For this reason, the lightest talk involving the responsibility of any financial concern has weight and a tendency to check purchases and increase sales of stock.

The action of the banks during the past month has a bearing upon this very point. It is a time when the surplus reserve should be at its highest and when the banks should accumulate cash in anticipation of the crop movement. On the contrary, the banks have this year gone on increasing loans and deposits; considerable numbers of banks carrying their reserve below the 25 per cent limit and letting it remain there until the end of June will see the smallest surplus reserve on record for that time coupled with loans well up to the largest on record.

There are two ways of looking at this. One is to say that the banks have encouraged loans, accepting indifferent collateral and making rates comparatively low because great interests connected with banks have been interested in securities and disposed to promote expansion.

The other method of stating the case is to say that the bank situation is not what it seems. That is, loans are of a character which may be very rapidly reduced. Money has been loaned freely, notwithstanding the low reserve, on knowledge that the July disbursements and syndicate payments will increase the volume of cash and pull down the aggregate of loans and deposits.

The chances are that a majority of the great bankers think they see their way to supplies of money for the autumn; hence, feel justified in the course which has been pursued. The effort to get out time money continues, and yesterday was the first day on which rates for call money were higher. Dear money at the close of this week would not necessarily mean dear money after the first. But it is essential that the banks during July should make preparations for autumn requirements if they expect confidence to be maintained.

June 28, 1901

The affairs of the Seventh National Bank were again the factor in the market. The declaration that the difficulties of the bank had been straightened out proved incorrect, and the formal closing of the institution proved over again that when difficulties with a firm or a bank become acute it is not easy to tide over all the problems that arise.

It is in character like the common announcement after a failure that the concern will pay creditors in full. Any concern which is able to pay creditors in full does not fail. The troubles of banks do not generally reach the point of official scrutiny without deep-seated difficulties.

The failure of the Seventh National was followed by declining prices, not because of the importance of the bank nor particularly on account of transactions of those who have done a large business with the bank, but because of the point made in this column yesterday; namely, that it suggested similar difficulties as yet unknown, but existing elsewhere and with the liability of cropping out unexpectedly.

Nothing is more certain than that a rising tide of speculation floats poor as well as good collateral. When the tide turns, the poor collateral is stranded, remaining in the unwilling possession of individuals or institutions because no market can be found, while the good collateral continues to float because its marketability enables it to be shifted from one person to another whereby the loss, when there is a loss, is minimized.

We do not know that there are other banks which are facing large losses through accommodation loans, but it is extremely probable that there are cases of that kind, which will be brought to the surface sooner or later through the locking up of capital, and with the effect of increasing financial anxiety perhaps at a time when there is anxiety enough. Knowledge that this is so explains the sensitiveness of the Street to financial rumors and suggests that, as the newspapers spread the facts bearing upon the Seventh National, the tendency to sell stocks will be increased, while the tendency to buy them will be temporarily lessened.

It is not known whether the market has yet seen its highest point for the period. Many well-informed people believe that it has not, in spite of the fact that the fullness of time for a speculative up-cycle has come. When it does come, however, one of the indications that descent has begun will be the recurrence of developments like those attending the Seventh National. Bricks here and there in the long row which represents financial conditions will fall, and their fall will cause others to topple over, making gaps in the line.

The greater the advance, the larger the volume of new securities, the greater the number of new stocks, the more numerous such difficulties will be, because of the greater number of unsound ventures. There has been great increase in capitalization, a vast number of new corporations have come into existence, and millions upon millions of new securities have been launched, if not distributed. All this is well known and in a broad sense is a cause for apprehension, not necessarily now, but in the future.

Offsetting the anxieties and the doubts which exist are favorable considerations. No small part of the prosperity of this country in the last few years has been due to good crops in the United States and comparatively poor crops abroad. It has been feared that the reverse might be true this year, but indications are that the winter wheat crop will be a full average and the spring wheat crop materially in excess of last year. It seems also probable that the French and German wheat crops will be below an average and that the crop year will begin with the available stocks comparatively small. This points to continuance of large exports of breadstuffs and to prices which will give the farmer a good return for his products. No one fact would be considered by Wall Street leaders as more important than that the balance of trade should be largely in favor of this country in the coming year. A year is a long time to look ahead, but present indications are that foreign trade will be large and profitable. If so, a long step toward profitable home trade has been taken.

It is hardly reasonable to expect railroad earnings to continue to increase, but if they hold their own, and this seems fairly probable, a comparatively high level of stocks can be maintained. Bank reserves are at a low ebb, but it is the opinion of sound bankers that by gain in cash and contraction in loans in the next two months the banks will be prepared to meet the fall drain without extraordinary dangers. Furthermore, that the large stock of money in the country will yield currency to this center whenever the demand for money here produces anything like abnormal rates.

Additions to the stock of money in the country have been enormous in the last four years, and the law which attracts money to the point where it gives the largest return seldom fails in its operations. There may be dear money in New York City next fall on account of the exhaustion of the surplus fund, but high rates will bring money here like a flood. Hence, the situation in its worst aspect, involving high rates for money and possibly lower prices for stocks, is very different from the situation of 1873, when the fundamental trouble was the lack of sufficient currency to do the business of the country.

There will be no general currency scarcity in the next few years. The rise and fall in the price of commodities will absorb money, or squeeze it out, as the case may be, but the ratio of the supply of money to the stock of commodities affords assurance that all that will be necessary to get a reasonable amount of money in Wall Street will be the squeezing process brought about through the machinery of money rates.

June 29, 1901

The failure of Marquand & Co. was an almost necessary sequence following the failure of the Seventh National Bank, or, to put the matter more fairly, the operations of Marquand & Co. caused the bank failure as well as their own. As the facts transpire, it may be found that operations were carried on through three institutions and that there came a time when a choice had to be made as to which should be sustained and which let go, with the conclusion that the Seventh National Bank should be the victim.

The failure of Marquand & Co. was followed by considerable buying of stocks, as the firm was short quite a line and the closing of accounts under the rule were chiefly on purchases. It must not be supposed, however, that the failure of this firm was due to their being engaged in a bear campaign. Their short accounts were only an incident representing temporary conditions.

The real difficulty with Marquand & Co. was their participation in the building of a coal road from Jefferson County, Pennsylvania, north to connections with Erie, Lackawanna and New York Central. About 150 miles of road were built, but the line had hardly reached the point of being profitable, and the bonds were slow in finding a market.

The road antagonized existing lines, and there was probably an effort by other railway corporations to interfere with its success. This illustrates the difficulty of establishing a new line where business must depend to a considerable extent upon terms which can be made with connecting but possibly hostile roads. The building of the Pittsburg, Shawmut & Northern road was the real cause of the downfall of Marquand & Co., and incidentally of the Seventh National Bank.

A good deal of interest has been felt in knowing whether other institutions were liable to be affected. Two other institutions have been regarded as possibly in danger, but the statement by the chairman of the Clearing House Committee that no further trouble was anticipated gave good assurance, because under existing conditions the Clearing House Committee is remarkably well informed as to the position of all the banks in the Clearing House.

This committee, through long experience in its work, has become able to judge very quickly when a bank departs from a high standard of management. The intention is to keep a close watch upon institutions for the purpose of detecting steps away from the right path. The policy then is to make personal inquiries of those in charge of such a bank, pointing out what appears to be wrong.

This usually has the desired effect, but if not, a policy is adopted involving examinations by one authority or another, and other official steps, which are calculated to correct difficulties or at least bring them to a head.

If this course fails, the bank begins to be discredited among other banks and the facts become known, increasing the difficulty of the bank in fault but saving others from commitments which might result in large loss.

It may be said now that the affairs of the Seventh National have been under scrutiny for two months, and the fact that its condition did not improve was, in all probability, the reason why the Clearing House banks did not give it assistance when its troubles came to a head.

When, therefore, the Clearing House Committee says in an official way that it does not look for further trouble, it means that the difficulties which may have existed with other banks in the Clearing House have been remedied or are in a fair way to be remedied. This does not mean absolute assurance of safety, because rumors and anxieties may make too great demands on deposits and resources, but the chances are the other way.

The financial difficulties this week have had one good effect. They have led the large money lenders to take steps for preventing extreme rates over the first of the month. Day before yesterday and yesterday high rates were expected, but money was supplied and borrowers had practically no difficulty in securing all the funds needed.

Money will begin to come out again on the 1st, and disbursements will be larger than usual. Hence, by the 6th a considerable proportion of the funds which have been drawn in the last day or two will again be in circulation.

Then will come the opportunity and practically the necessity for the banks to accumulate reserves in anticipation of fall requirements. If this is not done, it will be difficult to start any extended bull campaign. If it is done, the market is very likely to get strong and active on the feeling that there will be six weeks of plain sailing in which time large operators may hope to reduce their holdings, while small operators will hope for opportunity to make successful turns on the long side. The action of leading stocks was suggestive of better prices at once.

NOTES

[1] Cf. Mitchell, pp. 68–70.

[2] Jay Cooke and Company failed in 1873 when Cooke was unsuccessful in his attempt to market the bonds of Northern Pacific. Cooke was financing the construction of the railroad and used his own funds as well as the proceeds from bond sales. The bonds were sold in Europe and the United States. When the money market tightened in New York and capital imports stopped, Cooke was unable to secure funds through bond sales and was forced into bankruptcy. Henry Villard, and other capitalists associated with him, purchased control of the Northern Pacific in 1881. In 1883 Northern Pacific stock suffered a drastic decline when Charles F. Woerishoffer engaged in a stock market contest with the Northern Pacific party. Villard was forced to resign as president of the Northern Pacific on January 4, 1884.

[3] For a history of the price movement in Northern Pacific common and preferred stock during the corner see Frank Crawford Bell, Jr., "The Northern Pacific Corner," unpublished Master's thesis (University of Tennessee, Knoxville, 1961). Bell's account of the corner is among the most scholarly presentations of the episode.

[4] In 1895 Great Britain refused to submit to arbitration a long-standing boundary dispute between Venezuela and British Guiana. Secretary of State Olney on July 20, 1895 sent a note to the British which stated that the boundary differences should be settled by arbitration and any forcible rectification of the boundary by Great Britain would violate the Monroe Doctrine. The note was strongly worded, stating, "today the United States is practically sovereign on this continent, and its fiat is law upon the subjects to which it confines its interposition." When the British government refused the idea of arbitration on November 26, 1895, in a reply to Olney's message, President Cleveland took a serious view of the matter and in a message to Congress on December 17, 1895, asked that body to authorize a commission to determine the facts in the case and to ascertain the duty of the United States with respect to support of the findings of the commission. The fear of war between the United States and Great Britain caused a panic on the New York Stock Exchange on December 20, 1895.

[5] This editorial was included as Chapter XXXI in S. A. Nelson, *The ABC of Stock Speculation* (New York, 1902). It was not credited to Dow.

[6] Nelson included an abridged version of this editorial in *The ABC of Stock Speculation,* and credited it to Dow. See pp. 224–226.

CHAPTER SIX

July 9, 1901 — December 31, 1901

THE equity market was somewhat weaker in July and August of the year 1901. United States Steel common stock, which sold at 52⅜ in June, fell in July to 37. Atchison fell during the month of July from 89⅜ to 67¾, and Rock Island during the same period of time dipped from 158½ to 130.

A strike by the Amalgamated Steel, Iron and Tin Workers at the United States Steel Corporation and damage to the oats and corn crops due to a prolonged drought in the western agricultural states were influences of a depressing nature. In September the assassination of President McKinley shocked the nation and caused a small financial panic on the day following the assassination.

By the autumn of 1901 it was apparent that the copper market was "oversold" and that the price of seventeen cents could not be maintained. Amalgamated Copper was forced to reduce its dividend with the reduction in copper prices, and the stock fell from 120 to a low point of 60½ in December, at which time copper sold at thirteen cents. The collapse in the stock of Amalgamated Copper caused investors to lose confidence in the industrial list, and the industrials were weak from September through the close of the year.

July 9, 1901

During the summer, money always flows from the interior to New York. The influx usually begins in April and culminates in July. Between the middle of July and the middle of August, money begins to go south and west to move crops. The outflow generally continues until about the first of October, halts a little there, and then appears again in November. In 1900 the high point in surplus reserve came in the second week in August. In 1899 it occurred the third week in August.

In 1898 the high point was the last week in June, and the reserve ran down quite rapidly in July. In 1897 the high point was the third week in July. Carrying the comparison further back merely strengthens the statement that at some date between the middle of July and the middle of August the bank reserve begins to run down on account of the movement of money to the interior.

The outflow varies in different years, but is always large. The growing wealth of the West does not prevent a large movement of money from this country [New York]. Western cities have more money to lend, but the growth of western business makes more demand for that money. It is the surplus of the West which moves to and from New York, and the growth in surplus keeps pace with the growth of cash. Hence, there is no reason to suppose that the demand from the interior will be any less this year than usual.

If the New York banks have loaned here the money of the West, it is reasonably certain that when the West calls for its funds the banks will require payments of these loans, and unless money for the replacement of these loans is found elsewhere, the effect will be to squeeze out weaker borrowers and bring stocks in the market.

It is possible that money may be obtained from abroad, but the foreign situation in this respect is not assuring. It has often happened when a money situation has seemed difficult that a way out has been found. This year may furnish another illustration, but prudent people will wish to see this way open somewhat before greatly enlarging their commitments.

July 13, 1901

The money situation is certainly unfavorable. Low reserves and large loans are not unusual at this season. Furthermore, if, as is supposed, large loans have been made to important banking interests, it is hardly probable that these loans will be disturbed as long as smaller loans can be called. Hence, the probability of the disturbance of ordinary loans is perhaps greater than usual. The only way for the banks to obtain money for the crop movement is to squeeze it out of loans or to draw it from other centers by the attraction of rates [high interest rates]. The action of the market suggests that the squeezing process has been preferred and that it is under way.

The amount required for the crop movement varies in various years. Fifty million dollars has been considered an approximate amount. This is not a very large amount in view of the large holdings of specie and the large totals of the Clearing House banks. Indeed, it is a question whether the 25 per cent reserve is not more than is required for safety in view of the large total. Assuming that $50,000,000 may be required, it is very different to take this money from a cash total of $250,000,000 from what it was to take it from a cash total of $150,000,000, as would have been the case in 1885.

. . . One point may be of importance in the near future. A rising market always brings bad collateral into loans. When prices begin to recede, when banks begin to fail, and when scrutiny begins to be applied here and there, errors of judgment are discovered and institutions have to go through a process which sometimes results in restored health and sometimes in financial disaster. Investigations of this kind are going on and probably are responsible for a portion of the reports of something hanging over the market. It would not be surprising if there were some unfavorable financial developments, but, in saying this, we are reasoning from general principles and are not undertaking to forecast any specific outcome.

. . . .

July 24, 1901

It is a common thing to hear it said that, for example, St. Paul is selling 100 points higher than it sold in the 1893 panic and subsequent depression and that, therefore, its price is now 100 points higher than it will be in the next depression. This is perhaps a rather extreme form of statement, but the argument implied is in universal use among those who believe in the bear side of things.

It is, of course, true that prices do not move uninterruptedly in either direction, but almost always in a series of waves or swings. It follows that the prices of a boom are always a good deal higher than the prices of the subsequent depression. It is also true that the wave movements, being frequently determined by the necessities of holders, are temporarily independent of values. The one thing certain is, however, that over a sufficiently long period of time to equalize the purely wave movements, values determine prices, and earnings or earning capacity are the ultimate test of values. Therefore, over a long period of time the ratio of earnings to market price in the case of a given stock will more or less tend to constancy. Of course, when a company is paying dividends, the rate actually paid is an important factor in making the price, but the margin over the dividend has a great deal to do with determining the yield to the investor. For example, Northwest is paying the same rate of dividend on its stocks as St. Paul, viz.: 7 per cent on the preferred and 6 per cent on the common. Yet Northwest preferred sells 30 points above St. Paul preferred, and Northwest common some 35 points above St. Paul. The reason is that Northwest shows an earning capacity of 16 per cent on both its stocks, while St. Paul shows an earning capacity of 12 per cent. The rates of earning capacity to price thus appears:

	St. Paul	*Northwest*
Price of preferred	185	215
Price of common	158	192
Earned on stocks	12%	16%
Earned on market price preferred	7%	7½%
Earned on market price common	7½%	7%

There is sufficiently close correspondence in the last two items to prove the case for the two companies concerned. In a general way it may be said that over a long period of time the market prices of stocks will bear a reasonably steady ratio to the earning capacity of the railroads. Where a company is paying dividends, the ratio expressed in the percentages above will be somewhat smaller than where no dividends are being paid.

Now, in comparing present prices for stocks with those of the last great depression it should be remembered that the question is essentially one of earnings on capital. In the seven years that have elapsed since 1894 each mile of railroad has become more productive of gross earnings, and a permanent growth has taken place. Where no increased capitalization of mileage has taken place, the permanent growth is reflected properly in the market price of the stock. Further, besides turning out more transportation per mile of road, the railroads have learned to cut down the cost of transportation, so that a return even to the low gross earnings of seven years ago would not mean a return to the old net earnings. Here is another element of permanent growth.

On the whole, it is doubtful if market prices today are, measured by earning capacity, relatively higher than they were in the depression of 1894. In the days when St. Paul preferred sold at 130 and the common at 80, the road was earning 6 per cent on the common stock. The ratio of earnings to the market price then was actually smaller than it is now; in other words, stocks then were relatively higher than at present, in the case of St. Paul, at all events. Louisville & Nashville used to earn from 2 to 3 per cent in 1894 to 1896, and the stock sold around 50. Now it earns 8 per cent and the stock sells at par. It is relatively lower now than it was in those days, measured by this standard.

It may be true that earnings are going to fall some time or another to below the present level. When they do, values will also fall. But unless values fall, prices will in the long run be maintained, and they will only permanently fall when values permanently fall.

July 26, 1901

The market has had over two months of fluctuations over a range averaging about ten points. It could fairly be said either that stocks had shown excellent rallying power or that they had shown decided weakness. It is not probable that the market will continue to swing within recent limits. There will be the discounting of either higher or lower levels of value.

This makes it important to consider what there is to justify expectations of advance or decline. To put the matter in another way, what would a large operator see in the future to justify him in entering upon a campaign either way?

The argument in favor of higher prices includes the points following:

There has been no great creation of railway stocks in recent years, and while prices have risen, values have also risen, so that in many cases stocks are not intrinsically dearer, assuming present earnings to be maintained, than they were two or three years ago. The great railway properties have great value in their location, in the permanency of their business, and in the certainty of a general growth of the country. Such stocks may go in the future to very high figures.

It is a bull fact that the prosperity of the country in recent years both in its foreign and its domestic trade has greatly increased the investment fund of the country and provided means for large investments and large speculative commitments. Incidentally, the creation of industrial corporations has turned a great deal of former fixed capital into liquid capital, some of which is being used in the purchase of stocks. Public interest in the market has been greatly widened in the last five years by the creation of industrial securities during that time.

The continued increase in railway earnings is also bullish in its tendency. Each of the last three years has given increases over the previous year, and the gain thus far in 1901 compares favorably with the gain in preceding years. This maintains values. The gain in clearings is in the same direction. The volume of business is larger than before, although this is not necessarily saying that profits are also greater.

Crops are all that could be desired as far as winter wheat is concerned; spring wheat prospects are good and will soon reach the point of certainty. The cotton crop promises fairly well. High prices for products make good part of the loss in yield.

The great industrial corporations are generally reporting a good volume of business and profits which seem to assure the maintenance of current dividends for an indefinite time. The Steel Company made $26,500,000 in the first three months of its existence, which speaks well for the preferred stock of that company.

The great principles represented by community of interest seem to assure stability in rates. This has already been shown by the trunk lines and in the anthracite coal trade, and will receive a larger test under favorable conditions in the great combination of Pacific roads. Immense sums have been invested in order to secure these results and, in the opinion of those best able to judge, prospects for harmony and profitable business are good, with resulting increase in value of Pacific stocks.

The arguments in favor of lower prices include the following: The country has had nearly five years of prosperity and advancing prices of stocks. The experience of many years has shown that periods of prosperity and periods of depression alternate into cycles and that periods of prosperity seldom last much more than five years. The reasons for this may not be conclusive, but the probability that the future will be like the past has weight in many minds.

Prices of stocks are within an average of ten points of the highest figures reached in twenty years. The average price of the twenty railway stocks used in our table is almost three times as high as it was in 1896. It is over 30 points higher than it was a year ago. Prices, a year ago, were too low on values, but it can hardly be assumed that the value of stocks has increased 30 points in one year.

Prices are so high as to make an abnormally low yield on the dividends paid. Stocks like St. Paul, Rock Island, and New York Central give a smaller return on the investment than are given by many first-class bonds, which means that current prices have been made speculatively rather than by investors.

The gradual advance in the price of commodities and stocks, with the expansion of credit as a result of more active business and new commitments of all kinds, has absorbed the available supply of money, notwithstanding the increase in the volume of currency both by the acquisition of gold and the issue of national bank notes. The question whether the surplus reserves of the New York banks will support present prices during the fall drain of money is not beyond dispute. Neither is it clear that the situation abroad warrants belief that large supplies of money can be drawn from the other side. The commitments already existing in the form of stocks created but not distributed, will make further demands on the investment fund of the country for some time to come.

It is known that profits in some commercial lines have not kept pace with the increase in the volume of business. The statement of the Claflin Company, showing a very material falling off in profits compared with last year, is in point, and this applies to the whole cotton-goods trade. A material reduction in prices by the Woolen Company shows lack of satisfactory results there.

Labor is showing decided unrest. Strike after strike occurs, and while they have been thus far vexatious rather than destructive, their occurrence shows that the forces of labor and capital are developing friction which may lead to some disturbance which will be regarded as serious. When a body as powerful as the Amalgamated Association of Iron Workers thinks [it] wise to precipitate a strike involving thousands of men because the employing company will not insist that its employees become union men whether they wish to or not, it shows that the views of labor leaders are far advanced in the direction of compulsion and are likely to clash with the views of employers at many points.

The crops of the year are not likely to be up to the average. The excellence of winter wheat is admitted. Probabilities favor a good crop of spring wheat, but the damage to corn has been serious, and it is rare that corn improves in condition during August. The damage to oats has been great, pastures have suffered, and generally the evil effects of drought, particularly in Missouri and Kansas, are likely to be considerable. The cotton crop is uncertain, with the condition low rather than high.

Public interest in speculation has been checked by the panic in May and since by the difficulty of obtaining profits on the long side. Some of the large operators have become much less aggressive bulls, and some large commission houses are advising against accumulation of stocks. At present it would be difficult to secure enough outside buying to take any large speculative line of stocks. This, however, is something which might change with the change in conditions.

We have tried to state the arguments fairly and leave it for our readers to judge where the weight of evidence lies.

July 31, 1901

We have pointed out occasionally the correspondence of the advance in prices in the last few years with the advance which occurred between 1877 and 1881. There was no such striking interruption to the movement twenty years ago as that which occurred in the fall of 1899, but, otherwise, the similarity of advancing quotations, profitable business, growth of confidence, large foreign trade and the effect of financial legislation has been comparatively close. Another correspondence is now afforded by the injury to the corn crop, which was an important cause of the decline which began in 1881.

It has been customary to date that decline from the assassination of President Garfield, who was shot July 2. As a matter of fact, the high prices of that period were quite generally made in May, and the assassination, while a shock, was not in itself a cause for a change in the market from bull to bear.

Neither probably was the corn damage alone a sufficient reason. The turn came primarily because the measure of time was full.[1] If it had not been the assassination of President Garfield and damage to corn, something else would have occurred to precipitate the selling and the contraction which were the inevitable results of the expansion of previous years.

However, it was the corn damage which changed the balance of sentiment. The corn crop of 1880 was 1,717,434,543 bushels. The crop of 1881 was 1,194,916,000 bushels, a decrease of over 500 million bushels. It was pointed out then, as now, that the loss would be made good by higher prices. This proved true. The farm value of the corn crop December 1, 1881, was over $70,000,000 greater than for the preceding year, due to an advance in the price of corn from 39.6 cents in 1880 to 63.6 cents per bushel in 1881.

This, however, did not stay the decline in railway stocks. It can, of course, be said that conditions have greatly changed in twenty years; that railway corporations are stronger; and that there is less likely to have been overdoing with relation to resources than there was then.

Without disputing any of these points, it can be said, however, that the tendency to overdo in times of prosperity rests on a principle in human nature which makes a man always want to make money, no matter how much he has made. Hence, overdoing may occur on large capital and large resources as well as upon small.

However this may be, everybody knows that stocks began to decline in 1881 and went down more than they went up until 1885. As showing the immediate results of corn damage as the initial impulse toward decline, we give in the table following the prices of twenty stocks in July, 1881, with the lowest up to the close of the year 1881 and the amount of decline.

	July, 1881	*Aug.–Dec. Lowest*	*Decline*
Burlington & Quincy	165⅛	133½	31⅝
St. Paul	128⅜	102¼	26⅛
Northwest	131⅞	120⅞	11
Rock Island	144	131¾	12¼
C. C. C. & St. L.	96½	81	15½
Wabash common	59⅞	33¼	26⅝
Kansas & Texas	51⅝	34⅞	16⅞
Missouri Pacific	112⅝	98	14⅝
Texas Pacific	68¼	48	20¼
Northern Pacific common	45⅛	33¼	11⅞
Union Pacific	131¾	114¼	17½
Jersey Central	102⅝	87¾	14⅞
Lackawanna	125	119⅞	5⅛
Reading	61	119⅞	5⅛
Louisville & Nashville	108¾	90	18¾
Denver & Rio Grande	110½	66	44½
Western Union	93⅜	77½	15⅞
New York Central	146¾	130¼	16½
Erie	47¼	39¾	7½
Manhattan	26¾	17⅜	8⅜

While the corn damage was a factor of importance, it is evident that when the decline fairly started it was most pronounced in the stocks which had been overbulled and which lacked intrinsic value. This was pre-eminently true of Denver, Wabash, Louisville, Union Pacific and St. Paul. The decline in Burlington, which was the largest of all except Denver, was very directly due to corn damage.

It is an impressive fact on the instability of prices that, of the stocks in the above list, ten of the twenty have been in the hands of receivers since 1881, while only four or five have maintained an unbroken record of dividends since that date. And, of the entire number, only one company, Lackawanna, has maintained the same dividend during the time.

August 2, 1901

A correspondent writes: "Are periods of depression inevitable? Does not increasing wealth bring increasing stability in business? Will not combinations like the community of interest in railway affairs and the United States Steel Corporation in the iron trade tend to stability and to the avoidance of conditions which bring depression and panics?"

When Patrick Henry declared, "I have but one lamp by which my feet are guided and that is the lamp of experience. I know no way of judging the future but by the past," he laid down a proposition, which, while not scientifically true, has been found practically sound a great deal oftener than it has been proved to be unsound.

Theoretically, it is probably true that as wealth increases in a country, its business becomes more stable; that study of economic law has established principles which are acted upon with confidence and with good results, and that it is possible for a combination to do what a group of scattered interests could not do. The logic of the case points in the direction suggested by the inquiry.

Nevertheless, when it comes back to experience, we are inclined to think that the millennium of business, of finance and of transportation has not been reached and that actual results will be in kind if not in degree much as they have been in the past. There will be important gains in some directions, but they will be offset by losses in others. One difficulty will be overcome, but the measures used to remedy that trouble will create new troubles, which will have some of the effects of the old.

Take the case of banking in England, for instance. In the panic of 1793, more than one hundred banks failed. In the period of financial distress from 1810 to 1817, more than six hundred banks failed. The panic of 1825 brought a smaller number of bank failures because the principles laid down in the bullion report of 1810 were better understood and banking had become safer. In 1837 there was a commercial crisis, but the banks had learned wisdom and there were no bank failures. In 1847 there was a bank panic which was stopped by the modifying of a law which was responsible for the difficulty. Ten years later the same thing occurred again, and nine years later, in 1866, there was another bank panic in England, since which time, while there have been bank failures, there has been no general bank panic such as existed thereto.

Here was a case of a rich, well-developed country which had a series of panics of both financial and commercial character. Stability and wealth did not prevent them, but increasing knowledge gradually showed bankers what might and what might not be done, until bank panics have been practically eliminated from the financial difficulties of England. Banking was something which could be regulated by law founded upon knowledge of conditions. But this could not be done with reference to general business, because of its extent and variety.

The improvement in bank conditions, therefore, did not and could not bring freedom from periods of depression in trade, which have been as distinct since 1866 as before. The ups and downs of business, with the contraction and expansion in profits, has been as pronounced in England as it has been in this country since 1866. A comparison of index numbers showing the prices of commodities indicate that periods of depression have run quite evenly in point of time and extent here and abroad.

It is true that English railroad stocks became much more stable in the matter of fluctuations something more than twenty years ago. There came a time when the growth of railroad business reached a point which assured maintenance of dividends irrespective of the fluctuations in trade. After this became evident, railway stocks did not decline materially in periods of business depression. Exactly the same thing has occurred here. New York, New Haven & Hartford, Harlem, Boston & Albany and other stocks reached years ago the point where they were held for investment regardless of the rise and fall in the surplus over the dividend. The same thing is going on now with reference to Lackawanna, Northwest and other stocks, where dividends are becoming so secure as to make investors indifferent to the rise and fall in net earnings.

We think stability in prices of stocks will come more through increasing stability in value than as the result of combinations, although combinations may be useful in hastening or strengthening stability in values. In industrial stocks the difficulties will be greater and the results less uniform, because competition can be more easily brought about.

If all corporations were rich and conservative, prices might be expected to become stable and periods of depression might disappear. If all individuals were rich and conservative, panics and hard times might disappear. But as long as corporations and individuals differ greatly in resources but are alike in the desire to make money, there will continue to be elemental conditions likely to produce instability, and enough toppling over to produce cycles of depression.

Falling prices are produced by falling profits. Falling profits are caused by an excess of supply over demand. Excessive supply is always the result of overdoing, and overdoing is generally the result of haste to be rich. Until some link in this chain is broken, we think the lamp of experience will continue to flicker.

August 3, 1901

When business is very prosperous, employers generally prefer to admit even unjust demands [of labor] rather than lose the profits to be obtained by keeping plants at work. When, however, the business outlook becomes less certain, manufacturers in some cases are willing to see strikes, partly, at least, on the ground that an unsuccessful strike may enable the manufacturer to take off the addition to cost which he was forced to put on when labor had the best end of the controversy. It does not appear that the country has reached a point in this cycle of development where employers had rather have strikes than not, but it may be true that concessions which would have been made a year and a half ago will not be made now.

. . . .

August 14, 1901

We give in tables following the advances in leading railway stocks in the 1879 period and in the present period to date.

The 1879 bull period lasted from the 17th of April, 1877, until May, 1881, although, in a few cases, higher prices were made in 1882 than in 1881. As a whole, however, May, 1881, saw the top of the bull swing.

It may be remarked incidentally that some of the most successful bull leaders saw nothing in the spring of 1881 to indicate that the market was near top, and when the corn damage came in July and August, they explained that the loss would be made good by other tonnage just as is done now. Mr. Gould and Mr. Vanderbilt fought the decline for three years before they could get out of the stocks which they had at the top or were obliged to buy on the way down.

The advance from 1877 to 1881 was the largest that had ever been seen in the stock market up to that time, and many people believed that it would be impossible for stocks to ever go back to low figures. It was pointed out time and again that the Grangers as 7 per cent dividend stocks were worth the money and that stocks like Erie, Reading and Wabash had overcome their difficulties and would gradually reach a dividend basis. Union Pacific was considered worth every bit as much as St. Paul, and insiders were the largest holders of the stock at high prices.

People say now that the market of 1881 was manipulated and rested on an insecure foundation. Undoubtedly it did. Everybody can see it now, but the point is that some of the wisest and ablest could not see it then—there were those who did. Mr. Keene, Mr. Woerishoffer, Mr. Cammack, Rufus Hatch and others took the bear side in the summer of 1881, but they were the exceptions, and their statements as to the real situation were denounced all through 1881 and 1882 as the inventions of unscrupulous bears who wanted to enrich themselves by destroying the value of the property of others.

The bears replied by pointing to the advance in prices and by claiming that there had been no increase in values to justify such a gain in quotations. The rise was remarkable, as will be seen by the table following:

Stock	*Low, 1877*	*High, 1881*	*Adv.*
Central of N.J.	6	112	106
Chic. & Northwest	15	136	121
Chic., Bur. & Quincy	94	182½	88½
Cleve., Col., Cin.	19½	101⅝	82⅛
Del. & Hudson	25½	115¼	89¾
Erie	4⅜	52⅛	48¼
Illinois Central	40½	146½	106
Lake Shore	45	135¾	90¾
Lackawanna	36	131	95
St. Paul	11	129½	118½
N.Y. Central	85¼	155	69¾
Phila. & Reading	20	62¼	42¼
Wabash	1	60	59
Union Pacific	59¾	131¾	72
Western Union	56	129⅛	73⅛

Turn now to the present period. The rise began in August, 1896, and has lasted, except for the interruption in 1899, five years. The advances have been very large, as will be seen by the table following:

	Low, 1896	*High, 1901*	*Adv.*
Atchison common	8¼	91	82¾
Atchison preferred	14⅛	108	93⅞
Balt. & Ohio	10½	114½	104
Chic., Bur. & Quincy	53	199⅞	146⅞
Chic., Mil., & St. P.	59⅞	188	128⅛
Chic. & Northwest	117½	215	97½
Chic., Rock Is. & P.	49¼	175¼	126
C. C. C. & St. L.	19½	92½	73
Del. & Hudson	114½	185½	71
Del., Lack. & West.	138	244	106
Erie	10¼	45½	35¼
Illinois Central	84⅛	154¾	70⅝
Louis. & Nash.	37⅛	111¾	74⅝
Missouri Pacific	15	124½	109½
N.Y. Central	88	170	82
Northern Pac. common	12¼	* 700	687¾
Southern Ry. preferred	15½	88⅞	73⅜
Union Pacific	3½	133	129½

* Highest at which stock sold regular way in corner.

The question is whether the advances have been justified to an extent which warrants expectation that this time prices will hold. It will not be disputed that most, if not all, of the properties named give far better value for the present price than they gave for the price twenty years ago. There has been almost a generation's growth in business. There has probably been more money put into some of the properties since 1881 in betterments than was put into them previously for construction. Where were hamlets in 1881 are now cities. The fall in the rate of interest shows how values have increased.

Yet he would be rash who would say that the railroads of the country have grown beyond the effects of hard times; grown to a point where fluctuations in earnings affect surplus, but do not endanger dividends. Some roads have reached this point, but more have not. There has been no time up to the present when a large advance in stocks has not been followed by a large decline, not in every stock, but in stocks enough to establish the tendency of the market. Is there good reason for thinking that values have reached a point in enough stocks to nullify what has been speculative law hitherto?

August 15, 1901

We printed yesterday a comparison of prices designed to illustrate the general features of the great boom of twenty years ago, and also figures showing the extent of the rise in the "boom" that began in 1897 and reached its highest point this year. The prices disclose substantial similarity of movement in the two periods. We further pointed out that the decline which followed the 1877–81 boom surprised a great many people who were then supposed to be well informed on values.

In considering the analogy between the two periods, however, there are some things that should be remembered. The bull period of the last four years has brought to light a good many equities that must be regarded as somewhat solid in character. We made the other day a comparison between St. Paul's position this year and that of twenty years ago, which showed that the company has but slightly increased its capitalization as measured per mile of road, while the bonded debt per mile had actually decreased. The effect of this, of course, was to give the stockholders of the company practically the entire benefit in one form or another of the growth of business in the territory covered by the road. The United States has not stood still in the last few years, and, as everybody knows, St. Paul has been able to increase its dividends by degrees, so that the company is now paying 6 per cent, with an earning capacity that is not less than 13 per cent, on both classes of its stocks. The surplus income has gone into the property for the reduction of grades, the straightening of line and the increasing of equipment.

Today the road is so much the better off, not merely because a certain amount of earning capacity is thus set free for dividends, but also because the improvements that have been made will permit of material economies in operation. What we have shown to be true in the case of St. Paul is true also of many others of the large railroads whose stocks stand at high prices. It is certainly true of Northwest, Illinois Central, Pennsylvania, Union Pacific, Northern Pacific, Burlington, etc., in greater or less degree.

The result is that these companies are facing the depression that many people expect under conditions vastly more favorable than those which existed in 1881. Furthermore, it is a good many years since there has been any large building of competitive mileage, so that these companies have received most of the benefit accruing from the general increase of business. The mileage that has been built in the last few years consists in the main of small connections and branches. Thus, if depression comes, it will not find a large number of new roads forced to cut rates in order to get enough business to pay operating expenses and fixed charges. Every year that goes by, moreover, tends to protect more and more the companies already existing from this kind of competition, for it is becoming increasingly difficult to get terminal facilities in the big cities. In other words, railroad property is becoming more stable every year.

There is another point that should not be forgotten and that is the great advance that has taken place in the practice of transportation in the last few years. Some six or seven years ago we used to give a good deal of space to discussion of what were then known as "Hill methods" in railroading. Then they were new and by many people were regarded as fanciful if not indeed unsound. Now they are universally recognized as representing the highest practice in the industry, and they have been adopted by almost all large railroads in one way or another. These methods result in continuous pressure on the ratio borne by conducting transportation expenses to gross earnings. They do not in the least interfere with maintenance questions but bring economies, the wisdom of which cannot be questioned. Assuming that the railroads are bound to lose a certain proportion of their present volume of gross earnings, they will be able to shut off a good deal of what would twenty years ago have been loss in net earnings. In other words, their earning capacity has been permanently increased by these methods.

The great question is to what extent the railroad companies will lose in gross when depression comes. That they will lose something of the present volume of gross earnings is likely. Very few people will deny that the business of the country ebbs and flows to some extent over a period of years. It has been flowing strongly for four years, and many of the signs of high tide having been reached are apparent. It will probably be found, however, that there has been a marked change in the position of most of the large railroads as compared with twenty years ago. In those days, the speculation was mainly in such stocks as Northwest, Delaware & Hudson, Illinois Central, Lackawanna, St. Paul, Union Pacific and Lake Shore. The majority of those railroads now occupy a position where there is little or no speculation in their stocks, which sell at very high prices. This means that they have finally come to the point where they are considered no longer subject to the tide movements, at least so far as their dividends are concerned. It is clear, for example, that uncertainty regarding the dividends of such roads as Lake Shore, Northwest, and perhaps in lesser degree Lackawanna and St. Paul is now very slight. The stocks that now occupy a prominent speculative position are such as Atchison, Union Pacific, Southern Pacific, Missouri Pacific, Reading, etc. In the boom of 1897–1901 these stocks have done about what Northwest, Lackawanna, Lake Shore, etc., did twenty years ago. Upon these stocks no doubt will fall the principal brunt of the coming depression—if we have a depression. It is not at all likely that Pennsylvania, St. Paul, Northwest, Illinois Central and the like will suffer to anything approaching the same extent as in 1881–84.

August 23, 1901

The panic of 1893 and the subsequent depression which passed away in 1897 disclosed widespread weakness in the railroad situation and resulted in at least one-quarter of the railroad mileage in the country going into bankruptcy. Of course, it also disclosed commercial and financial weakness in other places besides the railroads and brought about the collapse of several industrial concerns. At the time the panic struck, however, there were comparatively few industrials that were the subject of speculation in Wall Street, and, of the few that were dealt in there, some escaped destruction. The Sugar Company, for example, was able to go on and pay its regular dividend through the panic and depression until the Arbuckles started the trade war.

Since the panic of 1893 there have been created a tremendous number of industrial companies, practically all of which have been capitalized on a most liberal basis. Merely to enumerate the names and capital of these companies would go a long way towards filling a page of the *Wall Street Journal*. Many of these are quoted in the market, and their stocks are freely bought and sold in one form or another. Meanwhile, there has been extremely little creation of new railroad securities, first, because there has been very little building of independent new roads and, secondly, because the companies have been very conservative as a rule in their financing of their own new mileage or improvements.

It is clear, therefore, that, as has been pointed out several times here, the next depression is very unlikely to leave many permanent marks on the railroad map of the country. It is most improbable that the railroad receiverships will amount to as much as 10 per cent of the present mileage. On the other hand, it is equally clear that the full force of the depression is rather likely to be felt by the industrial companies which have been created in the last three or four years, and the capitalization of which has been set at large figures.

Of course, where a company has but little bonded debt of any kind and where the management is good, absolute bankruptcy need hardly be feared, because the reduction or even the omission of preferred dividends in no way involves a receivership or a reconstruction. An industrial company, however, just as well as an individual manufacturer or trader, can become embarrassed through its "current liabilities" in connection with its business, and the effect is precisely the same in such a case so far as the stockholders are concerned as if it defaulted on its bonded debt. Thus the question of ability in management of an industrial company is perhaps as important to the stockholder as is the question of capitalization.

The problem, therefore, of determining the ultimate worth of industrial companies depends upon the extent of ability in the management and upon the extent of capital obligations.

In view of the admittedly large capital obligations of industrial companies at present existing, it is clear that in the depression, when and if it comes, the matter of management will play a most important part in sifting out the successful from the unsuccessful companies. As the event proved, this question was of great importance in determining railroad values in the last depression. If Northern Pacific had then had the management that it now has, it might perhaps have survived. So also might Baltimore & Ohio.

It is the industrial companies in the main that will undergo the "trying-out" process in the next season of adversity when it arrives, but no one can tell now what this process will develop in the case of individual companies, because from the nature of things it is impossible to judge accurately at this time the character of the management of these companies or the extent to which general conditions will affect their business. What the depression of 1893–97 did towards establishing the values of railroad stocks, the next depression will probably do in the case of the industrials. Some have already been tested, but the vast majority have yet to undergo the proof.

August 24, 1901

While everything favors further moderate advance in prices, it must be remembered that the season of the year is one not ordinarily healthy for speculation in stocks. It rarely happens that a strong market in the late summer is not followed by a considerable decline some time in the fall. The reason of this is usually the general withdrawal of money from financial centers to move the crops. There is usually a tightening up of money rates all over the civilized world in the fall, and a process of this kind always brings to light whatever weakness, speculative or otherwise, may exist in the situation. If there is any weakness in the situation, the autumn rise in money rates can hardly fail to disclose it. Even if everything is sound financially, an advance in money rates usually has the effect of checking speculation for the rise, and sometimes checking it in a rather violent manner.

People who believe that last spring marked the "high tide" of our prosperity for the time being, and more particularly marked the combination [culmination] of the boom in stocks, expect that some time this fall the market will break to a lower point than that recorded in the July break. If it does not, it will offer rather strong evidence against the theory of "high tide" having already been seen; if it does, it will tend somewhat strongly to confirm the theory. As there is already quite a little evidence in favor of the said theory, it may be said that there are some grounds for believing that the autumn decline, when it comes, will take prices to a lower level than that from which the present rally started.

Of course, these views represent merely an effort to guess the future in the light of the known facts, and nothing more can be claimed for them. Inasmuch, however, as people who trade in stocks have to base their operations on guessing the future in some such way, they will perhaps be wise to act on the theory that at some time in the next sixty days the market is likely to have a decline of greater or less dimensions. The rally is now some three weeks old and amounts to the best part of six points from the bottom. So far as precedent is any guide, and so far as the known facts bear upon the future, the advance will probably not last many weeks longer or go very many points further.

August 30, 1901

In the campaign of 1896 one of the favorite catchwords in the mouths of Mr. Bryan's supporters was the expression "without the consent of foreign nations." This expression was used with special reference to the free coinage of silver by the United States, those who used it being of the opinion that a simple thing like that could and should be done without the consent or support of other countries. The suggestion that the United States could not do it alone was flouted as most unpatriotic in its character. Most people now understand that there are some things that one country, no matter how powerful, cannot do alone. The principle, however, from which arises the falsity of the aforesaid expression is not as clearly seen in other cases.

There are many people who have a vague idea that such things as the Boer War, the Russian famine, the German industrial collapse are developments in some way or another favorable to the United States, and that our people derive benefit in some occult fashion from the misfortune of others. It is of course true that a war makes temporary demands for provisions and perhaps for other things in the way of munitions such as horses, mules, etc. It is of course true that a famine in Europe creates a strong demand for American wheat. But the tremendous waste of wealth that takes place during a war and the depression that follows upon a famine certainly do not have a lasting beneficial effect in any direction.

The fact is, and it is recognized by all intelligent observers, that from a business point of view the world is becoming more highly organized every year. This means that every part of it is more or less affected by serious injury to any other part. This is essentially true of all forms of business, but particularly so in the case of financial matters. A crisis at one money center is felt at practically all the other money centers. Most people remember, for example, the effect of the Baring panic in New York. Were such an unfortunate event to occur today, its effect would probably be even greater than it was eleven years ago. The effect of our panic in 1893 was felt all over the world in the same way. Financial relations between the principal centers are continually being drawn closer as time goes on.

The bearing of this principle on the present situation is tending to strengthen the belief that we have seen the high tide of prosperity, financial and commercial, in this country for the time being. There has been, as everybody knows, a severe check to the industrial prosperity of other countries. The Boer War has had a tremendous influence on Great Britain's trade already, and it will take some time for its effects to pass away. The overexpansion of industry in Germany has already resulted in marked commercial and financial depression, which also will pass away only after the lapse of considerable time. European countries generally, in fact, have apparently entered upon a period of dull trade, the reasons being different in different places, but the effect being pretty much the same all around.

The United States has had four years of extraordinary prosperity and in those four years has made a tremendous stride in the race for the world's markets. Four years of uninterrupted progress is, however, as history shows, a pretty long spell of sunshine. What grounds are there for believing that our experience this time will differ essentially from our experience in the past? Human nature remains the same from decade to decade, and one of the very few laws of human nature in business to which exception cannot be found is that progress is made by leaps and falls.

Depression has already overtaken the other civilized countries, all of which have had their "boom" as we have had ours. Is there any good reason to believe that what has happened to them and what is happening to them now, that what has always happened to us in the past, will not again happen to us this time? In other words, is there any reason to believe that the United States will not have in the next two or three years a reaction from the great prosperity of the last four years?

If there is any such reason, it is not apparent on the surface of things as they stand today.

August 31, 1901

There is a general similarity in all "booms" and in all periods of depression. The character of these movements is like a snowball running down an inclined plane and gathering snow as it runs. The movement is slow at the start, becoming quicker as progress is made and usually being quickest of all just before it ends.

When the character of the motive power is considered, it is evident why this should be the case. "Booms" are made by the gradual but increasingly rapid growth of confidence among the people. In 1895 and 1896 confidence was at a low ebb in financial and commercial circles in this country. Nobody wanted to take much risk in his business, and nobody planned very far ahead for that reason. Everybody wanted to see his money again as quickly as possible. This condition of affairs reached a climax in the "Bryan campaign" of 1896, when for a short time business men and financiers did the best they could towards suspending business altogether.

The election of McKinley in that year destroyed the principal fear that had so completely shaken people's confidence in the future. Mr. McKinley was elected in November of 1896, but it was not until the summer and fall of 1897 that the growth of confidence became really notable. This growth was very slow and very disappointing to people in Wall Street at that time. During the latter half of 1897, however, and practically all through 1898 confidence grew more and more rapidly, and in the first three months of 1899 it had become well grown. Then came a check to its growth from the "industrial collapse" and later from the "Boer War," and the effect of these had not passed away when the campaign of "1900" had to be faced.

Mr. McKinley's re-election in 1900, however, gave it renewed growth, and in the six months following his election, if the stock market be taken as a fair index, the "boom" made more progress than it had made in the preceding three years. It went on practically without a check till the "Northern Pacific corner" in May. That event resulted in a decline, temporary, it is true, but of a magnitude and severity surpassing anything recorded in the annals of Wall Street.

Some people ask why there should be a reaction from the boom of the last four years, seeing the growing prosperity of the country at this time. Those who believe that such reaction is coming, and in fact has already begun, answer this question by saying that people are shaken somewhat in their confidence as to the future, partly by the events of last May, partly by the corn crop failure, partly by the steel strike, and partly the depression abroad, and that there is in progress a process of contraction of confidence which will closely parallel the process of growth between 1897 and 1901.

It is not an easy thing at any time to weigh and measure confidence very exactly. No one, however, will deny that the stock market furnishes very clear proof that a different state of things exists in this respect than existed last May before the drop in prices arising from the "Northern Pacific corner." Certain it is, moreover, that the loss of the corn crop has materially shaken a good many business men's confidence in the purchasing power of people in many parts of the country where the loss of corn will be most severely felt. The steel strike has beyond doubt effected a considerable disturbance in the iron trade and has made it very difficult for people in that industry to see their way ahead.

Of course, it can also be said with truth that in parts of the country where people are not directly affected by corn, by steel or by Wall Street, there is no loss of confidence. This is true, for example, of the Northwest, where a bountiful wheat crop is assured. Nobody there is worrying about the future as yet. With all due allowance for this, it is yet a significant fact that, whereas three or four months ago all was harmony in commercial and financial circles, there are now some discordant notes that threaten to become louder as time goes on. It is possible that the discord will only be temporary and that confidence will again be restored where it has been shaken, that bountiful crops next year will repair the damage done this year and, in short, that everything will be as it was last winter. History, however, shows that confidence is a tender plant and that when it is most advanced in growth it can least well stand any injury. No one can say that last spring confidence was not well grown.

October 1, 1901

The London financial papers make it clear that the reports in regard to the foreign situation lately current have not been exaggerated. The depression is most pronounced in Germany and is a natural reaction from the boom which was in progress there up to the summer of 1900. The collapse in trading companies, the weakness in the iron and coal trades and the losses that have occurred through depreciation in shares have created a degree of uneasiness which is felt throughout the country.

The country banks of Germany are refusing to discount paper with anything like the usual freedom. The Imperial Bank of Germany is acting very wisely and has increased its discounts materially in the last few months. Nevertheless, the situation is such that it is impossible to get money on the less desirable forms of security. Unquestioned security, as is usual at such times, is in such demand as to create an oversupply of money for this class of investments. This explains the rise in German bonds and the decline in the rate of discount in the open market. The result must be a period of liquidation and contraction lasting a considerable time and gradually bringing about restoration of confidence.

French industrial ventures recently have not turned out very well, and some important Russian investments have caused losses. Russia is working through a period of depression, although the situation is perhaps a little better there than it was. Belgium is experiencing the results of overtrading, and Austria is having conditions which are certainly not better than an average. The depreciation of the notes of the Bank of Spain has affected trade in that country, and the situation is made worse by the danger of war with Morocco.

Trade in England continues to be affected somewhat by anxieties and uncertainties growing out of the South African war. The easy condition of the London money market is due partly to the employment of a good deal of French money and partly to dullness in the Stock Exchange and in commercial circles. It is expected, however, that money will be dearer soon, as gold will be required for Egypt, South America and the United States. The point of chief uncertainty is how much gold will be taken by the United States.

The depression in trade which exists abroad is very suggestive in its bearing upon this country. The interests of the world are so bound together that it is no longer possible for any of the great powers to live unto themselves. It has almost invariably happened in the past that the beginning of a period of prosperity in Europe has been followed by growing prosperity here. The reverse has been equally true. The index numbers representing the average price of many commodities, which are kept in various countries, show a remarkable tendency to rise and fall together. The turning of the tide in one country is generally only a few months earlier or later than the turn in another.

The following table shows the international movement of trade as expressed by changes in the average prices of commodities, using the Bureau of Economic Research index number for the United States, that of the London *Economist* for Great Britain and that of Conrad for Germany.[2] The differences in the numbers are due to the differences in the number and character of the commodities used:

Year, U.S.		*Yr., London Economist*		*Yr., Conrad, Germany*	
1881–2	117	1881–2	111	1880–1	110
1885–6	90	1885–6	92	1885–6	94
1890–1	95	1890–1	102	1890–1	106
1896–7	70	1896–7	86	1896–7	82
1889–0	93	1889–0	97	1889–0	100

It appears from the foregoing that the high point in the price of commodities was reached in Germany in 1880–81, while it was not reached in London or the United States till the succeeding year. The low point in the tide came in 1885–86 in each of the three countries; so also with the recovery in 1890, the low point in 1896 and the ensuing recovery up to 1900.

As we often say, because a thing has happened, it does not follow that it will happen again, but the recurrence of price movements is such and the evidence that substantially the same movements occur in different countries at the same time is so strong as to be worthy of attention if not belief in its application to the future.

October 2, 1901

We have received the following inquiry: "If the bull market ended last May and we are in a period of decline, ought prices to go off a good deal this fall?"

Mr. Jay Gould said once that the first requisite for successful speculation was patience. Most operators realize that they have cut short their profits, frequently and needlessly, by the lack of patience. A great movement in the market does not usually come suddenly. The market, while manipulated in a narrow sense, is, in its large sense, created by conditions. The prices of stocks act as a sort of skirmish line, out in front of the developments that have actually occurred, and in the direction of those which are expected to occur. When they get too far out, they have to fall back. Then, when the facts become clear, they move for a time with a rush.

When the tide is nearly in or nearly out, there is a period of slack water. When the business tide is nearly in or nearly out, there is a period when it is impossible to say definitely that conditions have changed in a large way either for better or for worse. Some conditions may have changed and others not, with the balance doubtful.

This makes a corresponding situation in the stock market. Prices go off on that which is unfavorable and recover again on that which is favorable. The net change during such a time may be small, even if the market is fairly active and the gross changes are quite large.

We know very well now that the bull market of 1879–80 culminated in May, 1881, yet a few stocks were higher in the summer of 1882 than they were in the spring of 1881, and many stocks went back to near their best price in the midsummer advance of 1882. This was because the conditions which made the market of 1879 did not come to an end all at once, and, while there was enough that was unfavorable to make stocks very weak at times in the early winter of 1881 and spring of 1882, there was, nevertheless, enough left that was favorable to give the market periods of very decided strength.

Exactly the same thing occurred at the turn of the market in 1890–92 and again at the turn in 1896. The last low point in the market was August 8, 1896, with the average of twenty railway stocks 41.82. But notwithstanding the improved conditions and the bull speculation that came with the first election of President McKinley, general conditions did not change rapidly enough to remove all doubt of a lasting change, and in April, 1897, the average was only 48.12, a gain of

6.30 in seven months. When the fact of a radical change became clear, the movement of the market became rapid. The gain from April, 1897, to August, 1898, was from 48.12 to 70.15, or 22.03 points.

We are not prepared to say that last May marked the high point in the bull period, but we can say that if it did, the action of the market since has been entirely normal, and, whenever the high point does come, if it has not come already, it will be followed by just such a period of prolonged fluctuations within a narrow range as we have been having this year.

If last May were the top of the rise, the market will swing as it has been swinging since then until the accumulation of unfavorable facts increases the supply and decreases the demand for stocks enough to break the existing balance and cause a decline to a lower level, discounting bear conditions as far as they have developed.

There will then be rallies followed by another period of steady prices with a succeeding adjustment to conditions, whatever they may be. Even in an active bear period, the average loss in the average of twenty stocks is not likely to be more than 10 or 12 points a year. As the monthly swing of the market in active trading is often from 5 to 7 points, it will be seen that there is room for a great many fluctuations in order to produce an average fall of 10 points in twelve months.

The probabilities, therefore, are against large or rapid decline soon even if the market has turned. The changes are in favor of a series of swings which may be made profitable for those who sell [short] when the market is strong and buy when the market is weak. It may be even more profitable for those who have the patience to wait for a long swing, but unless the coming market is different from markets past, the waiting policy will be one requiring strong convictions and a large endowment of patience.

October 3, 1901

A correspondent writes: "You say that if general conditions are unfavorable, the stock market will decline; that business conditions are to be judged by trade developments, comparing those which are good with those which are bad in order to see which side is gaining weight. What do you consider the unfavorable facts in the present situation?"

The most important is the damage to the corn crop. The average condition of corn September 1 was 51.7, compared with 80.6 September 1, 1900, and 85.2 September 1, 1899. This indicates a loss of something like 800,000,000 bushels of corn, with a money value of perhaps $300,000,000. Such a loss is a factor of great importance in its bearing upon the purchasing power of the country as applied to commodities and transportation.

Second in the list is the unfavorable condition of business abroad, particularly in Germany. The boom of a year or two ago has given place to acute depression, with large decline in prices and a great loss of confidence in investments. Trade is not good in England, France or Austria. It seems to us that such conditions must react unfavorably upon this country in due time.

Some effects are seen already. Lower prices for goods abroad have stimulated foreign exports to this country, resulting in an increase in imports of merchandise at New York since January 1 of about $15,000,000. Exports of merchandise from New York have fallen off during the same time about $24,000,000, showing quite a radical change at the port of the largest entry. The total excess of exports for eight months has been about $9,000,000 greater than for the same time last year, but the ratio of gain has been decreasing.

Another important fact is found in the industrial reports which have been made public in the last few months. The Rubber Company made a report showing a very large curtailment of profits. Standard Rope & Twine made a similar exhibit. Republic Iron & Steel showed net profits for the year of only $309,098, or about one-quarter of the dividend on the preferred stock. American Car Foundry in the last four months has earned only about half as much as in the same time last year.

The reduction in the copper dividends is clear evidence of a smaller proportion of profits in that trade. Exports of copper were 90,747 tons in the first half of 1900, 69,335 tons in the second half of 1900 and 50,027 tons in the first half of 1901. This, with stationary production, shows conditions which made a reduction in copper dividends a matter of good business judgment, if not one of necessity. In other cases there has been decided cutting down of profits, and there are more to come out. The reasons given in various cases differ considerably, showing that the loss has not been due to any one well-recognized occurrence, but is the outcome of varied conditions.

The assassination of the President was a great shock to confidence in the sense that it was amazing that anybody could have been found disposed to assassinate such a President, and also in the sense that while President Roosevelt is undoubtedly sincere in saying that he proposes to carry out the policy of Mr. McKinley rather than any policy of his own, it is certain that as new questions arise and new conditions are presented, Mr. Roosevelt will be compelled to act according to his own convictions, and the result may be something quite different from what is now recognized as the McKinley policy.

Speculatively speaking, the high level of prices is an unfavorable fact. The average price of twenty railway stocks is 108.18, compared with 75.85 a year ago. This means that the favorable conditions which have brought about this level of prices must be maintained in order that prices may be maintained. Conditions ought to be very much better than they were at this time last year in order to justify prices being so much higher.

The list of the unfavorable might be materially extended, but this is enough to show that there are important changes for the worse compared with last year. There have been important changes for the better, and we will point out some of these changes tomorrow. Whether the improvement outweighs the deterioration must be a matter for individual opinion.

There is certainly one point in which the balance is unfavorable. A year ago there were only two factors which were regarded as disturbing. They were the damage to spring wheat and apprehension in regard to the presidential election. Apart from these, it was difficult to find anything that could be regarded as a big unfavorable factor. The situation is certainly worse in the sense that there is now no difficulty in finding conditions which are against the market at the present level of prices.

October 4, 1901

We gave yesterday some of the unfavorable facts bearing on the speculative situation. Today, the other side is presented.

The most important favorable fact in the existing situation is that the railway systems have gained greatly in the last twenty years by the growth of local business without having a corresponding growth in either competition or charges. Most of the present great systems were prominent twenty years ago. New York Central, Pennsylvania, St. Paul, Northwest, Burlington, Rock Island, Missouri Pacific, Union Pacific, Louisville & Nashville and Wabash were fully established systems in 1881. They have added mileage since, but it has been a filling-in mileage, and an extension mileage generally of a non-competitive and on the whole profitable character. Charges have been swelled normally, but not to equal the growth of business, and the stocks of these companies occupy an entirely different position as a result.

While the creation of railway stocks in the last twenty years has been comparatively small, the investment fund of the country has had a steady and, on the whole, rapid rise. The ratio of money seeking investment to the supply of investment railway securities has made a higher level of prices for investment railway stocks permanent.

Look at some of the facts bearing on this point. The stock of money in the country in 1881 was 1,114 millions. The stock of money in October, 1901, is 2,227 millions, an increase of more than 100 per cent. The gold output of the country in 1881 was about 31½ millions. Last year it was 71 millions. Bituminous coal production has risen in twenty years from 48 million to 175 million tons. Pig iron production has risen from 3,835,191 tons to 13,620,703 tons. Steel production has risen from 1,588,314 tons to about 11 million tons.

The value of the corn crop has averaged over 600 million dollars a year for twenty years. The value of the wheat crop has averaged over 300 million dollars a year for the same time; the oat crop nearly 200 milions a year; the cotton crop about 300 millions a year, and the hay crop over 300 millions a year for twenty years.

Population has increased from 50,155,783 in 1880 to 76,303,799 in 1900, represented in its business activities by an increase of about 100 per cent in the earnings of national banks and a very large gain in clearings at leading centers. The gain in clearings at New York comparing 1881 with 1900 was over three billion dollars. Foreign trade has made great strides. Exports of merchandise in 1881 were 902 millions and [in] 1901, 1,487 millions, with an enormous gain in the ratio of manufactured products.

It is not necessary to say more to show that the foundation under the investment markets of the country, as they exist today, is vastly stronger than the foundation existing at any time hitherto. Many railway stocks have come or are coming soon to the point of being strict investments. As such they will not be subject to declines as violent as those which have occurred in the past, just as bonds which had reached an investment basis ten years ago have not had large decline in the intervening time. A stock which has reached the point where its margin of safety above current dividends will allow for all the loss of earnings that is likely to occur in bad times may be regarded as protected against great decline by permanent change in conditions bearing upon it.

With reference to stocks which have not reached this position, it can be said that community of ownership seems likely to be a factor of large importance. Stocks which have been acquired for purposes of control are not as likely to come on the market and produce serious decline as are stocks held by speculators for a profit. It is beyond question that large amounts of stock have been taken out of the market for this purpose and are likely to stay out for an indefinite time.

Even where stocks are not held for this purpose, the steadying in rates which ought to accompany the working out of the community of ownership idea should help the earnings of other roads and thus tend to maintain values. More scientific methods of operation, concentrated ownerships and a broader view of railway management tend toward greater stability in value of railway stocks.

A favorable factor in the situation is the demonstration in the last few years that this country has reached the point where it can compete successfully with any other in the markets of the world. Prospects for finding a market for surplus products of iron, coal, leather and textiles, as well as cereals, in other parts of the world will help to steady the output of manufacturers with a helpful influence upon trade at large.

The industrial capitalization of the last few years is favorable in the sense that it has made financing easier and has enabled producers to improve their position with reference to economy in operation and distribution. Industrials have been overcapitalized, and this error will probably prove costly to those who have the securities, but the principle of combination is sound, and the reorganizations that will come in the next few years will probably bring out the good and exclude the evil to some extent in this method of carrying on the great industries of the country.

In a narrower sense, railroad earnings continue good, clearings continue in excess of those last year, money bids fair to be in reasonable supply, and the stock market has shown wonderful ability thus far to resist unfavorable developments.

October 9, 1901

The stock market is always to be considered from two points of view: The first, and most important, is its main tendency, which is always to be regarded as continuing for a considerable length of time. The second, and less important movement, is a reversal of the main movement and is very variable in extent and in time.

In a bull market, the best method of trading is to buy stocks on declines and hold them patiently for large profits. If the bull market be well established, it will do to buy on advances, because, if relapses occur, it can be felt that the next high level will recover the temporary loss and bring profits.

In a well-established bear market, the best form of trading is to sell [short] stocks on rallies and wait patiently for declines. If there is no doubt about the bear market, stocks can be sold [short] when they are down, but allowance should be made for probable rallies and the danger of being frightened into covering on such rallies. When the character of the market is in doubt, increased caution should be exercised.

It is difficult to say whether the market is now in a bull or bear period. During 1897, 1898 and 1900 there was no doubt on this point. A well-defined bull market was under way, and while there were disturbing elements from time to time, they were of a local character and did not change the main tendency.

The proof of the existence of a bear market or a bull market is afforded by the movement of average prices, which show whether one level is lower than another or not. A bear market always produces the result of a series of fluctuations, a falling average. This fall is sometimes slow and sometimes irregular, but the result is certain.

Now take the market since last May. It has been a series of swings over much of the same ground. Prices of railway stocks have not been as high as they were just before the May panic, nor as low as they were at the close, May 9. Until there is a new level, either high or low, it will not be certain whether the main tendency is up or down. One point, however, is suggested: The average has gradually come nearer to the low point instead of nearer to the high point.

The industrial average furnishes additional evidence. The high point of twelve industrials May 1 was 75.93. The close May 9 was 67.38, while the average is now down to 64.48 or distinctly below the previous lowest. It was almost inevitable that the industrial market should lead decline, because industrial stocks have been in a relatively weak position on account of the faults in their organization. For such stocks to fulfill their natural destiny is, however, evidence that railroad stocks, which may be above value, will have a tendency to take the same course.

What we have said hitherto applies to the main movement of the market. The subordinate movement presents a somewhat different view. The stock market seldom has uninterrupted advances or declines. Its gains and its losses are the net outcome of an irregular movement. Even in a bear market, days of advance are very frequent.

This is because there are always strong people long of stocks and hopeful enough to be willing to add something to their lines. It is because the seller of short stocks must become a buyer, while the holder of long stocks is not necessarily a seller. It is because whenever stocks become oversold, and there is difficulty in borrowing, somebody endeavors to start covering in order to make a turn out of frightened shorts. These, and other causes, combine to make more rallies in a bear market than there are relapses in a bull market, even where the total movement is about the same.

Furthermore, there is always a feeling on the part of traders when the market has gone one way for several days in succession that it ought to turn, and stocks are bought in anticipation of recovery. The buyers are sometimes numerous enough, and powerful enough, to make by their own purchases the rally which they anticipate.

The market is now in a position where professional traders think a rally is due. Such traders have bought stocks expecting such a rally, and the strength shown yesterday reflected this temper. The argument is that prices have fallen for more than a week and that there is nothing in sight to justify any serious break; hence, no matter what the market may do in the future, it ought to have temporary improvement. Taking markets as they run, this reasoning is sound. There are, however, always exceptions to every rule, and this may be one. One thing is clear: If the market does not rally soon, traders will throw over their long stock and sell short lines on the ground that when the market fails to do what it theoretically should do, there is some good reason therefor and they do not care to take the chances of opposing it.

October 15, 1901

. . . .

We have referred frequently of late to the foreign situation as forecasting a change for the worse in trade conditions here. There has been no improvement in Germany. Last week brought increasing depression and despondency. There was no improvement in trade conditions nor in commercial sentiment. . . .

French money continues to seek employment in London, partly as a result of new taxes and partly as a result of disappointment over industrial investments. An expert examination of 150 investment stocks dealt in at Paris is alleged to have shown losses in operation for the half-year ended June 30, of over $10,000,000. Russia has been passing through a period of depression for more than a year, and the short wheat and rye crops this year will be almost a national disaster in view of the conditions previously existing.

Regarding the great commercial nations as forming one industrial body, it is difficult to see how that a rather extreme case of injury or malnutrition to the leg, which we may call Germany, and the results of blood poisoning which appear elsewhere [in the body] can fail to affect the right arm, which we may call the United States. There are those who believe that the analogy is not complete, and that the youth and vigor of the youngest of the great nations will enable it to throw off disease and continue the superb health illustrated by conditions in the last two years.

This, however, is something which, while forecasts may differ, must become known as the result of demonstrated facts. Which leads to the point where we often stop with the statement that whoever wishes to read this riddle earlier than his neighbor must note steadily the important facts as they transpire so as to see the changes as they may come along for better or for worse.

October 18, 1901

. . . .

. . . A large proportion of the industrial stocks dealt in today are new creations—promoters' schemes brought to maturity in the forcing house of a business boom. These companies have not been tried by adversity nor felt the effects of hard times. That some of them have suffered great loss of profits in good times shows how vulnerable they were to competition, and certainly suggests that when competition and hard times come together, the effect will be serious.

These industrial companies are now somewhat in the position occupied by the newer railroad systems in 1881. In that period, St. Paul and Missouri Pacific were 7 per cent stocks, with good surpluses. Union Pacific was considered as strong as it is now. Atchison was an investment stock. Even Wabash preferred paid regular dividends. But when the day of trial came, earnings and dividends disappeared together.

There is something more than a possibility that when a history of this period is being reviewed in the *Journal,* it will be shown that industrial companies which paid 7 per cent in boom times subsequently failed to maintain earnings and gradually went through the process, first, of stopping dividends, then of issuing bonds, then of default in interest and, finally, of reorganization.

We do not wish to be understood as saying that all industrials are alike and that all have receivers awaiting them. Nothing of the kind. There is no taint in the word industrial. Some of the best stocks are industrials. . . .

The trouble with industrials is not that they are industrials, but that certain industrials have been created, not with reference to the capital on which a good return could be paid one year with another, but with a capital all out of proportion to either normal earning capacity or assessed value, a capital created with the idea that in a boom $50,000,000 of stocks could be sold as easily as $20,000,000, and with the dominating thought in the mind of the promoter that this added $30,000,000 was the one thing of supreme importance. Where this has been done, the penalty will have to be paid, and it will have to be paid chiefly by innocent stockholders who bought in good faith, but in utter ignorance of the value of what they were buying.

. . . .

October 22, 1901

Trade conditions abroad are of unusual importance, because depression in England and on the Continent is so likely to bring about a check in business here.

The situation in England hinges, to a large extent, on the war in South Africa. The loss of gold receipts from the Rand has not only reduced the supply of money, but has cut off the South African demand for English manufacturers and lessened the ability of England to make loans in countries where such loans would have resulted in increased purchases of English goods.[3] The great rise in coal, wages and other materials has led to a falling off in the profits of English roads and a resulting decline in railway stocks. There is little promise of improvement.

In the iron trade there has been very little demand for 1902 deliveries, leading to manufacturers having to shade prices. Foreign shipments of pig iron from Middlesboro for nine months of this year were only 402,601 tons, compared with 649,864 for the same time last year. The cotton trade shows a very narrow margin of profit, and there is talk of curtailment of production. The building trade has dropped off, resulting in a large accumulation of building materials, especially woods, and many speculative builders are in a very unpleasant position.

Investors in France have had very heavy losses on industrial enterprises in Russia. The French *Economist* estimates that French investments in industrial concerns in Russia, outside of Russian railroads, have been about $400,000,000 in the last few years. The fall in the shares of these companies in the last two years has ranged from 50 to 80 per cent, with an average of perhaps 50 per cent, or something like $200,000,000. The causes of these losses have been overenthusiasm, lack of sufficient knowledge, bad management and too rapid investment of capital in a short time. The Russian government is now placing orders with distressed manufacturers, and there is a strong hope that the loan to be raised in France next year will tide over the existing difficulty until Russian industrial companies can take care of themselves.

We have already pointed out the character and extent of the depression in Germany. The country is passing through a crisis which must continue for some time. One of the great disadvantages of Germany is that the savings of the country have been used up to a large extent and other countries are thus far unwilling to invest money there. It seems probable, therefore, that Germany will have to go through a period of dullness and depression, during which savings can accumulate, before there can be any lasting revival of business.

Meantime the admirable results obtained by the Bank of Germany are furnishing an object lesson to this country. Instead of yielding to the alarm that has been felt by smaller institutions, the Bank of Germany has made free use of its powers and has increased its loans very largely, and, as far as can be seen, without the slightest unfavorable result. Indeed, its action seems to have been the one thing which has stood in the way of complete demoralization. The bank in one recent week extended accommodations to borrowers to the amount of over 90 million dollars and this without creating a ripple upon the surface of the money market. The ability of the Bank of Germany to do what has been done grows partly out of the law which allows the bank to issue notes in excess of the authorized circulation and of the gold held to any amount it wishes by paying 5 per cent duty on the excess issue. The law authorizing the unlimited issue, instead of being a cause for apprehension, has had the effect of lessening apprehension and of saving borrowers.

It has furnished a very striking illustration of the soundness of the position taken by Mr. Stickney in his address before the Bankers' Convention, in which he declared that swapping credits was the function of the modern commercial bank and that failure to continually exercise this function was sure to do incalculable mischief; furthermore, that the capacity to continue exercising the banking function had the effect of maintaining confidence and sustaining values during a commercial crisis. It is certain that the achievements by the Bank of Germany in the last few months, and the effect of the policy it has pursued, will be made the basis of very careful study by bankers in other countries.

Meantime, with distress in Russia, great depression in Germany, heavy losses in France and trade depression in England, it is a grave question whether commercial prosperity can be expected to increase in this country.

October 25, 1901

. . . .

There has been no instance since 1860 when a well-defined bull period has lasted less than four years. To assume two years ago that the rise had culminated in April, 1899, was to admit that the bull period has lasted somewhat less than three years, and this seemed to throw normal calculations out of joint. The event proved that the decline from September, 1899, to June, 1900, was a relapse and not a change in the main tendency; hence that those who believed in the spring of 1900 that the divergence between prices and values must be settled by advancing prices instead of declining values were right.

Now the measure of time for the bull market is full. The high level of the period, judging by the past, should occur this year. Prices have had a great rise within a year. The average of twenty railway stocks is 37 points higher than it was at the low point in the first half of 1900, and it is almost that much higher than it was exactly two years ago.

. . . .

October 29, 1901

Cycles in business may not be subject to scientific demonstration, but the theory has for a century worked well in practice. The reasons given why business should increase for a number of years and then, for a number of years, run backwards may or may not be sound. But action based on belief that this will occur has been sound. When the turn comes, there is always something to help the movement along, no matter whether the tendency is up or down.

Assume for a moment that the turn in the market came last spring. What has happened since of a depressing character? First, the Northern Pacific corner and the panic of May 9; then the loss of more than one-third of the corn crop; then the strike [United States Steel Co.]; then the assassination of President McKinley; then serious damage to cotton; then a series of unfavorable statements by industrial corporations; then trade conditions threatening the copper market, with a great falling off in copper exports and depression in trade abroad. Now come indications of a material decrease in exports and of decrease in railway earnings.

The market has stood up well under these blows because the momentum of good trade has carried business along on a sufficiently large scale to give increased clearings, increased railway earnings and, in many lines of business, increased profits.

Holders of stocks have not been disposed to sell, and the absence of liquidation has kept the market from important declines. Probably the bulk of the people interested in stocks are now more hopeful than despondent and disposed to consider purchases for long account wiser than short sales. This is always the public state of mind after a long period of advance, just as the public is always very slow to come into the market after a long period of decline.

We think, however, that those who do not wish to be governed by sentiment, but who are concerned solely in weighing the evidence for or against prices, will admit that the blows which the market has received since last spring have been numerous enough and heavy enough to raise the question whether they are not the accompaniment of a period of falling prices.

Take the question of exports and the shipping trade, for instance. The grain rate from New York to Liverpool a year ago was 4d. It is now 1¾d. The provision rate, which was 20s., is now 6s.3d. The flour rate per ton, which was 17s.6d., is now 5s., while the cotton rate has dropped from 50 cents to 17½ cents. Rates to Havre and Hamburg have had a proportionate decline, amounting to from 40 to 70 per cent.

The remarkable fact is that these rates do not bring cargoes. It is stated in the shipping trade that hundreds of vessels are idle because cargoes cannot be obtained and that the depression in the shipping trade is greater than it has been for years. Part of this loss of tonnage is due to the falling off in the corn crop. Exports of corn since July

1 have been 16,133,401 bushels, compared with 50,573,349 bushels for the same time last year, or only about one-third this year of the amount shipped last year. The short crop of corn has made the use of other feed products necessary and will result in smaller shipments of hog products. Indeed, it is impossible for the corn crop to fall over 800,000,000 bushels without producing widespread loss of tonnage, of profits and of buying power in many directions.

The depression in the shipping industry is not confined to the Atlantic coast of the United States. It is felt abroad as much as here. There appears to be an oversupply of tonnage in the world, with the singular additional fact that almost every great shipyard in the world has plenty of work on hand for months to come. This means that the profits of the last two years have resulted in orders for ships which cannot be profitably employed when they are completed.

English ship-owners have sold a great many vessels in the past two years and have invested the proceeds in the building of new ships. A large proportion of the new tonnage is in the form of cargo ships and very large tramp steamers, requiring deep water at ports, and being, therefore, limited to certain ports. In addition to this, termination of the South African war will release a fleet now employed in government transport service.

All this is in line, which seems so important at this time. The ocean-carrying trade has not gone to pieces and reached what the London *Economist* calls the "most serious condition ever known at this season of the year" without reason. That reason has been a check to consumption, originating in Germany and spreading over the world. The effect has not been felt here as a whole, but when the relation between supply and demand is such that a fall of 50 per cent and more in ocean rates does not move cargoes, the situation certainly calls for careful study with reference to the next important development, which, as far as this country is concerned, might be considerable exports of gold at the time of year when gold ought to be coming this way.

October 31, 1901

All trade rests on the ability of the consumer to consume. Consumption is never checked by lack of desire, but always by inability to procure. Inability to procure is because consumers are not able to dispose of what they have to sell. This may be farm products, mineral products, transportation or labor in its various forms.

The margin between the proceeds of the day's work and the cost of the day's living is so small in a vast number of cases that very small curtailment in the sale of labor must bring immediate curtailment in consumption. Furthermore, the world is now so bound together that when contraction occurs on a large scale in any country where civilization has created manifold wants, the effect must be felt in other countries.

It is fully recognized that there has been a great falling off in the ability of consumers to buy goods in Germany and Russia, and to a lesser extent in Austria, Belgium, France and England.

The immediate effect in Germany of a falling off in the consumptive demand was an accumulation of goods, which the owners sought to force into consumption by lowering prices. This had the effect of reducing profits and, to some extent, the closing of establishments, or a reduction of output where the output could not be profitably sold. This had two sequences: first, creating further falling off in demand, because those who lost employment lost a considerable part, also, of their power to buy, and, second, putting lower-priced goods into competition with goods manufactured elsewhere, causing a lowering of prices in other markets in order to prevent the loss of business.

This is exactly what is going on in Europe, and while the consequences have not been heavily felt here thus far, they are certain to be felt unless there should come marked recovery in conditions abroad before the widening circle of competitive prices is fully felt here.

Nor are indications of this wanting. The classified trade statement of the country for September and for nine months is instructive. Obviously, the effect of existing trade conditions abroad would be to increase exports to this country, where high prices still prevail, which would mean here an increase in imports of merchandise.

For nine months imports of merchandise have increased 22 millions, but the increase in September alone was 7¼ millions, or nearly one-third of the whole amount. Naturally, there would be an increase of imports of goods ready for consumption. We find that for the month of September alone the increase was over one million dollars. It is certain that raw materials would be marketed in this country when home markets declined. And we see an increase in imports of raw materials in September of 4¼ millions. No one would question that with the prosperity which has existed in this country for several years, importation of luxuries would expand. The increase in importation of luxuries for nine months has been over 13 million dollars, or almost half the total increase.

The table of exports is equally instructive. With manufacturing abroad depressed and prices low, we could not expect to continue large exports of manufactured goods. It is no surprise, therefore, to see that exports of manufactures for nine months declined 41 million dollars; nor, in view of the stoppage of building abroad, that exports of forest products should have decreased three millions.

People must eat, and, outside of India and China, do not often starve in great numbers, hence we continue to sell agricultural products and have, in fact, exported in nine months 56¼ millions more than in the previous year, but here, again, the falling off in ability to buy is shown by a decrease in exports of agricultural products in September of nearly five million dollars.

The tariff affords partial protection to the manufacturers of this country against the inroads of foreign goods, but while this country can maintain its home market to a large extent, it has been demonstrated that the manufacturing capacity of the country has outgrown the home market and that anything like the full employment of labor requires markets abroad.

Specialties manufactured in this country can be sold abroad to a greater or less extent at the manufacturer's price, but staple goods, manufactured in all countries, cannot be sold by American manufacturers in foreign markets except in competition with other goods offered in those markets. Hence, to be sold at all, they must be sold at a price which may not be profitable to the manufacturer here in view of the higher labor cost; or, if sold at a low price, will give occasion for grave criticism in regard to the different prices charged to consumers abroad and consumers at home.

In whatever way the situation is regarded, it is difficult to escape the conclusion that unless there should be rapid and strong recovery in conditions abroad, the effect of the conditions now existing will be felt here in increased imports, decreased exports, a reduced demand for goods of domestic manufacture and curtailment of either the wages or the hours of labor, with the attendant consequences.

November 2, 1901

An operator of large experience writes: "Your articles are written from the standpoint of a man who tries to foresee what may happen in the future, but are you not giving the public too bearish impressions for the present?"

This is one of the points which we have tried to make clear. An operator, to have been supremely right, would have changed his position on the market only eight times in forty years. The turning points in the market in that time have been 1861, 1867, 1872, 1877, 1881, 1885, 1892 and 1896. This means that the main movements of the market are not the current fluctuations, but the tidal influences produced by slow changes in conditions. The long look ahead is vital to every operator who tries to trade on conditions instead of upon current tendencies.[4]

But during a four- or five-year up-swing the market does not advance every day, nor does it decline every day in a bear period. The market seldom moves more than three or four days in one direction without a reverse movement. The average seldom moves more than five or six points without a counter movement of two or three points. There are those who always trade on the middle, or five-point movement. There are others who prefer the one-point movement from day to day.

No view of the market can be taken which will be right with reference to each of these movements at the same time. Therefore, a trader should make up his mind to which class he wishes to belong and should consider current news and current views with reference to that position.

We have lately raised the question whether the market was not near one of its main turning points. If so, it must be a turn down, as the last bull turning point was in 1896. We have pointed out various reasons why such a turn may be at hand, and these reasons, being chiefly citations of fact, have not been disputed. The disputed point is whether the reasons which are against a turn at this time are powerful enough to outweigh the reasons in favor of expecting a turn.

We are not able to tell the outcome, and the advice which we have given has been uniformly that those interested should study the situation, watch the facts, add up the totals and be able to judge for themselves. If the market is at or near a turning point, it behooves every stock operator to endeavor to discover the fact in order to reverse his operations and avoid the losses that often occur when transactions are made in opposition to the main tendency.

But should an operator sell short stock immediately if satisified that the market had turned? There is no one day when winter suddenly changes into summer, no one hour in which a man changes from young to old. Great changes are almost always gradual. In the past, when the main tendency of the market has changed, there has generally been a period during which fluctuations were small, a little run in one direction and then a reverse. In 1896 the market turned slowly and lost its advance in a most discouraging way during the first eight months of the bull period. In 1881 the market hung along during the summer and did not get a decidedly bearish tendency until fall. The midsummer rise in 1882 carried some stocks above the highest of 1881.

There is every reason to believe that the turn when it comes in this market will be slow, with many recoveries and with special stocks showing a strong response to such favorable developments as may occur. There is little ground for supposing that with a declining period at hand the immediate declines will be large, and it is certain that such declines will be followed by rallies, some of which will probably be very unpleasant for bears, as well as very encouraging for those who remain long of stocks.

The whole point in the case is that whoever believes the main movement has changed should regard those rallies as affording opportunities for profit on short sales. He should sell on such rallies and only on such rallies, and should then cover short sales on moderate declines. There are those who try to work the market both ways, but most people get better results by adhering to the side which they think represents the main tendency. If that be down, be a consistent bear. If it be up, remain a bull.

There is a great deal in the present situation that is favorable. The wealth of the people, the demand for investments, the confidence of great interests, the increased permanent earning capacity of railroads, the combinations intended to avoid needless loss of profits will all act for a time, at least, as barriers against great declines. We do not believe that any artificial combination can resist natural laws, nor that any group of capitalists can stand against the temper of the people, but they can erect breakwaters, which for a time will appear to be stronger than the tide. The breakwaters now existing are bullish, and they will undoubtedly do good service before they are overwhelmed.

November 9, 1901

The advance in prices has brought some increase in public buying. Office traders scattered over the country have quite generally bought a few stocks on the tendency. On the other hand, people who have been carrying stocks during the summer have in many cases taken the opportunity to realize. The books of some of the large commission houses show comparatively small net changes compared with a week ago.

There has been shifting of holdings rather than accumulation of stocks.

The sellers have included in many cases rich men who have marketed stocks which they have been carrying for two or three years. They have sold because they doubted whether there would be enough improvement in the situation during the coming year to justify expectation of a further sustained rise in stocks. The large operators continue to be non-committal, saying that one stock or another may be cheap, but their bullish views are half-hearted, and the public is not yet buying enough to make public operations a safe lead.

There are, of course, many confident bulls, including men of wealth, experience and skill in the market. Their bullish views rest upon two foundations. The first is a belief that the great banking houses still have schemes to be carried through and securities to sell, which insures their general support of the market and co-operation in advances when opportunity offers.

The other foundation is a belief that great increase in the wealth of the country in the last few years has created an absorbing power large enough to prevent any large decline in stocks. They hold that the farmers are rich, that mechanics are prosperous, that merchants have made money, that manufacturers have had and are having profitable business—all of which means continuance of large tonnage for railroads and profits for industrial corporations.

They hold that while the diameter of cycles has been tolerably uniform in the past, conditions are so unusual as to create the probability of a greater diameter for this epoch; that is, instead of the period of advance being from 1896 to 1901, which would be normal, it will be from 1896 to some date in the future, perhaps two or three years hence.

These views may be right. No one can say with certainty that they are not, and they certainly should be weighed by everyone who deals in stocks. No one will dispute that if the country continues to advance in prosperity and railroad earnings continue to increase, establishing higher actual values, prices will respond to that increase.

We think, however, that people should remember, also, that the market always looks strongest at the top and that this is true of a period as well as of a day. A business boom always appears soundest at its highest point. Coming changes in conditions appear in small events, not influential in themselves, but important only as they show changes. A small rotten spot in an apple is not very important, but if left alone, it may destroy the apple. There are always rotten spots in business, but if conditions are growing better, the bad spots gradually disappear and become smaller and fewer instead of more numerous and more important.

We think this describes the existing situation. The bad spots are to be watched. If they fade away, it will be well for the market. If they increase and become numerous, it will be evidence, no matter how the market looks on the surface, of a coming radical change in the tendency.

The vital spots to be watched at present are, among others, railroad earnings, gross and net, bank clearings at the principal centers, the money situation here and abroad, the exchange market here, and particularly at Paris, the reports of industrial companies, the volume and ratio of exports and imports, failures and the amount of liabilities and assets; trade conditions abroad, particularly in Germany and England; prices of staple commodities, particularly in Germany, and the tendency to increased competition in railway and in industrial lines where profits have been or are abnormally large.

These are all matters which can be watched, which the large operators always do watch to a large extent, and which combine to create the main tendencies of trade and speculation. If all these, or most of these indicators give favorable results, it will be well for the market.

If some of them are unfavorable and more become unfavorable, it will be bad for the market, no matter what temporary manipulation or sentiment may do. This is not a matter that can be told with certainty in any one day, because such conditions do not change suddenly, but they must be watched day after day and week after week in order to perceive the movement that is actually going on. To read this rightly is to foresee the course of stock prices.

November 14, 1901

In commenting, a few days ago, upon the fact that the average prices of railway and of industrial stocks have been moving apart instead of together, we gave reasons why railroad stocks should show increased strength. It is perhaps equally pertinent to point out some reasons why industrial stocks have declined or may decline in the future.

The industrial list occupies, to some extent, the position held by railroad stocks twenty years ago. Many of the railroad lines then had a great deal of new mileage, built to occupy territory and constructed far in advance of requirements. Railroad construction companies were paying large profits, and the spectacle of railroads built by capitalists for the purpose of being unloaded upon corporations which these capitalists controlled was not so common as to excite remark.

The inevitable happened. When business became bad, roads could not carry their increased charges and pay dividends, nor in some cases could even the charges be met, making collapse in prices sure.

A large proportion of the industrial stocks quoted today are of recent creation. A considerable percentage of the number represent combinations put together for the purpose of enabling promoters to make large profits by buying separate properties cheap and selling them dear in the form of stock of the combined companies.

Capitalization has proceeded boldly on the theory of capitalizing earning capacity instead of valuations, and this, while attractive from the standpoint of the promoter, necessarily stands upon the principle that values must change with earning capacity, and as the amount of capital cannot be readily changed, the changes in value must be represented by abnormal fluctuations in the price of the stock. As these stocks have been brought out and sold to a greater or less extent in good times, there is little doubt of what will occur in bad times.

The possibilities of this sort are illustrated by the following statement recently made by a man prominent in the iron trade. He said: "Some years ago, I bought a nail plant for $18,000 and in one year made out of that plant a profit of $30,000. I put this profit into extensions [additions to plant] and borrowed $20,000 more, which also went into the property. A few years later that plant was sold by the Sheriff for $7,000. The buyer left it idle for a while, but then started it up and in 1899 sold it to the Steel and Wire Co. for over $200,000."

This is perhaps an extreme case, but Mr. Carnegie had the same thought when he declared that "iron was either a king or a pauper." What is true of iron, is true to a greater or less extent of other trades. In practically every kind of manufacturing business, the difference between good times and bad times is relatively much greater than it is in railroad business because the variation in profits is so much greater.

It stands to reason, therefore, that people who own industrial stocks which they know to have been issued on an inflated basis will be very careful not to keep them, if they are able to sell them, a day after they think the tide in business has turned. The railroad boom of the last year has doubtless seemed to be a dispensation of Providence to people who had large blocks of industrial stocks for which a market was earnestly desired.

The depression in trade abroad has, doubtless, intensified the desire to sell during the recent strength in railway stocks and fully explains why with the railroad list less than four points below the highest, the industrial list should be ten points below the highest; explains why, with the railroad list nearly 30 points higher than it was a year ago, the industrial list should be less than one point higher than it was a year ago.

There are two additional reasons which are working against the industrial market. The first is the steady increase in competition, and the second, the probability of legislation against monopolies during the coming winter. It is an economic certainty that any combination which makes a profit enough to be able to pay dividends on a capital very greatly in excess of the value of the plant, will encounter competition from those who see that they can make a substantial profit on the actual capital required at prices for goods materially below those necessary to permit the combination to pay on its inflated capital. Proof of this point is afforded in many lines of business at this time. Competitors have sprung up and are springing up, and while some of them will not succeed, they as a whole will bring down profits to normal returns on a fair investment.

It has been known for some time that President Roosevelt believes further safeguards are needed to protect both the public and the investor against possible injury from combinations which may be called trusts on account of the extent of their control of the business they are in. It is too soon to say just what will be recommended, but it is fairly safe to say that some recommendation will be made and will be followed by, at least, an attempt to amend the anti-trust law. The actual enactment may do no great harm, but discussion will create apprehension and the tendency will be unfavorable on that account.

The best feature bearing on industrials is the widespread recognition that they have come to stay and are to be regulated and not destroyed. Regulation, or voluntary reorganization, or amendment putting capitalization upon a fair basis, with dividends gauged to suitable allowances for depreciation and [also gauged] to the volume of earnings in an average of good times and bad, will ultimately bring many industrial stocks to be worthy of favor and confidence.

November 16, 1901

We have frequently said that the turn in the tide of affairs would be shown by events which could be watched and the results noted. One of these events is the condition of foreign trade.

It has seemed impossible that there could be serious depression in trade abroad without its having some effect here. The effect seems certain to take the form of equalization. Theoretically, with bad trade abroad, this country could not go selling goods abroad as it could when conditions abroad were better. Theoretically, with business abroad depressed and the home market reduced, there would be increased effort on the part of foreign manufacturers to sell goods here where prices are high. Hence the evidence of an adjustment of conditions would be an increase in imports and a decrease in exports by the United States.

The October trade statement just issued bears out the theory in the case. Imports of merchandise increased in that month $10,780,823, while exports decreased $17,749,222; a comparative change for the worse as far as this country is concerned of $28,530,045 in one month.

In order to show the progress of this movement, we give in the tables following the exports and imports of merchandise in each of the ten months of this year compared with 1900.

Exports	*1901*	*1900*		*Changes*
Jan.	$136,323,601	$117,597,148	Inc.	$18,728,453
Feb.	112,957,014	119,426,985	Dec.	6,469,971
March	124,473,643	134,157,225	Dec.	9,683,582
April	120,754,170	118,722,580	Inc.	1,981,610
May	124,567,911	113,427,849	Inc.	11,140,062
June	102,774,263	108,651,957	Dec.	5,877,694
July	109,452,510	100,452,807	Inc.	8,999,703
August	108,027,868	103,575,965	Inc.	4,451,903
Sept.	106,986,864	115,901,722	Dec.	8,914,858
October	145,640,458	163,389,680	Dec.	17,749,222

Imports	*1901*	*1900*		*Changes*
Jan.	$69,307,680	$75,897,102	Dec.	$ 6,590,022
Feb.	64,501,699	68,833,941	Dec.	4,332,244
March	75,882,834	86,522,456	Dec.	10,635,624
April	76,698,131	75,510,262	Inc.	1,187,869
May	78,642,703	71,653,525	Inc.	6,989,378
June	68,404,657	61,001,692	Inc.	7,402,965
July	73,082,535	63,659,692	Inc.	9,422,843
August	73,132,138	61,820,488	Inc.	11,311,650
Sept.	66,822,532	59,568,600	Inc.	7,253,932
October	81,411,857	70,631,034	Inc.	11,780,823

It will be observed in the table of exports that the steady increases which were a characteristic of 1900 over 1899 ceased with the beginning of 1901. Results then became irregular, decreases and increases alternating, but with the tendency becoming clearer in September and October, when there were large comparative losses in two consecutive months. It should be said, however, that quite a large portion of the October loss was due to the smaller movement and the lower valuation of cotton.

The table showing the movement of imports is more definite in its character. Decreases in imports which had been pronounced in 1900 ceased in March 1901, and there has been no month since in which imports have not been larger than in the previous year. The tendency is further shown by the fact that the amount of excess over last year has been rising. It was but little more than a million dollars in April, but was 11¾ millions in October. This is precisely what could have been expected from existing trade conditions and what will probably occur in months to come until conditions here and abroad are more nearly alike.

The excess of exports of merchandise for ten months amounts to 464 millions, a decrease of about 36 million compared with last year. It is not probable that the total exports will be as large this year as they were in the previous year, and in estimating the trade balance, allowance has to be made for overvaluation of exports, undervaluation of imports and the heavy volume of carrying charges, all of which are against this country.[5]

November 28, 1901

We have received the following: "I am told that in 45 weeks out of 52, stocks can be bought cheaper on Monday than on any other day in the week. Is this so, and if so, why? Is there a recognized low day or high day, and what day is it?"

It is a tolerably complete answer to say that if Monday were uniformly the low day of the week, it would soon cease to be, because everybody would buy on Monday and it would become high day instead of low. Theories of this kind and dreambook reasoning are common with speculators who look upon the market as full of mysterious mechanism instead of being chiefly an attempt to discount expected changes in values. All sorts of events are twisted into reasons for or against buying stocks. Some of them stand for a time the test of trial, but then mysteriously go wrong.

The reasons why such theories exist, why for a time they seem to be sound, and why they inevitably go wrong, is that they form parts of the general law of chances. The foundation of this law is that events equally liable to happen tend to equality in occurrence. If a thousand black balls and a thousand white ones were put in a bag, a person drawing therefrom would, in a large number of drawings, take out just as many black ones as white ones.

It is equally true that there would be times when he would draw a considerable number of black balls without drawing any white ones, and then enough white ones to restore the balance. A sufficient number of tests would permit the construction of a table, showing the probabilities in favor of drawing any number of either color consecutively.

This in some degree has a bearing upon the number of strong days or weak days which may occur in the market. Many other influences enter into the case, but such influences over considerable periods of time neutralize each other and are interwoven into the general law of the recurrence of events equally liable to happen.

In a bull market, Monday might be expected to be rather stronger than other days because it might be supposed to get the accumulation of orders over Sunday. On the other hand, Saturday might be considered as unfavorably affected by the market being open only two hours instead of five hours. It is doubtful, however, if these modifications would have in the long run much influence. Examination over a time long enough to allow the various combinations to repeat themselves, would show that each of the days in the week was about equal to every other in the point of being high day or low day.

It would also appear that each day had runs of being either high or low. There might be a dozen weeks in which Monday would be low day. If this occurred, it could be accepted that within a short time Monday would cease to be low day and some other would take its turn in bringing up the average. This fact is what produces theories like that which has interested our correspondent. Somebody has observed a run of low Mondays and has been inclined to think they might be a permanent factor in trading. They were simply illustrations of the working of the general law, and the lesson to be drawn from them is not expectation of continuance, but certainty of change.

There is only one unchanging rule in speculation. That is the certainty that values determine prices in the long run, and that the fundamental effort on the part of everybody who tries to make markets is to foresee values and to make money by adjusting prices thereto.

In bringing this about there is often manipulation against values. The large operator who believes that a stock is going a few months hence to be worth a good deal more than the present price has to acquire a line of that stock in order to make money. He may make the price weak to induce others to sell him stock. It is difficult to tell at the start whether manipulation is in the direction of values or against them, but it usually becomes clear within a short time. So when prices are up and a large operator wishes to sell, he makes the market look strongest when he knows that an advance has been carried too far. This is a matter for individual study and opinion. Fortunately, values, especially of railroad stocks, can be determined much more accurately than heretofore, and this puts the outsider in a better position, as, while his view of value may differ from that of other people, he can, at least, act on his own opinion.

Theories of trading are of little use because of the difficulty of applying the law under which they act. It is simpler and safer to trade in one of two ways: Either be sure of knowing the value of the stock held and stand upon it as an investor, or trade blindly on news or tendencies or sentiment with a two-point stop order for protection. Each has its advantages and its disadvantages, but either method will be likely to give better results than any system of fortune-telling.

December 5, 1901

Napoleon once said, "To have patience is to have success." General Grant, in reply to a question as to what he thought was the first essential in a military commander, replied "patience." Mr. Jay Gould declared that patience was absolutely essential for any man who wished to be a successful operator in stocks. Anyone who has traded much can obtain confirmation of the value of this testimony by looking over the record of his transactions and seeing how often he has run from profits by being unwilling to wait.

The explanation is that people are not willing to apply to speculation the principles which they recognize elsewhere. Nobody who plants corn digs up the kernels in a day or two to see if the corn has sprouted, but in stocks most people want to open an account at noon and get their profit before night. If a man is bearish, he wants the market to go down at once to the point where he is disposed to cover, and then, as soon as he has taken the other side, to go straight up.

When this does not occur, people lose patience and close their accounts about the time that the move they anticipated fairly starts. If an operator is bearish on judgment, he often sees in temporary advances evidence that he is wrong, and he reverses his position. He is governed by fluctuations instead of by his judgment of the facts.

All this bears very closely on existing conditions. Operators who study the situation can hardly escape conviction that prices are high. They see that the market has gone up most of the time for five years, and they find no records in the past where advances without serious interruptions have continued for a longer time. They see an unfavorable condition of affairs abroad and know that such changes, when they come in several countries, are likely to spread to others. They see a loss in crops larger than has occurred in any previous year. They see gold go out when gold ought to be coming in, exports decreasing and imports increasing, congressional agitation against trusts, a stir in the Northwest against railway combinations, railroad earnings at a point which makes decreases a probability, and the issue of new securities in magnitude hitherto unknown.

This is surely enough to make bull operators pause. It calls for the most careful scrutiny of the reasons offered in favor of further large advance. The reasons given are that railroad earnings show increases still, and that community of ownership will maintain railway profits at a level higher than heretofore. It is shown that general business in this country is prosperous, with large profits in many lines of trade, and with demand exceeding the supply in great trades. The conclusions drawn from this are that prices are made by values and values are still rising. To this is added the fact that great houses hold many securities and can probably be counted as on the long side of the market.

The respective weight of these facts should be judged by every man who proposes to deal in stocks other than on current tendencies. If he decides that prices are too high, he will prefer the short side, or he may decide the other way, but whatever the decision, the exercise of patience is likely to be necessary.

If the market is going materially higher, time will be required in which values can be established sufficiently to justify bull speculation. If the market is going down, it must be remembered that many people think otherwise and that time will be required for the weight of unfavorable facts to disintegrate and break through the structure of confidence that has been built up by the five years of success on the long side.

Momentum is just as real in the stock market as it is in physics. The momentum which carried prices down from 1892 to 1896 was so strong as to keep the market heavy and frequently weak for eight months after the turn in the tide came. The momentum which carried prices up from 1877 to 1881 was so strong as to give the market striking powers of recovery up to midsummer in 1882.

Exactly the same thing will occur in this period when the high point is reached. The market will decline stubbornly and rally frequently, just as it has done since May. This will continue until bull confidence has been fully established.

The man who is a bear today should patiently wait until the market has risen considerably from the lowest and until indications are that bull efforts have been exhausted. He should then sell stocks [short] moderately and wait until prices refuse to go lower. Then he should cover and await an opportunity to repeat the operation. The man who is a bull should wait until the market has had considerable decline and becomes firm at a low level. He should then buy and wait until he sees no prospect of further rise and then take his profit.

Both of these requirements involve the exercise of great patience. It is weary work waiting for high points or for low points, and it is about as weary waiting for an expected move to work itself out when small counter-moves are continually coming in and threatening to defeat the expected move altogether. This is wherein the greatness of patience consists, and it marks the difference between the man who succeeds in getting large profits on his ventures and the man who does the right thing, but who fails to reap the full benefit.

The success of great operators comes very largely through taking the right position and holding on in good report and in evil report, when the market looks right and when it does not, regardless of disturbing rumors and indifferent to threatened dangers, looking chiefly to the development of value in that particular stock, until the desired result has been reached.

There is a large operator in this city who bought quite an amount of a certain stock about ten months ago. He has held it against all sorts of difficulties and doubts. Most of his associates in the campaign have become discouraged and have sold. He today has a profit of more than $500,000, representing chiefly the yield on his stock of patience.

December 11, 1901

The large advance in the average price of commodities in the last few months, and particularly the gain in November, is not favorable for the country at large. An increase in the cost of living, reflected by a rise of three points in 350 commodities in one month, means, among other things, a shrinkage in the savings of the people at large. This month brought no corresponding increase in wages or profits, taking business as a whole; consequently, it meant just so much more out of gross income as the cost of living. This means a shrinkage in buying power and will result in a falling off in demand for commodities. This will check the rising tendency in prices, but will not restore savings.

It will, however, tend to increase the demand for higher wages, and this, in turn, will affect manufacturing lines. The chain which, starting with the farmer and the miner, passes through the links represented by merchants, manufacturers, trades and other non-producers has two links where breaks occur.

They are the ability to borrow money on credit and the employment of labor. One of the surest marks of the coming of bad times is the falling off in the employment of labor. As labor does not voluntarily deprive itself of employment, the cause of lack of employment must be found in inability to borrow money on favorable terms by those who depend on borrowed money to carry on lines of business in which labor is employed.

Hence the importance of anything which largely increases the cost of living and of any financial policy which tends to make money scarce enough to threaten a restriction of credits. There are now possibilities along both these lines, but there is ground for hope that they will not become acute enough to make a radical change in the industrial situation for months to come. Men whose interests have led them to look at the industrial situation with the utmost care look for a good degree of prosperity during the first half of 1902.

December 14, 1901

We have received the following inquiry: "You seem to feel sure that the next few years will bring falling prices for stocks. What great factors in the situation justify such a belief?"

We think there are three. The first is the operation of the law of action and reaction. The second relates to the great mass of industrial stocks created in the last few years. The third is the position of the United States Treasury.

The law of action and reaction in trade is founded on principles of human nature. People like to buy stocks when they go up, not, as a rule, when they go down. The prosperous farmer buys more land, the prosperous miner puts his profits into additional claims; the prosperous manufacturer builds larger mills. When things go well, the tendency is to expand, to increase risks and to incur higher fixed charges. When prices of commodities rise at intervals for a considerable time, merchants increase their stocks of goods to take advantage of the next rise. When this goes on over the country, it produces a business boom like that which occurred in 1879 and 1880, again in 1892 and again in the last few years.

After such a period of expansion, there invariably comes a time when prices recede, demand falls off, goods depreciate and profits disappear. As this process goes on and one loss after another has to be taken, sentiment changes from high hopefulness to shaken confidence, and then runs into anxiety and depression, ending in confidence in nothing.

The period of depression is usually longer than the period of advance because decline is resisted and people hang on to what they have, hoping for the best as long as they can. Better methods, more wisdom and greater conservatism have a tendency to lessen the violence of the advance and the severity of the decline, but neither can be wholly eradicated from business affairs until human nature is greatly modified.

It is certain that the pendulum which has been swinging up since 1896 will from some point begin to swing back. No one can say with certainty when the high point will be reached, but the higher it goes above normal, the nearer the time when the reverse movement will set in. Dun's index number, which was 94.15 at the end of 1892, was 72.45 in 1897. It has now risen to 101.37, the highest of recent record. As this number covers the price of 350 commodities, the extent of the advance is impressive.

During the past few years, stocks representing a par value of thousands of millions of dollars have been created to represent industrial properties. These stocks are an absolutely new quantity in the financial situation. They represent, for the most part, a very high degree of inflation. They have been received by people whose chief thought has been to turn them into cash. Persistent efforts have been made to distribute them among investors, but the magnitude of the amount, the knowledge of overcapitalization and the lack of information in regard to the properties have kept the public from buying largely, except in stocks which have had a wide artificial market and where the public, buying as speculators, have become investors from necessity.

Great blocks of industrial stocks remain in the hands of promoters, syndicates and bankers. They have drifted into loans. These stocks have been given a quotation, have been mixed with other collateral, and in this way are carried on borrowed money. Disturbance in the money market must cause discrimination against this class of collateral, and borrowers will be required to give other collateral or take up loans. This will increase the demand for money on this class of stocks and, as it becomes difficult to get, will lead to increased efforts to market such stocks.

Lenders who find themselves caught with unsalable collateral will be obliged to carry it, thereby reducing the accommodation which they can give to other borrowers and thus indirectly reducing credits by curtailing the facilities for exchange of credits. Ultimately, this mass of new securities will be digested, but there will probably be times in the next few years when the digestive system of the country will seem to be considerably out of order.

The United States Treasury is absorbing money at a rate which would be disastrous were not steps taken to restore this money to circulation at short intervals. The method of restoration is to purchase bonds, or to place the money in deposits secured by bonds. Bonds, therefore, are essential either way. Bonds are becoming scarcer and must grow scarcer every year. It is possible that Congress may cut down revenue or increase expenses. There is, however, opposition to cutting down the revenue by important tariff changes on account of the disturbing effect of tariff agitation on general business. Some reduction of internal revenue will undoubtedly be made, and increase in expenditures will grow out of the Nicaragua Canal, irrigation in the far West or other government operations on a large scale.

The government will probably endeavor to keep the Treasury from doing serious harm, but legislation is always slow, and danger might come before relief measures were fully worked out. The possibilities involved will have a tendency to bring about action calculated to prevent danger, but until there is much action, danger from this point must be recognized.

We do not think any of these considerations have a bearing upon the immediate market. They are only to be regarded as great forces, slow in operation, but irresistible when fairly under way. They are the kind of forces which great operators watch carefully and go with, instead of against, in planning operations to extend over a long period.

December 19, 1901

There is a market theory that stocks, after a December decline on realizing, should have a January rise on the investment of the money coming out in interest and dividends. The sentiment is quite strong now, and stocks are being bought in anticipation of such an advance.

We are quite willing to admit that the action of the market at any one time of the year is no indication of what it will be at the same time in another year, except where there is a well-established cause for this action each year. The market almost invariably has a period of advance in some portion of July or August for the good reason that crops are measurably determined at that time and stocks are bought in anticipation of the earnings which crops assure.

In the same sense the January disbursements are a recurring factor of importance. A great deal of money comes out, and, while probably the larger part is used for living purposes, there remains a considerable sum which is put into securities for either speculation or investment. There is, therefore, some reason for expecting a January rise.

We have compiled in the table following the average price of railway stocks in December and January for each of the past sixteen years. We have taken the low point in December and the high point in January, with the date of each, and have indicated, also, the relapse in January occurring when the high point came early enough in the month to give time for any decided setback. Where no such decline is given, it may be assumed that none of importance occurred. The average is of twelve stocks down to the year 1897 and for twenty stocks after that time. The column of figures under the words December and January show the dates of the month when the prices were made:

Year	*Dec.*	*Low*	*Jan.*	*High*	*Jan.*	*Relapse*
1885–1886	22	77.04	4	86.30	25	80.28
1886–1887	20	86.46	19	89.95	24	86.55
1887–1888	13	80.38	9	83.38	24	81.38
1888–1889	5	81.88	14	87.13	24	85.88
1889–1890	4	90.25	28	93.16	—	—
1890–1891	8	76.77	13	85.82	26	82.58
1891–1892	7	88.15	1	91.19	19	88.11

Year	Dec.	Low	Jan.	High	Jan.	Relapse
1892–1893	19	85.76	21	90.38	—	—
1893–1894	29	71.39	31	75.38	—	—
1894–1895	27	71.23	4	71.81	28	68.68
1895–1896	20	70.10	31	74.82	—	—
1896–1897	18	49.98	19	53.19	—	—
1897–1898	4	60.76	29	65.90	—	—
1898–1899	5	71.21	26	82.70	—	—
1899–1900	22	72.48	2	78.87	11	75.95
1900–1901	8	87.21	12	97.85	19	93.56

The most conspicuous fact brought out by this table is that in fifteen of the sixteen years there was from a moderate to a large advance from the low point in December to the high point in January. In three of these years, however, very little of the rise occurred in the month of January, the high point of the month occurring once on the 1st, once on the 2nd, and once on the 4th of the month.

In four of the sixteen years the advance amounted to nine points or more. The move amounted to six points twice and to five points three times, with the remainder less than five points. In one year, 1895, there was no January rise. In nine of the sixteen years there was an average decline after the high point in January, ranging from two to six points.

The rise had its start in December seven times in the first third of the month, three times in the second third, and six times in the last third, including in the latter the fractional rise of 1895. The culmination of the advance came five times in the first third of January, five in the second, and six times in the last.

The advance this year appears to have started in the second third of December. In past years, when the advance has started in the second third of December, the January culmination came once on the 9th, once on the 19th, and once on the 21st. In nine of the sixteen years, the average rise from low in December to high in January did not exceed five points.

We think the nearest approach to practical utility in this is the demonstration that there is about an even chance that the high point in January will not exceed the low point in December in any year by more than five points in the average. If, therefore, that part of the move which comes in December shows a rise of two or three points from the lowest in December, there is something more than a possibility that the January part of the advance will not be very great.

Whether it is much more than a possibility must be judged by the conditions which exist in January.[6]

December 20, 1901

. . . .

The movement of the market is always in swings. The center point stands for close approximation to values. When prices go down, the momentum carries them too far, and when they go up, the same thing occurs; hence reaction in both is inevitable.

The same thing is true with regard to small speculative movements. If the price of a stock is run up two or three points, it very generally swings back about half of the amount of the advance. There are exceptions where changes in value or a fixed speculative purpose makes an abnormal movement, but in a free trading stock there is more than an average chance that any primary movement will be followed by a reactionary movement of at least three-eighths of the first swing.

This fact is illustrated very forcibly in our table showing the course of the market since 1885. The average responds almost as regularly as individual stocks to this rule. Charts showing movement of prices will be found to afford interesting confirmation.

. . . .

December 21, 1901

Momentum is one of the great factors in speculation. Momentum is the result of a conviction impressed upon great numbers of people that the tendency of the market is in a certain direction. Such people, consequently, act in that direction in either the purchase or the sale of stocks. When there has been a bull market for three or four years, the public becomes convinced that the long side is the right side. Hence when stocks decline, the public buys, and this buying, with the help of manipulation, makes frequent rallies even after the tide has fairly turned down.

The market for the past eight months furnishes an interesting illustration of each of these forces. There has been one event after another which has brought decline, but from each the rebound has been practically equal to the loss, and now after ten periods of decline and ten periods of advance the market is less than six points below the price prevailing May 1, the highest thus far of record. The table following gives these movements in detail:

	Average 20 stocks
May 1, top of boom	117.86
May 9, panic	103.87
Drop in 8 days	13.99
May 10, recovery	110.06
Advance in 1 day	6.19
May 14, second panic drop	104.54
Drop in 4 days	5.52
June 3, rally from second drop	115.69
Advance in 20 days	11.15
June 11, corn damage	114.39
Drop in 8 days	1.60
June 17, rally from crop report	117.65
Advance in 6 days	3.26
July 15, confirmed corn damage	106.35
Drop in 28 days	11.35
July 18, rally from crop damage	111.50
Advance in 3 days	5.15
August 5, cotton and corn damage	104.86
Drop in 16 days	6.64
August 26, rally from crop news	111.69
Advance in 21 days	6.83
Sept. 13, President's assassination and death	105.30
Drop in 18 days	6.39
Sept. 21, rally after death of President	110.82
Advance in 8 days	5.52
Oct. 7, copper and crop damage	106.20
Decline in 16 days	4.62
Oct. 26, rally	110.88
Advance in 19 days	4.68
Oct. 28, copper slump	109.60
Decline in 2 days	1.28
November 11, rally	114.56
Advance in 14 days	4.96
November 14, copper, etc.	112.35
Drop in 3 days	2.21
November 22, rally	115.21
Advance in 8 days	2.86
December 16, cotton, copper, etc.	110.96
Decline in 24 days	4.25
December 19, rally	111.96
Advance in 3 days	1.00

	Average 20 stocks
20 active railroad stocks, Dec. 19, 1901	111.96
20 active railroad stocks, Dec. 19, 1900	91.51
Advance	20.45
Same stocks, December 22, 1899	72.48
Advance in two years	39.48

This table is interesting from another point of view. It shows the probability that secondary movements will equal practically half of the primary movements, whatever the former may be. After the May drop of 14 points the recovery amounted to 6.19. After the June rise of about 14 points, the decline amounted to 11.00, while from this decline of 11 points there came a rally of 5.15. The changes since June have been so nearly alike as to indicate a close balance of forces each way. It will probably be found that whenever the market has another large primary movement, the secondary movement will be not less than three-eighths of the first swing, while it may be much more.

The table can hardly be said to show that the disintegrating process has made great headway. What is shown on this side is that the market has had one blow after another. Obviously, they have prevented the advance which would otherwise have occurred; as, if the market has held its own with this weight, it would probably have gone higher without it.

If the market continues to receive blows which break prices down, the time will come when rallies will fail to maintain the average level of prices. On the other hand, should there be conditions which prevent fresh blows, it is reasonable to suppose that the force which has held the market thus far will be strong enough to carry it higher.

It is practically certain that the market will receive blows in the future, but their frequency, extent and effect cannot be foretold. Good judges of markets and of trade conditions believe that the country will have a good degree of prosperity during the first six months of the coming year, but that is about as far as conservative predictions run.[7]

December 31, 1901

. . . .

The increase in the value of eighty stocks for the calendar year has amounted to over $760,000,000. The decrease in value of twenty-five stocks has been about $150,000,000, leaving a net gain of $610,000,000 in what may be called the active and semi-speculative list [of the New York Stock Exchange]. This does not take in hundreds of other stocks, which have advanced to a greater or less extent, nor hundreds of bonds which have risen materially. It makes no reference to the intangible firm ownerships [sole proprietorships and partnerships] which have become tangible [by assuming the corporate form] through conversion into stocks and takes no account of the increase in wealth which has come through advance in values of products of all kinds. These additions would multiply manifold the sum representing increased values in speculative stocks.

When we remember, therefore, that wealth is quite distinct from currency and that resources chiefly represent credits, it is easy to see how the enormous increase in credits has served to establish the demand for investments which is making prices hitherto unknown for the high-class investment stocks, and is sustaining prices generally at so high a level.

Even the increase of $600,000,000 in the value of semi-speculative stocks is a factor of importance in maintaining the price of these same stocks. The man who owned a thousand shares of Atchison common at the beginning of 1901, representing $42,000, and who now has the same thousand shares representing $80,000, has added $38,000 to his marginal resources during that time. The same thing in many stocks, and especially when multiplied by the increased credits produced in other ways, shows a volume of credit which cannot be measured or appreciated.

While this is of the highest importance at present, it must be remembered that credit falls as rapidly as it rises and that it is possible for credit resources to be swept away, not only by decreases in actual values, but by any loss of confidence which restricts operations on a large scale. Credit is and must remain the basis of business, the basis of speculation and the foundation upon which values rest. Saying that it ought not to be so does not change the facts. The facts, however, should be continually borne in mind when expansion of credits has produced either abnormal values or abnormal prices.

NOTES

[1] Note that Dow believes the turn in the market came because "the measure of time was full." As a result, contraction was one of "the inevitable results of the expansion of previous years." This is reminiscent of the famous dictum of Juglar that "the only cause of depression is prosperity."

[2] Dow has again used the index numbers compiled by John R. Commons and published by the Bureau of Economic Research. See Dow's editorial of September 13, 1900, above.

[3] Gold production of Africa (of which about 80 per cent came from the Rand) totaled 3,532,488 ounces in 1899. Due to the Boer War only 419,503 ounces were mined in 1900 and 439,704 in 1901.

[4] Henry Hall commented on this editorial in *How Money is Made in Security Investments* (New York, 1908), p. 101: "In confirmation of the cycle theory, allusion may be made to the assertion of a financial writer of repute in New York City, a few years ago, that 'an operator, to have been supremely right, would have changed his position on the market only eight times in forty years; the turning points have been 1861, 1867, 1872, 1877, 1881, 1885, 1892 and 1896.' It is singular that 1864 should have been omitted from this summary; but the remark agrees in substance with the ten year cycle theory."

[5] Cf. Mitchell, pp. 252–263.

[6] Note the similarity of Dow's statistical approach in this editorial to that later employed by Wesley C. Mitchell.

[7] Cf. Mitchell, pp. 65–66. Mitchell covers the same period of time and concludes: "So strong was the business situation, however, that none of these depressing influences had more than momentary effect."

CHAPTER SEVEN

January 1, 1902—June 20, 1902

THE year 1902 opened with considerably less enthusiasm than that which accompanied the speculative stock market activity characteristic of January, 1901. Stocks sales for January, 1902, on the New York Stock Exchange were less than 50 per cent of the volume reported in the same month in 1901.

Several recently promoted industrial combinations were in difficulty, and the failure of the National Asphalt Company and the Crude Rubber Company tended to make investors and speculators cautious. During the year 1902 New York Stock Exchange volume was nearly one-third less than the reported figure for the previous year, so it was obvious that the public remained out of the market.

However, general business continued excellent, and the year 1902 surpassed all former years in this respect. The United States also augmented home production by large imports for the year as a whole. American farmers enjoyed most generous harvests as contrasted with the short corn crop of 1901.

A suit against the Northern Securities Co. by the state of Minnesota in February was quickly followed by similar action by the state of Washington. On the federal level President Roosevelt instructed Attorney-General Knox to institute legal action against the company. This copious legal activity caused a severe decline in stock prices. Attorney-General Knox filed his suit early in March, and this had a depressing effect on stock prices through the month of June.

Likewise in February an agreement was reached by which the firm of J. P. Morgan & Co. would purchase control of a number of British and American shipping lines plying the North Atlantic. This was the ill-fated International Mercantile Marine Company, scheduled to include complete ownership of the White Star Line, the Leyland Line, the Atlantic Transport Line and the Dominion Line. An interest was also to be acquired in the Holland-American Line and in the Red Star Line.

While purchase of the shipping lines was not to be completed until later in the year, the gigantic combination, embracing most of the ships operating in the North Atlantic, caused hostile criticism in Great Britain, as it was thought that British supremacy on the seas was threatened.

In April John W. Gates ("Bet-a-million Gates") cornered the stock of Louisville & Nashville but sold out to J. P. Morgan, which gave rise to rumors that Morgan intended to combine the Louisville & Nashville properties with the Southern Railway. However, the combination never came about, and Louisville & Nashville passed under the control of the Atlantic Coast Line.

Also in April the anthracite coal miners under the leadership of John Mitchell demanded an eight-hour day and sixty cents a ton for mining coal. This was rejected by the coal operators. Thereupon, in May the bitter and lengthy coal strike of 1902 began and continued through October.

On the last day of April a sharp drop occurred in International Power, which was quickly followed by a complete collapse of the so-called Webb-Meyer specialties. During May the stocks involved declined as follows: Dominion Securities Company from 118¼ to 16; Hackensack Meadows Company from 79½ to 8; Storage Power from 10¼ to 3½, and North American Lumber and Pulp Company from 39¼ to 5.

Nine editorials in this chapter should be especially interesting to financial analysts, since they are among the earliest examples of modern financial analysis. They are dated February 25, 26 and 28 and March 1, 6, 13, 14, 18 and 22.

January 1, 1902

An evenly balanced penny tossed in the air is equally liable to show heads or tails. This is just as true after the penny has come down heads a dozen times in succession as it was at the beginning. Yet anybody who proceeded on the theory that there would be an indefinite run of heads would find himself wrong, except under very unusual conditions. A run on heads is followed by an equal increase in the proportion of tails, notwithstanding the fact that each is equally liable to appear on any one toss.

Reasoning upon the course of the stock market produces somewhat similiar results. Cycles do occur. The reasons given for their recurrence may be faulty, but it has been for a century better to pay attention to the fact of recurring cycles than to the arguments showing why such cycles ought not to occur.

When a cycle is demonstrated to be under way, it is comparatively easy to guess at the course of the market, especially if the cycle has two or three years more to run. The time of difficulty is when the turning period draws near, because cycles differ in length and it is impossible to say whether the turn will be a year or two sooner or later than the average.

It seemed probable a year ago that 1901 would see the high average point in stocks. The period was complete in years and in prices. It is not certain that the high point was not seen at the beginning of May last year, but it seems rather probable that a higher average will be made in the next few weeks than the highest of 1901. This will establish a somewhat longer up-swing than usual, but it can probably be shown that the buying of railway properties for the purpose of concentrating ownerships came so late in the cycle as to produce special strength.

The vital question is whether the top will come in 1902. There are arguments for and against the theory that the high point will come this year. The argument that the rise will go further is founded upon existing prosperity. It is shown that many great manufacturing interests have orders enough to keep their works profitably employed during the year.

It is held that community of interest in railway affairs by maintaining rates will prolong the period of railway prosperity. It is argued that with the increased wealth of the country there will be increased stability in traffic and a better general average of profits in trade. Admitting trade to rest upon credit, it is obvious that the larger the reserve funds of merchants and manufacturers, the safer, within reasonable limits, will be the condition of trade, because of the larger ratio of reserve to credit.

The country is unquestionably far richer than it was four years ago, and this wealth will tend to promote stability. Placing the currency on a gold basis will remove much of the cause for anxiety which existed in the first half of the last decade, and this again will tend to keep the fabric of credit unimpaired.

The demonstration that this country can sell goods in the market of the world on even terms with other manufacturers will exert an important influence upon business by making the employment of labor more certain. Nothing throws business out of adjustment faster than the curtailment of consumption which comes with the lack of employment for labor.

The two weak spots in the commercial chain are credit and labor. When labor is well employed, consumption goes on; when consumption is checked, goods accumulate, money is locked up in unsalable products, and credit begins to be affected. Indications are that labor will be profitably employed this year, and this stands for much in the general forecast.

No especially disturbing conditions are in sight; no presidential election; no tariff agitation in Congress; no conditions that seem serious as far as the rest of the world is concerned.

Termination of the Boer War will greatly improve affairs in England and will help the world by resumption of the Rand additions to the stock of gold. Signs of trade improvements appear in Germany and in Russia. War rumors abroad have a sense of rest. Altogether, conditions as far as they can be foreseen and the momentum of present prosperity combine in favor of the maintenance of large profits and good values for securities this year.

What can be said on the other side? First, that the market always looks strongest at the top; that conditions always seem best just before they change; that the very appearances which exist are the fruit of highly developed confidence.

Nothing is surer than that the cause of the termination of business booms is the expansion which grows out of the boom itself.[1] Business men who would not buy goods except for immediate use when prices are below the cost of production do not hesitate to make large speculative commitments when prices show great profits on the cost of production.

Furthermore, it is a principle of human nature that the desire to do more runs ahead of the ability to perform, no matter how much that ability may be increased. The larger the reserves on which credits can be based, the larger the credits that will be based thereon. This does not appear in statistics, but most men who will look into their own business at this time will find that they have expended and are expanding on prosperity to an extent, which, when applied to the whole country, contains serious possibilities.

It has often been shown that conditions can change almost in a day. Appearances were most hopeful in the spring of 1899, yet the incident of a cut in the price of wire nails brought a change in the iron trade like the result of a frost upon a garden of flowers.

Cancellation of orders is a very unfortunate practice. But a change of conditions at this time would probably bring cancellation of orders on a scale which would have a radical influence upon profits for the year. We do not know that such cancellations will occur; but the fact that they may occur must be placed by the side of the orders that exist.

We have seen in the industrial market during the past year signs of a coming change. Railway stocks and particularly the investment stocks are at the highest prices known. But the industrial list as a whole does not show improvement in prices compared with a year ago. The records of copper, sugar, rubber, lead and other properties of this class tell the story of competition, reduced consumption and curtailment of profits.

Here and there are more serious developments. The Asphalt Trust has collapsed. Trading corporations have been embarrassed. Investors have suffered heavy loss. Trade reports from the South have become adverse. The cotton crop is short, yet prices are materially lower than they were a year ago. The farmers of the middle and western states are short by comparison of the value of 700,000,000 bushels of corn. Clearings at leading cities which were showing increases of 50 per cent have dwindled to increases of 10 per cent.

Even railway earnings are showing smaller gains. Exports of merchandise have decreased; imports are increasing. The Treasury locks up money and gets it back into circulation only by the purchase of bonds at prices which show the government's enormous loss. The banks find it more profitable to sell their bonds than to maintain circulation, and notes are being retired.

Where does the balance lie? We think there is momentum enough to carry activity and strength in stocks somewhat further, but that the load to be lifted is growing heavier and that the lifting leverage is becoming weaker, with the probability that if the high point in the stock market has not already been reached, it will be reached this year.

January 14, 1902

Indications favor a fair supply of money here for the next two months. The chief doubt grows from the large short interest in exchange, which makes further gold exports a possibility, if not a certainty. Money will come to this center [New York], but some will be absorbed by the Sub-Treasury, and, if more is sent abroad, the surplus reserve may remain comparatively low and keep money from being very cheap.

The surplus reserve is now $12,958,450, compared with $22,398,050 in 1901, $16,707;350 in 1890 and $28,263,075 in 1899. The movement of the surplus reserve in the first three months of the year is tolerably regular. In 1897 the high point in the surplus was made the third week in January, from which there was a decline of $13,000,000 down to the second week in April. In 1898 the high point of the reserve was the fourth week in January, followed by a fall of $15,000,000 to the first week in March, with a subsequent increase continuing up to the second week in June.

In 1899 the high point of the reserve was the fourth week in January, succeeded by a loss of over $20,000,000 to the third week in April. In 1900 the high point did not come until the second week in February, from which the reserve dropped $25,000,000 to the second week in March, with a recovery of about $12,000,000 up to the end of April. Last year the high point of the reserve was the fourth week in January, with a fall of about $24,000,000 to the first week in April. This suggests an increase in reserves in the next two weeks, and after that time a more or less rapid fall during February and perhaps March.

Indications at London are that the supply of Rand gold in the next few months will not be extremely large, even if the Boer War comes to an end in the meantime. The moment that the supply of gold materially increases, Continental nations will endeavor to secure a proportion of the increase. More gold will bring a more hopeful spirit and predispose people to engage in new enterprises.

The great Continental banks have gained gold moderately in recent years, with the exception of Russia, which has been a large loser. In the last three years France has gained about 26 million pounds and Austria-Hungary 16½ millions, while Russia has lost 31 millions. This has been due to the heavy payments by Russia on account of public works and outlay in the Far East. Russia will endeavor to raise a large loan in France as soon as conditions are favorable, which will presumably reduce French holdings of gold somewhat.

The French banks bid fair to continue to employ balances in London, as they secure a better return there than at home. The German banks during the past year have needed all available supplies of money, but the German situation is improving, and money will probably go from Germany to London this spring. All this points to comparatively cheap money at London, although large sums will continue to be required in South Africa, no matter whether the war stops or goes on. After the war closes, there will be heavy outlay for bringing home troops, for the rebuilding of public works and for the compensation of loyalists in South Africa.

General trade conditions abroad are involved. Germany shows improvement, but it is improvement from very bad conditions and is not yet pronounced. Prices have fallen heavily, great numbers of people are out of work, and the debris of unwise speculation appears on all sides. Nevertheless, the people are taking a more hopeful view, and in some lines of trade there is beginning to be confidence.

France is at a standstill. The losses have come largely from unwise investments in industrial enterprises at home and in Russia. More recently, the fall in copper has hit French capitalists and French investors quite severely. This has caused general unwillingness to take new risks, but the supply of money in France is still large, and it is only a question of time when confidence comes back. The French loan caused temporary overspeculation. Everybody knew the loan would be a success, and consequently applied for more than was expected to be allotted, and this locked up money, while the manipulation of the loan caused some losses. But this is only a temporary condition.

Trade conditions in Austria-Hungary are depressed, but are no worse than they have been for some months. The Russian situation continues unfavorable. Development has gone ahead altogether too fast, and it will take a long time for consumption to overtake the production that has been laid out, although this difficulty is being remedied for the time being by the collapse of ventures which have run out of capital. A very considerable part of the money that has gone into Russian industrial undertakings in the last few years will be lost.

It is obvious that conditions abroad differ materially from those which exist in this country. Europe has usually been ahead of the United States in the beginning and in the termination of a business boom. Whether the depression abroad will be followed by depression here this time remains to be seen. But the foreign situation is certainly calculated to afford the ultra-optimists of this country food for thought.

January 16, 1902

. . . .

Whenever railroad earnings begin to show any material decline, people will realize with a rush that the return on some railway stocks which pay dividends is less than the return on the first mortgage bonds of the same companies. This is an abnormal condition. It is the other end of the scale from the period when staple goods can be bought below the cost of production. Such conditions are not apt to last at either extreme.

January 22, 1902

A correspondent writes: "How do you reconcile your rather bearish views on the market with your admissions that the country is in an extremely prosperous condition?"

If our correspondent will look over the files of *The Wall Street Journal* in 1896, he will find that a good deal of the talk about the market then was bullish, although the news was bad and conditions were bad. The event proved that the year 1896 was the time to buy stocks, and that they were cheap because of the unfavorable conditions.

It may be found that the reverse is true now, and that the market will begin to recede before the change in conditions becomes so distinct as to be generally recognized. The market turned in this way in 1881 and in 1892. Conditions were comparatively favorable in both periods for months after the high prices in stocks were seen.

It is perfectly natural that this should be so, because, while values support prices, manipulation usually advances them first, because the manipulators foresee the values which are to come. In other words, prices generally discount events, or what stock operators think events will be. Then, the facts come along and bring other buying or other selling as the manipulator anticipated.

Take the present situation, with good railroad earnings, large transactions and fair profits in most lines of trade. The people in special lines of business learn to foresee what is likely to come in their trade. They detect the signs of falling off, see prospects of diminished profits, of overbuying on the part of customers before the total result becomes evident through statistics. These people talk about coming changes, and if they are speculators, they try to take advantage of their knowledge, especially if they think that what is true with them is equally true with others.

Take the case of a great banking interest: It discovers that the public no longer takes the securities which it has to sell, that syndicates, instead of making large and quick profits, have quite a fight to make any profits at all; that their banking friends are getting [en]ded up here and there; are less anxious to make new ventures and are less desirable associates in new ventures; and that diligent manipulation of the stock market fails to bring buying outside of the semi-professional class.

With such a state of facts, will a great banking interest feel inclined to largely expand its own operations or will it adopt a very conservative policy and reduce commitments as fast as it can do so to advantage? The public sees nothing of this, but it is knowledge of this kind on the part of business men and of bankers that stops advances in prices and makes the wish to sell exceed the wish to buy at the time when justification for such a course is not widely evident.

Some of these conditions exist today. Great bankers who, a year ago, had no hesitation in advising the purchase of stocks, now speak very cautiously and say the market may go up a little, but it is not time to expect a great rise. Some of the great merchants are taking more conservative views and are calling for more careful scrutiny of credits, especially among customers who are known to be inclined to overtrade.

The continued strength of exchange; the loss of deposits by trust companies, the comparatively small midwinter bank reserves, the declining increases in clearings are all indications which point in one direction. It is true that orders in the hands of manufacturing corporations are probably larger than a year ago, and may give great prosperity during 1902.

But we had an illustration in 1899 of how the iron situation could change almost in a day. Mills were then full of orders, but it was found that many either had a provision for cancellation, or could be filled only under conditions which promised more difficulties than would result from cancellation. It is hoped that this will not occur, but it has occurred in the past and may again.

Modern business is done chiefly on credit. As long as there is confidence, everything is serene. But anything which impairs or seriously disturbs confidence might change the situation beyond the possibility of recognition within thirty days. No one can say that this will occur, but when prosperity has been running for several years, when the level of prices is high, and the return to investors is small, when the investment fund of the country has been well absorbed and new stocks have been widely distributed, when syndicates and combinations and excessive capitalization have gone on apace, it is wise for conservative people to think about the possibility of a change, and to put their financial houses somewhat in order, even if they find their precautions ahead of time.

January 23, 1902

. . . .

An unfavorable impulse seems most likely to come from either dear money, crop damage or a distinct check to business. Dear money is always a depressing factor, but it frequently effects its own cure. Crop damages are serious because unavoidable. A check to business is probable, chiefly because prosperity has gone so far and lasted so long. It, however, is something that can be watched and its arrival observed. Some sign of its approach is afforded by clearings, which instead of showing increases of 40 per cent are showing increases of 10 per cent and this outside of speculative markets.

A halt in a bull period almost always starts with something which lessens confidence in credits. When credits begin to shrink, business begins to contract, and as this throws labor out of employment, the great circle is established and generally runs until self-correction takes place.

. . . .

February 6, 1902

The increase in railway earnings in 1898 and 1899 reflected recovery from the business depression in previous years. The increase in 1900 was due to the general expansion of business, and this was a large factor in the increases of 1901.

The short crop of corn and the reduced crop of oats were expected to bring decrease in earnings this year, but thus far, this has not occurred, although it is the time when decreases were expected to appear. Corn receipts have fallen off, but the loss has been made up by increase in miscellaneous traffic.

The question now is whether miscellaneous traffic can go on increasing. Expansion once under way promotes expansion up to a certain point. The railway companies are responsible for a very large amount of new general business. When a railway corporation decides to expend millions of dollars on its property, it provides a great deal of work of all kinds.

When such requirements are made, not merely by a few roads, but to varying extents over 200,000 miles of road, the total reaches a sum which gives a great stimulus to producing interests. Such stimulus is felt, not only by the manufacturing concerns, which supply goods direct to railway companies, but by those from whom these manufacturers buy raw materials or partially manufactured goods, and tracing these supplies back to their source, involves widespread employment of labor and the united energies of tens of thousands of people, all of whom receive compensation or profit out of the railway outlay.

As long as labor is profitably employed, general business is prosperous, because the wages of labor pay for such an immense amount of supplies as to create the main market for all who have products or goods to sell. Whenever every consumer adds a little to his scale of purchases, the effect is felt in the retail trade everywhere, spreading thence through jobbers, manufacturers and railroads, around to the food producer, who in turn acquires the power of larger buying of that which others have to sell.

This expansion is the true explanation of the increased traffic which has kept the railroad companies thus far from feeling the loss represented by a shortage of more than 750 million bushels of grain.

How long can this expansion be expected to continue? It has already run longer than in years past. There has been more material to expand on. Larger resources, greater wealth, more people, magnitude in all directions have increased the magnitude of the forces which expand when expansion is in order. That perhaps will have a tendency to lessen contraction when contraction comes.

It is probable that the first check will come with something which will shake credit and lead to curtailment of output through fear. That has usually started contraction, and is undoubtedly a point to be watched. But, for the present, danger does not seem to be near. The fact that railway companies have recently been issuing bonds and stocks on a comparatively large scale means the expenditure of more money, and more stimulus to the forces which have been working for expansion. The orders on the books of the great manufacturing companies seem to assure large employment for labor for months to come.

Much, of course, depends on this year's crops. A serious shortage in any of the great staples will have a very important influence. Good crops, on the other hand, will strengthen confidence and make manufacturers and merchants willing to stand new commitments.

These are the conditions which have maintained earnings of late and which may maintain them in months to come. Fortunately, this is a point which can be watched. The majority of the great systems report earnings either weekly or monthly, and investors and speculators can see when there is enough change in conditions to bring important changes in earnings.

Sentiment is now affected very much by earnings, and the feeling is general that prices will not have a serious decline as long as earnings keep up. Should there come decreases, the effect upon prices would be considerable, because so much stress is being laid on this point.

February 8, 1902

We have referred recently to the effect of railway expenditures in maintaining the activity of general business. Some details on this subject seem to be pertinent. The total listings of stocks and bonds on the New York Stock Exchange last year amounted to $2,565,023,815. Of this enormous sum, $1,486,112,300 were listings of industrial stocks and bonds, while $1,078,911,515 were listings of steam railway and street railway stocks and bonds. Of this amount, $667,006,000 were steam railway bonds, and $284,584,515 were railway stocks.

Of these bonds and stocks, a large portion was issued for the purpose of replacing other securities, and another portion was on account of issues already listed, while, of the amount issued for new capital, part was for purchases of existing properties, the payment of floating debt and similar uses. The remainder, used for extensions, improvements and betterments, represents the new money which the railway companies contributed to the general business of the country.

The amount of bonds and stocks specifically stated in the application to list as for the purpose of betterments and improvements, footed up something over $250,000,000. Some of this money may have been expended in the previous year, and before the bonds were issued. Another portion may be intended for expenditures in the future, but after making allowances of this kind, a very large sum is left which must have gone into the products and commodities which made up the outlay for railway supplies last year.

It seems clear that the policy of large expenditures out of capital will be continued this year. There have recently been issued or authorized bonds amounting to nearly $200,000,000 and stocks issued or authorized amounting to about $115,000,000. Not all these bonds and stocks will be used for betterments, but the amount intended for this purpose reaches very high figures, and shows in part the reasons for the confidence that is expressed in the maintenance of profitable business in many lines this year.

The magnitude of railway and industrial figures makes it easy to lose sight of what such amounts mean when brought into practical use. Suppose, of old money and of new money, the railway companies contemplate an expenditure of $300,000,000. That sum would represent the employment of a million men at $2 per day for six months of the year. It would represent at a cost of $15,000 each the building of as many locomotives as have been produced in the country in the last ten years.

The average cost of maintenance of way of a railroad is estimated at about $750 per mile. The sum under consideration would maintain the roadbeds and bridges of all the railroads in the country for two years without a dollar from any other source. The number of railway employees in the country in 1900 was 1,017,653, and their wages that year amounted to $577,264,811; hence the sum named would be sufficient to pay nearly three-fifths of the wages of all railway employees in the country for a year.

The operating expenses of the railway companies in the country in 1900 were $961,428,511, an increase from $725,720,415 in six years. The outlay for betterments on capital account is necessarily added to the sum. Hence it can be seen what the effect of the expenditure of between $200,000,000 and $300,000,000 of new money must be upon general business.

The effect will not be confined to railway properties direct, as large orders for materials and supplies given by railway companies will lead manufacturers to enlarge their plants, to buy new machinery, and generally to employ not only the money received, but their own capital and credit, in enterprises which further increase the total volume of trade.

The stimulus alone afforded by the expenditure of such great sums is no small item. It is probably well within bounds to say that the expenditure of $200,000,000 of new money by the railway interests of the country will produce an outlay in the various ramifications of the expenditure and the enlargement of credit connected therewith of not less than double that amount.

In the light of these facts and of the orders already in existence, and which are likely to be filed, the force under the business of the country today seems sufficient to maintain a good degree of prosperity through this year.[2]

February 14, 1902

. . . .

. . . If profits are too large, they will be brought down by competition. No corporation is beyond the reach of competition; and no corporation, not having a natural or legal monopoly, will be able to obtain unreasonable profits through long periods of time.

. . . .

February 15, 1902

In our compilations of railway earnings, it is generally shown that the percentage of increase in net is larger than the percentage of increase in gross. This is due to the fact that the cost of operation of a railroad increases less in proportion than the amount of business transacted, which, of course, leaves a relatively larger net return.

A large part of the expenses of a railroad are approximately fixed. The items of maintenance of way, maintenance of equipment and a considerable portion of the general expenses cannot be very greatly changed whether the volume of traffic is normal or abnormal. In good times the cost of conducting transportation increases materially, while in bad times it can be cut down, but the other items can be modified to only a small extent.

It has been estimated that from two-thirds to three-fourths of the expenses of a railroad go on independent of the volume of traffic. . . .

The year 1894 was a rather low point with railroad earnings. Comparison with 1900 showed an increase in gross earnings of 38 per cent, with an increase in expenses of only 31 per cent, this operating cost including a large outlay for betterments charged to operating expenses. The ratio of increase in earnings per mile for five years was approximately double the rate of increase of expenses per mile.

This was shown very clearly by the development of gross earnings of the trunk lines. Trunk-line mileage, comparing 1880 with 1890, increased about 82 per cent, while a number of tons hauled one mile increased 132 per cent. This increase in density of traffic permitted the roads to earn a great deal more money with a falling rate per ton per mile. The rates that may be charged by any road are governed very largely by the density of traffic, and it has been figured that with a tonnage available for 2,000-ton freight-train loads the cost would fall to about one mill per ton per mile—under given conditions.

At present, the lowest revenue per ton per mile in the United States is that of Chesapeake & Ohio, which works at 2.21 mills per ton per mile on account of its long haul of soft coal business. Wherever there is a real heavy tonnage of bituminous coal, the cost per ton per mile falls rapidly on account of the density of traffic.

In order to show the operation of this law of increasing returns, we give in the table following the increase in earnings, gross and net, of a number of prominent railway systems, comparing 1896 with 1900. The figures used are those of the interstate commerce reports:

Road	*Inc. Gross*	%	*Inc. Net*	%
Atchison	$ 5,339,985	20	$3,015,695	30
Balt. & Ohio	10,945,445	45	5,976,852	86
Bur. & Quincy	12,414,459	48	4,602,690	48
Can. Pacific	10,178,434	49	4,462,783	54
Ill. Central	10,681,246	48	3,142,427	38
Lake Shore	3,854,265	18	2,444,089	35
Louis. & Nash.	7,763,427	37	2,444,089[sic]	35[sic]
N.Y. Central	10,098,437	23	4,745,771	30
Nor. Pacific	9,975,693	49	7,784,410	99
Northwest	9,393,374	27	3,937,402	30
Pennsylvania	15,219,513	23	6,368,214	31
Rock Island	6,244,518	32	2,625,802	46
St. Paul	9,150,469	27	4,698,897	.04
South. Pacific	13,889,307	38	6,814,219	53

These figures show that in most cases the percentage of gain in net was larger than the percentage of gain in gross. This was conspicuous by the case with Baltimore & Ohio, Northern Pacific and Southern Pacific, with Northern Pacific a very striking illustration. St. Paul presents the abnormal feature of a good average increase in gross and no increase worth mentioning in net. This, however, was due to the well-understood fact that during this period St. Paul put net earnings into the property in wholesale fashion. This probably affords the explanation also in the case of Illinois Central and Burlington, neither of which shows in net the results of the increase in gross.

The effects of previous outlay on the property are shown in the case of Lake Shore, because of the known high condition of roadway and equipment. This is exactly what occurred. Lake Shore, with an increase of 18 per cent in gross, was able to gain 38 per cent [sic] in net.

This illustrates what will appear in due time in St. Paul, as the outcome of the large outlay on that property in the last few years.

February 18, 1902

The market is in a position where the balance of conditions is more even than usual. It is possible to make a good argument for or against advance in prices at this time. We enumerate some of the arguments each way in order that readers may judge for themselves.

The following are bull factors: The condition of the country is unquestionably prosperous. This is seen in most of the great trades and in the iron trade conspicuously. The great manufacturers are well supplied with orders insuring profitable business for months ahead. The consumption of staple products is large, and trade seems to be in a healthy condition. This means that people are making money, and that the investment fund of the country is increasing.

Great financial interests are still active on the long side. This does not mean that they are bulling stocks, but they are willing to take bond issues and finance new corporations on a large scale. Great syndicates do not underwrite securities without [unless] they have a reasonable hope that these securities will be taken by the public. They have more at stake than anyone else in reading both the public ability and the public temper in the matter of the absorption of securities. Their action indicates confidence in sustained values.

Practically the same thing is shown from another viewpoint by the great corporations. Directors of these companies are able men, in close touch with the situation at financial centers and in the section of the country traversed by their roads. They think it an opportune time to bring out bond issues freely, and engage in important financial rearrangements.

For eight months past, gross earnings have had an average increase of over 10 per cent, while net earnings have had an average increase of over 15 per cent. This represents a large addition to the actual value of stocks. If this addition were not discounted by the advance up to last May, it affords a basis for further advance.

The comparatively small declines in prices that have occurred on bad news shows a high degree of public confidence in security values. If the public is willing to hold stocks against bad news, it is not unreasonable to think that the public may be willing to buy more stocks on good news, or in sympathy with advancing prices. Prices speculatively are chiefly a matter of habit, and stocks are considered cheap or dear in a speculative sense mainly with reference to prices shortly preceding.

The improvement in the foreign situation has resulted in easy money abroad, and in facilities for renewing sterling loans, which is likely to prevent exports of gold in the near future. The recent large expansion in loans and deposits has been made by banks controlled by interests which are of necessity chiefly on the side of the up-building of properties and the support of prices.

The following may be considered factors against material rise: The level of prices is so high as to give a meagre return on a considerable portion of the investment stocks. There are stocks which return a good yield, but a large proportion of the list cannot be bulled on the return to the investor, but only on hopes of something by means of which accrued value may be returned to the stockholder. As the investor determines prices in the long run, when prices cease to be attractive to investors, they are high for speculators.

The period of expanding prosperity has been fully as long as the average, and while the greater wealth of the country and the greater buying capacity justify expectation of business on a scale larger than heretofore, unchangeable principles in human nature make it certain that great prosperity will bring overtrading sooner or later. The longer expansion has been in progress, the greater the probability of a termination of this growth.

Business shows some signs of curtailment. Clearings, which, a few months ago, were from 20 to 40 per cent larger than for the corresponding time in 1900, are now showing small gains, and in some cases no gains. The same thing is true of railroad earnings. Increases, which were running from 12 to 15 per cent, are now down to an average of perhaps 5 or 6 per cent, with some lines showing rather persistent decreases. While the volume of business is large, the profits in many lines have been reduced by the increased cost of raw materials, and net results to manufacturers and merchants are nothing like as large as the change in the prices of finished goods compared with a few years [ago] would indicate.

The issue of new securities during the past twelve months has been greater than could possibly be cared for by any normal increase in the investment fund of the country. If this fund had been fully employed, there would of necessity be a large accumulation of securities in first hands. This accords with the well-known fact that syndicates and underwriters, while still willing to undertake new ventures, have not succeeded brilliantly of late in selling bonds, and are still carrying very considerable lines. The decline in the market in 1899 was brought about partly by overloaded syndicates, and anything which tends toward that condition has an unfavorable side. It makes financial interests support the market at times, but it makes them certain sellers of stocks when opportunity is afforded.

This is illustrated by the action of the market for the past eight months. Declines have been checked, but every advance that has come has encountered what has been called inside selling enough to check a rise and discourage the public. With all the favorable facts, all the good reports, and all the gains in earnings, the average price of twenty stocks is still two points lower than it was at the beginning of May.

While the public is not disposed to sell on declines, it does not appear to be willing to buy persistently on advances. It realizes the high level of prices, and is quick to take profits and quick to cut losses short. It shows within a narrow range great sensitiveness to bad news. The market, furthermore, has been of a kind to increase this sensitiveness.

The large expansion of loans by New York banks carries with it the possibility of a large contraction in loans and deposits and the danger of money becoming scarce at inopportune times. Perhaps there is no immediate danger on this point. Probably contraction can be regulated so as not to cause disturbance. But the fact remains that the people look at the bank statement with a sense that it carries unfavorable possibilities, and whenever the reserves run down, prudent brokers begin reducing their commitments.

The weight of evidence can be compared by anybody for himself, but whatever the conclusion may be, the one point to remember is that values will determine prices in the long run.

February 25, 1902

The one sure thing in speculation is that values determine prices in the long run. Manipulation is effective temporarily, but the investor establishes prices in the end. The object of all speculation is to foresee coming changes in values. Whoever knows that the value of a stock has run ahead of the price and is likely to be sustained can buy that stock with confidence that as its value is recognized by investors, the price will rise.

In a bull period, extending over four to six years, it will be found in every case that the value of stocks has risen with the rise in prices, sometimes falling back, and at others running ahead, but in the main keeping not only the same general direction but moving over approximately the same points. If prices go up and values do not follow, prices will presently fall back, but if values do follow, prices are likely to advance again, and stocks may be cheaper at high prices in view of the values that exist than they were at low prices with the values then existing.

In order to demonstrate this fact, we have worked out a table showing how the rise in stocks in the last few years has been supported by the rise in values. We have taken the average price of twenty railway stocks at the beginning of the bull market in 1896, and also, as a general exponent of stock values, the earnings per mile applicable to dividends of all the railroads in the country.

This is a very conservative way of putting values, as it allows in many cases for large betterment outlay charged in operating expenses and deducted from net earnings, thereby discriminating against earnings on stocks. As a whole, however, earnings after the payment of all charges give in broad lines the amounts earned on stocks, hence, increase in this amount is equivalent to increase in the value of stock.

Prices and Values in the Year 1896

August, 1896, average price 20 railway stocks 41.82
November, 1896, average price 20 railway stocks 56.08
December, 1896, average price 20 railway stocks 49.98
July, 1896, surplus earnings per mile about 480
December, 1896, surplus earnings per mile about 510

Prices and Values in the Year 1897

January, 1897, average price 20 railway stocks 50.60
March, 1897, average price 20 railway stocks 54.21
April, 1897, average price 20 railway stocks 48.12
September, 1897, average price 20 railway stocks 67.23
November, 1897, average price 20 railway stocks 57.45
January, 1897, surplus earnings per mile about 510
December, 1897, surplus earnings per mile 612

Prices and Values in the Year 1898

January, 1898, average price 20 railway stocks 61.86
August, 1898, average price 20 railway stocks 70.15
October, 1898, average price 20 railway stocks 65.60
December, 1898, average price 20 railway stocks 74.99
January 1, 1898, surplus earnings per mile about 612
December, 1898, surplus earnings per mile about 800

Prices and Values in the Year 1899

January, 1899, average price 20 railway stocks 75.08
April, 1899, average price 20 railway stocks 87.04
June, 1899, average price 20 railway stocks 77.38
September, 1899, average price 20 railway stocks 85.55
December, 1899, average price 20 railway stocks 72.40
January, 1899, surplus earnings per mile about 810
December, 1899, surplus earnings per mile about 1,000

Prices and Values in the Year 1900

January, 1900, average price 20 railway stocks 78.86
April, 1900, average price 20 railway stocks 82.94
June, 1900, average price 20 railway stocks 72.99
November, 1900, average price 20 railway stocks 88.88
January, 1900, surplus earnings per mile about 1,000
December, 1900, surplus earnings per mile about 1,180

Prices and Values in the Year 1901

January, 1901, average 20 railway stocks 97.85
May, 1901, average 20 railway stocks 117.86
May, 1901, average 20 railway stocks 103.87
June, 1901, average 20 railway stocks 117.65
August, 1901, average 20 railway stocks 104.86
November, 1901, average 20 railway stocks 115.21
January, 1901, surplus earnings per mile about 1,180
June, 1901, surplus, earnings per mile about 1,240
December, 1901, surplus earnings per mile (estd.) 1,300

It is evident from the foregoing that while there have been periods when prices went materially against the tendency in values, there has invariably been recovery, and that the general move through five years has been similar, not only in the main tendency, but in the range of prices and earnings covered.

For instance, the average of twenty stocks started at 42, and the surplus earnings were about 480 a mile. While the averages remained between 50 and 60, surplus earnings per mile were between $500 and $600. When the average rose from 60 to 80, the line of value crept up from $600 to $800 a mile.

Then came a period of distinct divergence. The decline in prices during the summer and fall of 1899 was not caused by loss of value in railway properties, but by conditions which grew out of excessive underwriting of industrial properties early in 1899. The average of railway stocks dropped below 80, while surplus earnings ran up to about $1,000 per mile.

During this period we frequently called attention to this divergence and said that either prices must go up or values come down. The outcome was the great rise in prices from June, 1900, to May, 1901, bringing the average price up to 117, while the surplus earnings per mile rose to $1,200 a mile.

Since May, 1901, prices have been irregular, but have shown no net advance, averaging during the time a little above 110. We are not able to give the surplus earnings per mile of all roads since June 30, 1901, but, as net earnings increased materially during that period, it is very safe to assume that the surplus per mile at the end of 1901 was not far from $1,300 or more than 15 points above the average value of twenty railway stocks.

This established a condition somewhat like that existing early in 1900, when the line of value was above the line of price. If the past is any indication of the future, either railway earnings applicable to dividends must show a material decrease, or there must be another general advance in the prices of railway stocks.

February 26, 1902

We regard the table published yesterday in this column showing the parallel lines of value and prices during the last five years as of much suggestive value. It has been obvious to everybody that the large increase in railroad earnings in recent years has been the basis for the higher level of prices of railway stocks, but it has probably not occurred to most observers that this increase in earnings formed a line of values which has kept in close correspondence, most of the time, with the rise in the average price of twenty railway stocks.

In order to show this movement still more clearly, we give in the table following for all railroads in the country the rise in gross earnings per mile, in net per mile, and in the surplus per mile compared with the advance in the average price of twenty railway stocks:

Years	*Gross Per Mile*	*Net Per Mile*	*Surplus Per Mile*	*Average Price*
1896	$6,223	$1,850	$ 480	42
1897	6,228	1,884	612	57
1898	6,771	2,111	800	74
1899	7,161	2,272	1,000	72
1900	7,826	2,519	1,180	88
1901	Estimated		1,300	115

It is obvious that the rise in gross earnings per mile could not be expected to accord with the changes in prices, because out of gross earnings have to come expenses and charges as well as some betterments prior to the amount which would bear directly on dividends. In the same sense net earnings would not bear directly upon stock changes, because of the intervening charges and the variability of net earnings according to the policy of companies in regard to betterments.

When it comes, however, to earnings after charges, meaning, in this case, the earnings applicable to dividends, no matter whether actually disbursed in dividends or not, the correspondence cannot fail to attract attention.

It will be observed that surplus earnings per mile were 480 when the average price of twenty stocks was 42, and that the advance in 1897 and in 1898 was close as between the two. The divergence in 1899 was marked and furnished an extraordinary opportunity for foreseeing the course of prices. It was clear enough that if in 1898 surplus earnings of $800 a mile justified an average price of 74, that surplus earnings per mile of $1,000 in 1899 justified an average higher than 72. This was demonstrated very clearly in the rise which came in 1900 and 1901, when the average price reached 117 with the surplus per mile about $1,300.

The earnings in this case are those of all roads in the country, which makes the test at once more valuable and more severe than it would be in the case of a smaller number of roads. It seems probable from these figures that a list of representative systems could be made which would give a fairly correct exhibit of the earnings of roads in all parts of the country and thus permit test earnings showing the line of values to be worked out at all times.

It is probable also that the same principle can be applied to individual stocks, and that it will be found that extending over periods of time, the line of value moves in close accord with the line of price. Of course, there will be interruptions due to special causes, and undoubtedly one line or the other will at times be too low or too high, but the fact that a ratio seems to exist cannot fail to be of value to those who may work it out, and who may have their judgment as to the wisdom of holding or not holding specific stocks strengthened by the demonstration to be obtained in this way.

A holder of Union Pacific during the year 1900 would undoubtedly have been strengthened in his determination to keep his stock and try to get the full benefit of the rise if he had seen, as he could have seen, that the line of value kept steadily above the line of price during the whole of that time. This would have been very conspicuous, also in Atchison and in a number of other stocks where the facts could have been worked out. It seems to us that this method of testing values can be profitably employed, and we intend to present a variety of illustrations bearing upon this point.

February 27, 1902

We have received the following: "Has there ever been severe depression in prices of securities in this country when labor was fully employed?"

Periods of depression in business and in prices are invariably preceded by periods of good business and advance in prices. At such times, which usually last for several years, there is a gradual increase in the employment of labor until at the high point abundance of work, large production, large profits and high prices go together.

It is equally certain that periods of depression begin with overtrading, overproduction, overconfidence and general excess in all directions. Upon this condition of affairs comes some sudden shock. It may be an important failure; it may be some great catastrophe or national event; it is something which arrests attention and makes people stop and think.

They see that they are extended and begin to restrict operations in whatever line of business they may be in. Lenders of money restrict credits, merchants restrict purchases, creditors urge payments, and, as a result of this shrinkage, the demand for labor lessens a little in each case, but enough to make a large aggregate. This begins to be felt in reduced consumption, and this is the first turn of the wheel which brings about general contraction.

It is evident, therefore, that the bearing of the employment of labor upon the prices of securities is only that restricted employment is one of a number of causes operating to produce smaller profits; hence lower prices. As showing how closely the demand for labor follows the lines of expansion and contraction, which find their ultimate expression in the prices of securities, we give in the table following an exhibit of the percentage of labor employed in the United Kingdom in four decades as contrasted with the high prices and the low prices of stocks during the same period:

1860	Percentage of labor employed	99
1868	Percentage of labor employed	91

1872	Percentage of labor employed	99
1878	Percentage of labor employed	87
1881	Percentage of labor employed	98
1885	Percentage of labor employed	81
1890	Percentage of labor employed	98
1893	Percentage of labor employed	92
1899	Percentage of labor employed	98 [3]

Now compare this with the table following, showing the high and low points in the stock market, remembering also that the prices are those of American railway stocks in New York, while the employment ratios are those of labor in the United Kingdom. Our record of average prices does not go back to 1860, but with the war and the inflation of the currency, quotations of stocks between 1860 and 1865 could not be considered fairly representative. The starting point for modern compilations of stock prices was in 1868, when the reaction after the inflation immediately following the war was felt. The year 1868 was a low point, followed by the rise to 1872, from which time our figures run as follows:

1872	High point 60 stocks	76.57
1877	Low point 60 stocks	36.33
1881	High point 60 stocks	99.80
1885	Low point 60 stocks	41.25
1890	High point 20 stocks	78.03
1896	Low point 20 stocks	41.82
1901	High point 20 stocks	117.65

It will be observed that the low point in stocks and the employment of labor was in the same year—1868; the same at the next high point in 1872, the same at the next high point in 1881, the next low point in 1885, and the next high point in 1890.

In 1877 the low point in prices came a year earlier than the low point in labor, while in the last decade the low point in labor abroad came coincidentally with the panic in this country in 1893 rather than with the low point of labor here, which did not come until about 1896. The high point in labor abroad came in 1899 instead of in 1891 or 1892 [1901 or 1902] as it has done here thus far. The improvement in the United Kingdom started earlier and ended earlier than it has done here.

The illustration is important chiefly as a further demonstration of the point which we have often made; namely, that stock prices are generally an effect, seldom a cause; that they reflect the profits which grow out of changes in general business, and that the far-sighted speculator should watch not the stock market as it exists from day to day, but chiefly the great causes which are affecting general business, adding to or taking from the profits of railroads and industrial corporations. The manipulated and temporary swings of the market should be considered merely vantage points from which to go with the main tendency whichever way it may be.

The application for present purposes is that the time of the advance both in business and in prices has been full; that the amount of advance has been up to the normal; that there are some signs here and there of a receding tide, but that these signs are not definite enough to be conclusive. It is a time to be very watchful, but uneasiness should be regarded as the outgrowth of the high level and not the result of unfavorable developments which can be definitely located.

February 28, 1902

We have shown in recent articles that the line of values during the past five years has, during the greater part of the time, kept in close touch with the line showing the average price of twenty railway stocks. The present line of values compared with the past is fully up to the line of prices.

It follows that stocks are not to be regarded as cheap or dear in comparison with prices previously prevailing, but chiefly with reference to the values which may be supporting the prices which exist. The twenty active stocks in our list are as dear today, if present earnings were assured, as when they were selling at 42, or 73 points below the present prices, assuming those earnings to have been permanent. The reason is that the surplus earnings of all roads in the country were then about $480 a mile, while they are now about $1,300 a mile.

The increase in values as shown by the increasing surplus earnings per mile has not only kept pace with the rise in the price of stocks, but the ratio of advance has tended to unity, in spite of all manipulation and the special causes which have affected particular stocks.

In other words, investors who by holding or selling their stocks determined in 1896 that the value of twenty railway stocks justified a price of 42, or a percentage of 11.4 to the earnings per mile, now hold their stocks or sell them on a belief that the value of the twenty stocks justifies a price of about 115, or a percentage of 11.4 to present surplus earnings per mile. The variation in this percentage is shown by the table following:

Ratio Surplus Earnings to Average Price

1896	11.4
1897	10.7
1898	10.8
1899	14.0
1900	13.4
1901	11.4

It appears from this that when the ratio rose to 14.0 investors considered stocks cheap. When the ratio was 10.7, stocks were relatively dear. It should be remembered that our average of twenty stocks does not necessarily represent the absolute average value of all stocks, but it clearly does exhibit by its movement changes in relative values of all stocks, between one time and another.

We do not claim that this exhibit should be made a rule of action, and that stocks should be bought or sold on any given change as the percentage of price to surplus earnings. What controls prices on a large scale may not control the price of every stock at all times; but being long or short of a stock on well-established convictions relating to the value of that particular property, i.e. the broad facts of the relationship of values to prices, generally can be regarded as a supporting and confirming factor of great importance.

Under normal conditions, stocks move together, if at all, nearly related in conditions. Knowledge that the Granger group of roads was doing well would be very strong evidence in support of belief that each individually was doing well, and that a ratio of value applicable to all would be found approximately true in regard to each one.

There is one qualifying point not to be overlooked. This is that the stock market discounts expected changes in conditions. It is probable that stock prices will fall before changes in earnings become extremely pronounced. Hence, at a turning point, the rule of sustained values will be temporarily misleading.

Correction on this point will come about in this way. Prices have repeatedly fallen in the past year on a belief that a change in values was near. The fall has been arrested within a short time, in each case, because the change in values has not come. Values have been maintained and prices have recovered. This will continue to occur until change in values justifies not only the short declines, which we have seen, but a large decline, and continuing for a longer time. When the market declines and earnings decrease also, the need for watchfulness will be greatly increased.

When decrease in values comes, it will probably come slowly, and by degrees, just as the increase came by degrees. This means that prices will decline by irregular stages, just as they advanced, being supported all the time by the values which remain. So that holders of stocks, even at high prices, will probably have—where they have good value at the high prices—abundant opportunities to see the changes which are coming, and sell on the rallies which occur, even after decline in quotations is clearly justified by reduced values.

March 1, 1902

We have received the following: "Your recent articles showing the correspondence in the line of values and of prices have been instructive and interesting. Will you now tell us how to prepare a chart showing these lines with reference to individual stocks?"

The first thing is to trace the operations of the property selected for a period of years. Find the net earnings and deduct therefrom the fixed charges, which consist of interest on bonds, guaranteed interest or dividends, rentals, car trusts, and any other items of regular expense, which must be paid before there can be any dividend on the stock. Subtract this total from the net earnings; the remainder will be the sum applicable to dividends. Divide this sum by the operated mileage, and the quotient will be the surplus earnings per mile of that road for the year or whatever time may be covered by the figures used.

In making up the fixed charges, care must be taken to include all the items which belong in that account, yet not to include items which may be included in the total disbursements, but are not fixed charges. The accounts of roads are made up very differently. Some include taxes in fixed charges, others do not. Some put all disbursements into one total, while others separate the fixed charges proper from miscellaneous payments, which cover outlay for special purposes. Miscellaneous payments are not generally fixed charges, and a little practice in railway accounts will enable anyone to draw the line closely enough for practical purposes.

Distinction must also be made between the amount applicable to dividends and the amount paid in dividends. The basis to be used should be, not the dividends paid, but the dividends earned. It is a common thing for a railway company to pay in dividends only a part of the dividend earnings, using the remainder of the money for betterments and miscellaneous purposes instead of giving it to the stockholders.

In cases of this kind, all belongs to the stockholders, and is in most cases credited to them in the form of additions to profit and loss. Stockholders are usually reimbursed sooner or later for such outlay, either by extra dividends, distribution of stock or by the strengthening of the regular dividends through betterment of the property.

It does not appear to be of first importance in the price of a stock whether the money earned goes chiefly into dividends or partly into dividends and partly into betterments. The policy which under different circumstances is the one called for by good management is the one which will have the best effect on prices.

The line of value is always the line of earnings applicable to dividends, never the line of dividends paid. The price of the stock should then be compared at intervals with the surplus earnings per mile, and if a percentage test is desired, it can be had by dividing the surplus earnings per mile by the price of the stock. This will balance relative changes in value.

If surplus earnings per mile increase considerably, and the price of the stock does not rise, the percentage of value will rise, and will show that the stock is relatively cheaper than it was. If, on the other hand, the price of the stock rises out of proportion to the rise in surplus earnings per mile, the percentage of value will fall, showing that the stock is relatively dearer than it was.

The tendency of the percentage will be to work toward a true estimate of the value of the stock. There will be temporary variations, perhaps sometimes considerable in amount, but after such variations the movements will be toward adjustment either by rise of price or fall in value. As each can be watched with approximate accuracy, it is possible to see the tendency and take advantage thereof.

Fixed charges of roads in some cases are given monthly, in others, quarterly, and in others, only annually. Some roads have the excellent practice of indicating what the fixed charges are expected to be in the current year. In any case, it is easy to ascertain about what the fixed charges of a given road will be for the current year, either by application to the company, or by reference to the "guide to values" published in our columns. This permits applying the line of value to the successive statements of net earnings, thereby keeping the record up to date.

March 4, 1902

. . . .

Great combinations permit the application of scientific methods of business, both as regards theory and practice, on a scale which could not be considered or carried out by small concerns. This idea as applied to railroads through community of ownership and to industrials through combinations may prove of great importance to the country and, in an international sense, to the world by finding some approach to a scientific basis for carrying on business, just as a scientific basis has been found in banking, in railroad management, in metallurgy and in other lines where broader knowledge of cause and consequence have been made effective.

One element must not be overlooked. Leaders and the controllers of great interests may get these results, but it will be some time before the principle in human nature which has thus far produced undue expansion and undue depression will be eliminated sufficiently to avoid tendencies which will be in the aggregate strong in these directions.

March 6, 1902

Our recent articles bearing upon the lines of value and of price have brought a number of inquiries, one being whether the lines ran together during the period of decline up to 1896. We give the answer to this question today.

We have taken the surplus earnings per mile and the average prices of stock for twelve years. The movement corresponds very closely in character to that shown in the period from 1896 to 1901. The surplus earnings per mile in the table following are obtained by dividing the charges of all roads by the operated mileage and subtracting this sum from the net earnings per mile of all roads. The difference, or the surplus earnings per mile, is the amount theoretically applicable to dividends. We take the net earnings per mile rather than the net income per mile because of the extraordinary variations in the "other income" of the roads due to causes apart from traffic. Net earnings represent traffic conditions.

It would be impossible to make an average of prices of all stocks of all roads, because quotations could not be obtained. The average of twenty railway stocks has proved to be fairly illustrative of changes in general conditions. We give for each year two columns of prices. The first is the highest of the year, except where indicated by a star as the lowest. The second column gives the average price at the close of the year, intended to show the response of prices to earnings as they developed during the year. The right-hand column shows the ratio between the surplus earnings per mile and the prices existing at the close of the year. The table follows:

Year	*Surplus Per Mile*	*Highest Average*	*Closing Average*	*Rates Per Cent*
1890	746	78.03	61.96	12.0
1891	744	73.21	72.60	10.2
1892	721	75.68	67.74	10.0
1893	699	70.87	51.35	13.6
1894	471	63.77	51.86	9.0
1895	466	* 48.50	52.23	8.9
1896	496	* 41.82	51.33	9.6
1897	589	67.23	62.29	9.4
1898	825	70.15	74.99	11.0
1899	988	87.04	77.73	12.7
1900	1,243	99.28	99.28	12.4
1901	† 1,440	117.86	113.00	12.7

* Lowest prices of year. † Estimated.

It will be observed that surplus earnings per mile at the high point in 1890 were $746, from which they fell to $466 in 1895, recovering to an estimated amount of $1,440 in 1901. We think the estimate in this case is low rather than high. It is based on the supposition that net earnings of all roads increased on an average last year 10 per cent over the year before, and that the increase in charges did not increase 5 per cent. We think the increase in net will prove to have been more than 10 per cent and that the increase in charges will be less than 5 per cent, notwithstanding the large bond issues during the year. We wish, however, to have the figures under rather than over the mark.

The year 1890 showed the high point in stocks from 1885 to 1896. The average at the highest was 78.03, from which it declined to 41.82, the low point in 1896, recovering since to 117.86. The tendency of the figures to come together, comparing high and low with the surplus earnings per mile, is noteworthy. During the four years that surplus earnings per mile remained between $746 and $699, the high point of twenty stocks remained between 78 and 70. The next three years saw the surplus earnings per mile cut nearly in half, with the price of twenty stocks nearly cut in half, while even the figures tended again to unison. With the recovery since 1896, surplus earnings have almost trebled, while the average of twenty stocks has nearly trebled also. The column showing prices at the close of the year reflects in a number of cases temporary conditions. The decline in 1890 was due to the Baring failure, which caused a fall in the average of nearly 17 points; but, as values did not fall, prices recovered by the spring of 1892 nearly the full extent of the loss. The low point shown at the end of 1893 was due to the panic of that year and to the conditions which made it evident that surplus earnings per mile were falling, as was clearly shown in 1894.

The closing prices in 1895 and 1896 represented the level of conditions existing at that time, and since that date have shown, except in 1899, the progress of the bull market. The prices at the close of 1899 represented conditions growing out of the excessive underwriting of industrials in that year.

The fact that the investor makes prices in the end is clearly shown by the right-hand column in our table. Speculators depress prices, accidents and apprehensions bring temporary collapses, cliques carry prices too high, but the price at which the investor is willing to hold or to sell his stock comes out in the regular movement of the ratio.

At the high point in 1890, the ratio of price to earnings was 9.5 per cent. The Baring panic raised the ratio at the close of that year to 12 per cent, from which it fell to about 10 per cent in 1891 and 1892. The low point of earnings and prices showed comparative stability around 9 per cent, while in the bull period since 1898 earnings have gone ahead faster than values, large as the rise in values has been, keeping the ratio in the neighborhood of 12 per cent during this time.

The figures given today confirm the conclusions reached in previous studies. Values follow earnings. Manipulation makes temporary movements, but the main course of prices is simply a response to changes in values. Prices cannot be held up without [unless] values are up, and they cannot be kept down if supporting values are underneath.

If present earnings could be assured, stocks would be cheaper now than they were at the low prices prevailing three or four years ago. There is no assurance that earnings will be maintained, but it is hardly probable that they will decrease very rapidly, and they cannot do so without the fact being apparent. Hence, the holder of stocks at this time has a good basis in present values if they are maintained, and he will have notice of decreasing values when such decreases occur.

March 7, 1902

We have received the following: "Is it true that dullness in the market is almost invariably followed by decline?"

It is an article of faith with many operators that dullness is always followed by decline. The basis for this belief is that during certain periods this occurs, and the repetitions are regarded as establishing a rule.

The fact is, however, that the action of the market after dullness depends chiefly upon whether a bull market or a bear market is in progress. In a bull market, dullness is generally followed by advances; in a bear market, by decline. As bear markets as a rule last longer than bull markets, dullness is followed by decline rather oftener than by advance. There are exceptions, but they do not alter the general rule.

The reason why, in a bull market, dullness is followed by advance, is that a bull market is the exponent of increasing values. Values go on increasing, while the market rests, and prices start up because it becomes apparent to cliques or individuals that values are above prices, and that there is margin for rise. Exactly the reverse argument applies to declines after dullness in a bear period. Prices fall because values are falling, and dullness merely allows the fall in values to get ahead of the fall in prices.

The start after a period of inactivity is generally due either to some special event or to manipulation. In the former case, the reason for acting is obvious. In the latter case, manipulators begin by studying the situation and reach a conclusion that it will pay them to move prices. They then scrutinize the speculative situation, and learn something of the position of traders; whether they are carrying a good many stocks or not; whether they seem disposed to deal; whether margins appear to be large or small; and whether specialists have large-scale orders to either buy or sell.[4] This gives a basis on which manipulation begins. The public often follows the lead given, sometimes to its own advantage and sometimes to the advantage of the manipulators.

All this, however, is merely an incident in the main tendency of prices, which, as a whole, is in accord with the values which grow out of changes in earnings. Temporary movements in the market should always be considered with reference to their bearing on the main movement. The great mistake made by the public is paying attention to prices instead of to values. Whoever knows that the value of a particular stock is rising under conditions which promise stability, and the absence of developments calculated to neutralize the effect of increasing earnings, should buy that stock whenever it declines in sympathy with other stocks, and hold it until the price is considered high enough for the value as it is believed to exist.

This implies study and knowledge of the stock chosen, but this marks the difference between intelligent trading and mere gambling. Anybody can guess whether a stock will go up or down, but it is only guessing, and the cost of guessing will eat up most of the net profits of trading on pure guesses.

Intelligent trading begins with a study of conditions and a justified opinion that the general situation is either growing better or worse. If general conditions are improving, ascertain if the particular stock to be dealt in is having a fair share of that general improvement. Is its value rising?

If so, determine whether the price of the stock is low or high with reference to that value. If it is low, buy the stock and wait. Do not be discouraged if it does not move. The more value goes on increasing, the greater the certainty that rise in the stock will come. When it does come, do not take two or three points profit and then wait for a reaction, but consider whether the stock is still cheap at the advance, and if so, buy more, rather than sell under the assumption that the expected rise is under way. Keep the stock until the price appears to be up to the value and get a substantial profit.

This is the way the large operators make their money; not by trading back and forth, but by accurate forecasts of coming changes in value, and then buying stocks in quantity and putting the price up to value. The small operator cannot put prices up, but if his premises are sound, he can hold stock with assurance that large operators and investors will put the price up for him.

All this has been very easy in the last few years. It is not as easy now on account of the high level of prices and the fact that earnings at this level are perhaps as likely to recede as they are to advance. In estimating values at present, the high level of earnings and the high level of prices must be carefully considered with reference to the possibility that neither will be maintained. This makes it important to think about the short side as well as the long side, because the rules that apply to increasing values apply just as well to decreasing values. Values are the thing to watch under all conditions.

March 13, 1902

We have shown in recent articles how the average price of railway stocks and the surplus earnings per mile of railroads have moved together. At the high point of the market in 1890, the average price of twenty railway stocks was 78.03, and the surplus per mile of all roads was $746. In 1896 the average price of twenty railway stocks was 41.82, and the surplus earnings per mile at the close of 1895 was 466. Since that time, the average price of twenty stocks has risen to 117.85, and the surplus earnings per mile to a sum between $1,450 and $1,650 per mile. The percentage of price to earnings in 1890 was 12 per cent, in 1895, 8.9 per cent, in 1900, 12.4 per cent, and is now between 10 and 12 per cent, depending upon what earnings per mile prove to have been in 1901.

In order to see whether similar conditions prevailed in the bull period twenty years ago, we have worked out the surplus earnings per mile and the average price of twelve active stocks in order to show the movement from the high point in 1881 to the low point in 1885, together with the percentage applicable in that period. The results appear in the table following:

Year	*Surplus Per Mile*	*Average 12 Stocks*	*Rates Per Cent*
1881	1,521	117.52	12.9
1882	1,372	106.85	12.8
1883	1,265	96.79	13.0
1884	906	79.12	11.4
1885	702	66.15	10.6

The movement here shown is very similar to that which has occurred in the past eleven years. Surplus earnings per mile fell from $1,521 to $702, while prices fell from 117 to 66, a parallel quite as close as that prevailing in the period from 1890 to 1896.

The percentage showed exactly the same action by investors. The return in 1881 was 12.9 per cent, and in 1885 it was 10.6 per cent, just as in 1890 it was 12 per cent and fell in 1896 to 9.6 per cent and rose again to 12.7 per cent. It seems certain that the investor, in making prices for railway stocks in averages and over a period of time, acts on a conviction which establishes the normal percentage at 9 to 10 per cent in periods of depression and between 12 and 14 per cent in times of prosperity.

There is another interesting point. Surplus earnings per mile at the top in 1881 appear to have been very close to what they were in 1901. The surplus per mile in 1900 was $1,243. The net earnings of more than three-quarters of the railway mileage in the country increased in 1901 about 14 per cent. If all roads gained that amount, the surplus per mile would be over $1,600, and in any event a sum in excess of $1,500 seems an approximate certainty. The surplus in 1881 was $1,521.

The price of stocks furnishes another coincidence. The high point for twenty stocks in 1901, and the highest to date was 117.86. The highest average of twelve stocks in 1881 was 117.52. The stocks included in the 1881 average were Jersey Central, Northwest, Rock Island, Burlington, C., C., C. & St. L. [Cleveland, Cincinnati, Chicago and St. Louis], Lackawanna, Denver & Rio Grande, Delaware & Hudson, Erie, Illinois Central, Lake Shore and Louisville & Nashville, a good representative list of that date. St. Paul was omitted because of the stock dividend in that period, which had an effect on the price apart from earnings. The increase in the stock of Rock Island and of Louisville & Nashville had occurred prior to 1881.

The broad conclusion is that in a period extending from 1881 to 1901, the same general correspondence between average earnings and surplus earnings per mile has been maintained. In that period, surplus earnings per mile have been as low as $466, and as high as $1,531. Prices have moved up and down in the closest accord with this change in values.

There have been times when a temporary separation has occurred, but in every case values, as shown by surplus earnings per mile, have in due time exerted a controlling influence. A method of judging values which has proved sound for twenty years would seem to be worthy of consideration in looking at the probable tendency of prices in time to come.

March 14, 1902

In 1899, the average price of twenty railway stocks declined from the high point of 87.04 down to about 72. During this period, which covered about eight months, the earnings of railroads increased steadily and rather largely. The increase in net of about seven-eighths of the railway mileage of the country in the year 1899 was $46,000,000. More than two-thirds of this increase was made during the time that prices of stocks were going down. The cause of that decline was known at the time to be not any loss in the value of railway stocks, but the financial situation growing out of excessive underwriting of industrials in the early part of that year.

Since May, 1901, or a period of over ten months, the average price of twenty railway stocks has swung the greater part of the time between 108 and 114. There have been frequent alternations of advance and decline, but with very little net change.

During this period, railway earnings, gross and net, increased more rapidly than ever before. In the twelve months ended December 31, 1901, earnings covering about 166,000 out of 191,000 miles of road increased about $64,000,000. More than three-quarters of this increase occurred since there has been any rise of importance in railway stocks.

The situation differs, however, from that of 1899 in two respects. Prices have not had a large decline as they had then, and the level of prices is materially higher than it was then, but the feature of increase in value without increase in prices exists.

We have pointed out recently that prices are lower compared with surplus earnings per mile now than they have been at many previous times since 1896. Our figures used in estimating surplus earnings per mile at the end of 1901 were made low, so as not to overstate; but we think our first estimate of $1,440 per mile may prove to be so much below the truth as to be misleading.

Our statement of net earnings has shown a ratio of increase varying from 12 to 15 per cent. The [*Financial*] *Chronicle* report of increase in net earnings averages 14 per cent. There is little doubt that an increase of 13 per cent on all roads will be justified by the final figures.

The average net earnings per mile of all roads in 1900 was $2,519. An addition of 13 per cent would make the net for 1901 $2,846. The charges per mile of all roads in 1900 were about $1,276 against $1,284 in 1899, $1,286 in 1898, $1,295 in 1897, and $1,344 in 1896. Charges per mile change very little, and we think it fair to assume that the average for 1901 will not exceed $1,300 per mile. Should this be the case, the surplus earnings per mile would be $1,546 compared with $1,243 in 1900, and $988 in 1899.

Taking the net earnings actually reported on 166,500 miles, and assuming this indicative of the whole, the net per mile would work out

[to] $3,176, and this would give surplus earnings per mile of $1,776. We regard this as extreme, but believe that the figures will show a surplus per mile between $1,546 and $1,700 per mile.

In this case, the surplus earnings per mile have risen from $300 to $400 a mile with a very small increase in the average price of twenty stocks. There will therefore be a basis of value justifying rise in the market in case earnings are maintained as the year goes on, and other conditions, particularly those relating to money and crops, are such as to give assurance of continued prosperity.

It is reasonable to suppose that large operators will wish to be sure of the crop situation before undertaking any important advance; but if crops should be up to the average and there should be no serious change for the worse in general conditions, the situation in July and August would be favorable for promoting rise in railway stocks.

March 18, 1902

We have received a considerable number of inquiries bearing upon our comparison of the lines of value and price, and the following paragraphs are intended to be answers to some of these questions, many of them covering much the same points.

We have tested earnings in a variety of ways, using gross earnings per mile, net earnings per mile and net income per mile, but find the best results are given by surplus earnings per mile. Gross earnings per mile are too far removed from dividends. Operating expenses and charges have to be deducted, and there is room for too much variation. In using net income, considerable sums may be received from sources other than traffic in one year, and not in another, making an alteration in income not in accord with the true basis afforded by traffic.

Net earnings per mile represent actual traffic conditions, and when charges per mile are deducted, they leave the sum actually earned on the stock, or the earning surplus per mile. Prices must inevitably be more responsive to the sum available for dividends than any other one item, except perhaps that of dividends paid. In the long run, the dividend earned exerts a stronger influence than the dividend paid, as is afforded by the cases of Northwest, Lackawanna and other stocks at the present time.

Theoretically, capitalization per mile should be considered in getting at the relation of prices to earnings. We find in practice, however, that taking twenty stocks on one side, and surplus earnings of all the roads in the country on the other, the variation in capital has not been enough to materially alter results. If an examination were being made of the surplus per mile of a given road, as compared with the price of the stock of that road, changes in capitalization per mile would be important, and should receive allowance, although here the lowering of the price attending the increase in the capital would tend toward normal results.

Comparison of values and prices over the twenty-one years from 1881 to 1901 shows that the percentage of average price to average surplus earnings per mile has kept within a comparatively narrow limit. It has been down around 9 per cent and it has been up around 13 per cent, but its range in the main has been between 10 and 12½ per cent, showing the sentiment of investors as a whole upon the value of railway stocks.

A wide range is shown in surplus earnings per mile. In 1881 they were above $1,500 per mile. In 1895 they were as low as $466 per mile. At present they are again probably above $1,500 per mile. These large changes are due to the fact that operating expenses and fixed charges are comparatively stable items of expense, whether earnings are good or bad. Increase in gross earnings result in a substantial addition to surplus earnings per mile, while decreases in gross earnings fall heavily on surplus earnings per mile.

It is probable that fall in prices from the highest point, wherever that may be, will precede important decreases in earnings. Far-sighted men in and out of Wall Street will perceive coming changes in conditions before those changes actually arrive, and will discount their approach by sales of stock. If their forecasts are correct, and decline in prices is followed by decrease in earnings so that the level of prices thus created is about a fair level in view of decreased earnings, the process will very likely be repeated, perhaps again and again.

The point for the ordinary trader to consider is that when conditions begin to change for the worst, and business begins to shrink, contraction will be likely to go on, not for a period of months, but for some years. Hence, the outsider, as well as the insider, can foresee the probability of further shrinkage in prices and earnings and can take advantage of that fact. It has taken earnings five years to work up to the present level. It will take them several years when the turn comes to work down to the level of perhaps $700 surplus earnings per mile.

During this time there will be many changes, declines and recoveries, both in earnings and in prices, but with the contraction fairly started, shrinkage in the main is likely to go on. When the low point is reached, recovery will set in and come about in the same way, improvement extending through a period of years, rise in prices being backed up and supported by increase in values.

The great point in speculation is to think of the market in broad lines, in periods of four or five years, holding justified views as to the general tendency, with the expectation that changes in conditions in the direction in which such changes tend will bring fair profits by the slow but sure process of increases or decreases, as the case may be, in actual values.

March 22, 1902

We constantly receive requests from readers for a treatment of industrial securities on lines similar to those followed in the case of railroad securities in our "Studies in Value." There seems to be a desire for the establishment of some standards of value in the case of industrial securities, and some of our readers are apparently surprised that we do not devote more space to this matter. It may be well to explain just how the case stands.

The process of analysis depends in the main upon comparison. In dealing with the accounts of a railroad, the method adopted by us has consisted in the main of two processes. The first is the rearrangement, in greater or less degree, of the official figures so as to disclose in as striking relief as possible what we consider to be the vital features and facts. The second is comparison of the features and facts disclosed with similar features and facts of previous years in the history of the same company, so as to exhibit relative progress, or with corresponding features and facts in the case of other companies so as to disclose relative economy, efficiency or the reverse. Thus, the two requisites for an analysis which shall be of any value are, first, the existence of such figures as will disclose the vital facts, and second, the existence of similar figures for previous years or for other companies with which fair comparison can be made.

Now, it is evident that in the case of most industrial companies one or the other of these requisites is lacking. In the case of new companies, which are, of course, in a large majority at the present time, there is no past with which we can compare. How, for example, can the U.S. Steel Corporation undergo comparison with anything? Again, far too many industrial companies fail to make such a showing in the way of reports as would enable us to extract the vital facts of their business even for a single year. Consequently, how can we or anybody else arrive by a process of analysis at the actual value of their securities? The best thing that we can do is to make a very rough approximation and then qualify that.

It is strictly true to say that it will take some time to disclose the value of most of the industrial securities recently created and floated on the market. Time is an absolutely necessary factor for the reason that we have described. Even if every industrial company made a proper report, which unfortunately is not the case, and is very far from being the case, we should have to wait at least some time before we should feel any confidence in estimating the intrinsic value of industrial securities.

Many people are impatient with us because of what they evidently consider our "ultra-conservatism" on this point, but if we are to deal with facts, we must take them as we find them.

Without the two requisites that we have mentioned, namely, sufficiency of information and a basis for comparison, an investor must be in the dark as to the actual value of an industrial security. As these requisites are lacking in the case of most of the industrial securities now being dealt in, it is clear that investors are in the dark as to their value. Consequently, one can only speculate as to what this value may be. In other words, of necessity, the vast majority of industrial securities at the present time are to be looked upon in the light of a "speculation," and not in the light of a strict "investment."

This is not to say that a great many of them may not have investment merits of the first quality. Time may prove this, and undoubtedly will prove it in the case of some. But until time elapses, the investor cannot sift out the good from the bad, nor can anyone sift it out for him. To say that a stock must be looked upon in the light of a "speculation" is not to say that it has no value, but it is to say that it has an indeterminate value. When a security has a value that can be determined, it can be looked upon as an "investment," and if its value is above the market price, it becomes a good investment.

We are trying to make these points clear because from time to time managers of companies have felt aggrieved because we have described the securities of their companies as "speculative," and they have apparently understood this to mean that they had no value. A stock is speculative until its value can be demonstrated; as soon as this can be done, it ceases to be speculative, in one sense at all events, and becomes an investment, taking rank in one of the many classes into which investments are divided. The essence of an "investment" is the fact that its value is known. The essence of a "speculation" is in the fact that its value is unknown.

April 3, 1902

There are two kinds of money in the stock market at any time, both seeking employment. There is "investment" money, so to speak, which is looking for safe return of income, and "speculative" or "venture" money, which is looking for quick profits. There is in the country a good deal of money that is sometimes speculative money and sometimes investment money, according to sentiment and the general conditions of business. In times of depression after panic, this money is mainly investment money, while in times of prosperity and expansion, it becomes very largely speculative or venture money.

In other words, a great many people sometimes speculate with their money and sometimes invest their money. It is very safe to say that at this time last year there were more speculators in the United States than at any time in its history, at all events so far as the stock market is concerned. The volume of venture money probably was larger at that time in proportion to the whole than ever before. Nor can it be said that in spite of the crop failures and accidents of last year there has been actually accomplished a very great change in sentiment in this respect as yet. The peculiar condition of the bond market shows that the public has not up to the present time entirely lost the desire to "get rich quick" which exhibits itself in speculation in stocks.

Consider, for instance, the case of the Burlington & Quincy joint fours. Here is a bond jointly guaranteed by two railroads whose stocks stand at high prices, or rather did stand at very high prices previous to their exchange into the stock of the Northern Securities Co. The quoted price for Northern Securities stock now means high prices for the stocks of Northern Pacific and Great Northern owned by the company. Yet the syndicate which underwrote a large block of these Burlington & Quincy joint 4 per cent bonds was obliged to extend its term of existence beyond the limit originally prescribed because it could not sell its holdings of the bonds. So far as appearances go, moreover, it has not made very great progress in this direction since this extension of time. Everybody knows that if the Burlington & Quincy joint 4 per cent bonds are not good, a condition of things must be presupposed which would make existing values of railroad stocks ridiculously high. In other words, if railroad stocks are worth anything like their present prices, the

Quincy joint fours are good beyond peradventure. What, then, is the reason for the bonds being so slow of sale?

The reason is that the public has not yet come around entirely to the point of regarding its money mainly as investment money, but still looks upon it very largely as speculative money. On the other hand, it is not actually using this money for speculation or, at all events, not for new speculation at this time, and apparently will not do so unless business conditions are evidently such as to assure a considerable extension of the period of general prosperity. It looks very much as if the public's sentiment respecting its money were undergoing a change rather gradual in character and as if the tendency from now on might be less in the direction of speculation and more in the direction of investment. In other words, the chances rather appear to favor a better market for bonds.

The position of the Burlington & Quincy joint 4 per cent syndicate is by no means exceptional. Several other instances will readily suggest themselves to those who are familiar with the bond market at this time. There is undoubtedly a considerable supply of bonds—and good bonds at that—in what might be called intermediary hands, mostly first hands. When people begin to realize that it is no longer possible to "get rich quick" by speculating in stocks, they will begin to think about putting their money where it will earn something, and they will choose bonds for this purpose. Consequently, an improving market for bonds may be looked for as speculation in stocks falls off.

One of the great differences between a period of depression and a period of expansion is a matter of sentiment. A man who has money that he is willing to speculate with feels himself rich. When he looks upon his money as something to be carefully invested and saved, he does not feel himself rich but rather the reverse. It is not that in times of depression everybody actually is so much poorer than in times of prosperity. It is largely that people feel themselves poorer and govern their actions accordingly.

It is the judgment of many who have carefully studied the situation as it exists today that from now on people are likely to regard their money as something to be carefully saved rather than as something to be speculated with for large profits. It must not be forgotten, moreover, that the public undoubtedly has a good deal of money tied up in more or less speculative enterprises at this time. The U.S. Steel Corporation alone accounts for a good many millions in this way. Nevertheless, the public is by no means entirely tied up in this class of security. It still has a good deal of money which in due time will probably seek more or less strict investment.

April 4, 1902

The process known as "watering" capital means essentially the increasing of capital, not primarily for the acquisition of new property or for cash, but to represent an earning capacity existing, supposed to exist or expected. In a reorganization commonly so-called capital is usually cut down to bring it into proportion with an ascertained earning capacity. Reorganization, however, simply means adjustment of capital to earnings, which, of course, can be done in either direction. It is also true to say that capital is watered not so much to afford a medium for the distribution of earning capacity as it is because speculative conditions offer an opportunity for disposing of the watered capital for cash.

The most remarkable example of capital watering in corporation history is undoubtedly the U.S. Steel Company. This company, as everybody knows, was formed a year ago by the union of some ten corporations, practically every one of which was itself a somewhat similar formation. The Federal Steel Company, for example, was a union of the old Illinois Steel Company and the Minnesota Iron Company on a very liberal basis of capitalization. The American Steel & Wire Co. underwent what amounted (according to recent disclosures) to at least a double watering in the course of its formation. The other companies, including even the Carnegie Company, all experienced a similar process. In the final formation of the Steel Corporation, each and every one was watered once more on a large scale. It is not easy to determine without a long and troublesome examination the exact amount of the watering that was done, but it appears that whereas the ten companies now mainly comprising the U.S. Steel Company had about $220,000,000 bonds, $250,000,000 preferred stock, and $460,000,000 common stock, the Steel Company now has in one way and another, close upon $350,000,000 bonds, and over $500,000,000 each of preferred and common stock. Thus, it looks as if the final watering amounted to substantially $300,000,000 of stock and $100,000,000 of bonds.

It must be understood that we are not using the word "watering" in an offensive sense, but merely as describing the process of extra capitalization.[5]

Thus, it is clear that of the Steel Company's capitalization of about

$1,400,000,000, including obligations of subsidiary companies, the odd $400,000,000 represents practically the final watering. It is impossible to determine how much would be represented by the previous waterings. It may be noted, however, that the market value of the enterprise at this time is practically $1,000,000,000. This, as has been seen, represents more or less the capitalization of the constituent companies previous to the final watering. Assuming the figures for the year ending March 31 as representing the results in an extremely favorable year, it appears that what may be called the gross profits, in other words, the profits before allowances made for depreciation, etc., were about 11 per cent on the market value of the enterprise and on the value of the constituent companies previous to formation of the Steel Corporation.

Practically, the water in the Steel Corporation capital represents what may be called the price of promotion and organization of the company in its final development. The bulk of it represents necessary profits paid to promoters and others in order to secure the organization and flotation of the combined enterprises. In the case of the Federal Steel and of the Steel & Wire, more than one set of profits has necessarily been paid. In all cases, at least one set of profits has had to be provided.

All this, of course, is admitted by everybody, and the answer that is made to criticisms based on the facts recited is that the advantages secured are sufficient compensation for the price paid. In other words, it is claimed that the strength secured by concentration of organization and by integration of the industry from the ground up, will enable the company to earn and pay a substantial return on the capital issued for promoters' profits. This is the view held by the company's friends, and they support their contentions with strong arguments.

Those who do not agree with them say that the burden of providing a return on capital sunk in promoters' profits will place the Steel Company at a material disadvantage as compared with those of its competitors who have not been obliged to pay as heavy a price for organization as has been paid by the Steel Company. Time will show which view is right. If it be true, as has been persistently rumored, that the Steel Company is about to raise $50,000,000 of new cash capital for "general purposes" within a year of its formation, the company's critics will feel themselves considerably strengthened in their position. Pending final official information on the point, however, we are still bound to presume that the company is not seeking fresh capital for use upon existing plants at this time after having been in existence for only one year, and after having paid in that year $20,000,000 in dividends on the common stock.

April 22, 1902

It is probably safe to say that on the recent advance the stock market, as a whole, reached and passed the high level made a year ago. Our compilation of averages clearly indicates this—even after allowing for exceptional movements in a few stocks, such as Chicago & Northwestern, Jersey Central and Louisville & Nashville. Thus, the expectations of those who regarded the level of last year as likely to prove the high-water mark of the "boom" are disappointed. The recurrence, moreover, of active speculation on a large scale is a matter for some surprise, considering the situation. The questions that need more particularly to be answered at present are two, viz.:

1. Is the present speculation being conducted on a safe scale? and—
2. Are prices relatively high as measured by values?

It is the business of "financial criticism," as discussion of market prospects is termed, to supply some kind of answer to these questions, and at present the field of criticism is occupied by two rival camps or schools—both a little inclined to be hysterical. On the one side is the school which looks upon recent operations as unlicensed piracy and Wall Street as a den of intoxicated gamblers, and on the other side is the school which "points with pride" to predictions fulfilled, and scoffs at the fruitless warnings of the other school, incidentally arguing it almost a matter of good citizenship to buy stocks, as who should dare to impugn even by the implication of inaction the great prosperity of the country? Meanwhile, there are some facts which are not in dispute, and to recall these facts may not be unprofitable.

The banking situation is unquestionably extended in degree much greater than a year ago. Moreover, borrowing by sterling loans has been conducted on a very large scale, and syndicate operations about to be undertaken will tend to increase the tension in this respect. There cannot be said to be very much more than standing room in the money market at present, and the tide of the exchange is getting strongly against this country. Yet a very large speculation is in progress. A clique of powerful and daring western speculators and half a dozen "pools" of sorts are busy in the market, actively engaged in "booming" their respective specialties. The Street is full of "tips" on this, that and the other stock, and it is characteristic of the existing state of things that many of these "tips" actually prove correct. With every desire to say pleasant things, even the most complaisant of "critics" cannot but admit that the answer to question number one must be in the negative. Speculative conditions at present are very far from sound.

As regards the second question—whether prices as measured by values are relatively high—it is necessary to distinguish. Values make prices, and earnings make values. It is true that the percentage of increase in earnings in the last year is larger than the percentage of advance in prices. If current earnings were assured of continuance, stocks on an average would be relatively no higher than they were in 1896. But can we be assured of continuance of earnings on their present level?

Earnings make values, and, in the long run, crops make earnings. It is too soon, of course, to speak with any certainty as to this year's crops. Yet it is now common knowledge that conditions are not promising anywhere in the West. The ground is relatively dry and winter wheat, except in places, is not in good condition. The seeding conditions in the Northwest are unfavorable.

Now, good crops are imperatively needed this year to stave off a reaction from the "boom" which has run over five years. Everybody knows that poor crops would result in a general check to business and a very severe check to speculation. The next six weeks will be a period of vital importance in the winter wheat regions, and after that, supposing spring wheat and corn seeding to have progressed favorably, there is the crucial month of July to be passed.

Again, there is the very serious matter of litigation to be considered, which has now put a stop to very far-reaching plans, and may have even more important results. It will be many months before this matter is finally cleared up.[6]

Thus, the future is full of uncertainties, and, with speculation rampant, railroad stock prices averaging three times what they were six years ago, banking credits widely extended, large foreign borrowings and uncertainty as to crops, there is much to be said for the attitude of those who think it wise now to sacrifice possible speculative opportunities in order to secure safety. After all, Wall Street is one of the few places where it not infrequently pays to refuse the hand tendered by opportunity, and one does not lose money when one misses a chance of making a profit.

More than at any time since the "boom" began does strict conservatism now seem to be the only safe policy, so far as the stock market is concerned.

April 30, 1902

In these days, when "water" in capitalization is so common, it is customary to hear a line of argument designed to justify the existence of "watered" capital, which is about as follows:

"The value of capital in the case of an industrial company depends not upon the extent to which that capital represents actual cash put into property, but the extent to which property owned can earn a return on capital outstanding. In other words, earning capacity and not actual cash outlay is the test of capital value."

This is, of course, in a sense true, but it is entirely untrue in so far as it denies the importance of actual cash cost in its bearing upon capital value. The demonstration is extremely simple, but many people may perhaps find it new. Our proposition is that in industrial business, other things being equal, the value of capital will in the long run tend to be determined by cash cost of duplication of existing plants, and the valuation of capital in excess of this cost will tend to disappear.

In other words, in the long run, nature tends to squeeze the "water" out of capital valuations.

Suppose two factories or mills operating as competitors in the same industry, one of which is capitalized for $1,000,000 and the other for $200,000, the actual cost of erection of each mill being $200,000 and the earning capacity of each mill being in times of prosperity $75,000 per annum. The owners of the mill that has the larger capitalization can truthfully say that its capitalization represents earning power and is therefore justified. There comes along, however, a third competitor, who observes that the former two mills are making considerable profits, and he figures out that at a cost of $200,000 he can put up a mill of equal capacity to that of each of the others. He is able to raise his money by a syndicate which goes on the principle that it can make a 15 per cent return on a profit of $30,000 a year, or less than half the profit made by the mill with the $1,000,000 capital.

In other words, this competitor is able to go into the business and compete with the company of "watered" capital on terms such that he will make 15 per cent on his capital where the other will make but 3. He does so, and the event fairly justifies the enterprise. The mill with "watered" capital is compelled either to lose business or sacrifice profits, and its earning power simply disappears. In other words, nature squeezes out the "water."

This process in one form or another is certain to take place sooner or later in any industry that is returning a profit upon "watered" capital, because wherever capital valuation represents anything more than duplication costs, real patents or monopoly rights of some kinds, the excess valuation is simply a premium upon competition which is certain to come into the field. Thus, it is certain that where no monopoly, natural or artificial, exists, no permanent value can be safely regarded as resting in capital representing "water." It is, of course, difficult at times to estimate the amount of "water" in a company's capitalization, because as conditions change, the cost of duplication changes, monoplies are set up or existing monopolies disappear. Nevertheless, in the long run, certain it is that the natural forces of competition will destroy ultimately all value in capital that does not represent tangible property, including, of course, monopoly rights.

The next period of depression will almost beyond question have for its principal feature a large number of industrial company reorganizations, which will, if properly carried on, consist chiefly in the writing off of nominal capitalization representing promoters' profits, "water" in other forms, etc. This kind of capital is able to earn its living to only a very moderate extent and in the long run inevitably proves unable to do so. This period of industrial reorganization may be some distance off, for there is happily as yet no immediate indication of a serious setback in general trade save in the rather unfavorable crop prospects; but it is certain to come, and it is practically certain to disclose the existence of large quantities of "water" in industrial capitalization, which will have to be squeezed out. No industrial company can hope in the long run to return regular profits on capital representing dismantled mills, expired patents or promoters' profits. Of course, in times of prosperity, it can and does frequently show a large return thereon, but this is simply because the forces of nature do not work in a hurry, and require time for their full effect to be felt.

May 13, 1902

The one distinguishing feature of the stock market in the last twelve months has been its resistance to sudden and unexpected shocks and its recuperative power. It is worthwhile noting what it has had to combat in this way.

A year ago the market was thrown into sudden and most violent panic by the development of a corner in Northern Pacific and by knowledge that powerful banking interests were engaged in a bitter contest for control of that property. The decline in prices was probably more severe in May, 1901, than in any similar period in the country's history. This is well shown by our averages indicating the movement of the stock market, as follows:

May 1, 20 active stocks closed average	117.80
May 9, closing average	103.87
May 10, closing average	110.06
May 11, closing average	104.54
June 17, closing average	117.65

Thus, in spite of the financial tornado, the market was practically as high on June 17 as it was on May 1. It is safe to say that never before in the history of the Street was so sharp and sudden a panic followed by so complete a recovery. It may be well to note, moreover, that the closing averages by no means indicate the full force of the panic, as the market closed at a substantial recovery from the worst.

Having surmounted the Northern Pacific panic, the market was next called upon to face a severe disaster to the corn crop. Early in July the corn crop was cut in half by hot winds, with the result that the smallest crop in many years was finally harvested. One would have thought that, following upon the financial panic of six weeks previous and coming at a time when an enormous speculation seemed to have culminated, such a development would have wrecked the market completely. As a matter of fact, it did nothing of the kind. The movement, as shown by the averages, was as follows:

June 17, average closing price	117.05
Aug. 5, average closing price	104.86
Aug. 26, average closing price	111.69

Thus, the failure of the country's largest crop caused a decline of only about six points, and at the end of August the market was within six points, on an average, of the highest price touched in the boom.

Coincidently with the failure of the corn crop, moreover, there came the strike of the men employed by the United States Steel Corporation and other iron and steel companies, which, while it ultimately was a complete failure, yet nevertheless at one time threatened serious results.

These events did not exhaust the casualty list by any means. On September 6 President McKinley was shot at Buffalo. After a few days of anxious hope, the President died early on September 14. Yet the market reflected the shock to only a slight extent, as may be seen from the price movement as follows:

Aug. 26, closing average	111.69
Sept. 13, closing average	105.30
Sept. 21, closing average	110.82

Yet another blow was in store for the Street in the shape of a disclosure of the unsatisfactory copper position, with a collapse in the price of the metal and a heavy break in Amalgamated Copper stock. How sharp this break was may be seen from the fact that in September the stock sold at 120 while in October it fell to 83¼ and in December to 60½. This was a bad blow to confidence generally, and yet its effect was but transitory, so far as the market as a whole was concerned. This is well shown by the market movement as follows:

Sept. 21, closing average	110.82
Oct. 7, closing average	106.20
Oct. 26, closing average	110.88

Thus, after all these blows, the market was on the same average level as at the end of August and within less than seven points of the top of the "boom."

Then followed a lull in the procession of unfavorable events, and an opportunity occurred which was availed of by the Morgan-Harriman interests to settle the Northern Pacific dispute by the organization of the Northern Securities Co., division of control of Burlington & Quincy and retirement of Northern Pacific preferred stock. Under the influence of this, the market rose as follows:

Oct. 28, closing average	109.60
Nov. 11, closing average	114.56
Nov. 14, closing average	112.35
Nov. 22, closing average	115.21
Dec. 12, closing average	110.08
Jan. 2, closing average	115.85

Thus, between May 1, 1901, and the beginning of this year, the stock market faced:

1. The Northern Pacific panic,
2. The corn crop failure,
3. The steel strike,

4. The assassination of President McKinley,
5. The collapse in Amalgamated Copper,

and as the net result of eight months' operations held its ground within two points of the top.

Nor is this all. Early in the present year another severe blow was struck by the commencement of a suit on behalf of the United States against the Northern Securities Co., which raised question as to the entire railroad situation from top to bottom. This suit had the effect of checking indefinitely many plans of various kinds in connection with railroad combinations and created considerable uneasiness in railroad circles. Even this did not suffice to do more than temporarily check the market, as may be seen from the record as follows:

Jan. 2, closing average	115.85
Jan. 14, closing average	111.73
Feb. 10, closing average	115.88
Feb. 20, closing average	113.63
Apr. 3, closing average	117.13
Apr. 10, closing average	116.95
May 1, closing average	121.86
May 10, closing average	119.51

Thus, while a year ago the market was thought to be on dizzy heights, on the first of May this year, after the succession of blows above enumerated, it was actually four points higher, on an average, as a result of the twelve months' operations.

This exhibit of strength cannot be described as other than extraordinary. There are, however, two ways of looking at it. One is to regard it as evidence that the wonderful prosperity exhibited by this country in every kind of trade is still in full vigor, and that a continuance of advance in prices may be looked for.

The other way is to regard the market as having been so frequently checked and shocked by untoward occurrences as to leave it with diminished strength and, so to speak, lowered vitality. One thing, however, is clear, and that is that nothing that has yet occurred has been able to induce people to sell stocks in any quantity. It is undoubtedly true that the most careful and strenuous efforts have been made by the large financial interests to prevent any serious shock to public confidence, and this has been done because these large interests were themselves heavily concerned in the market.

So far they have been entirely successful, despite all accidents. At present their only anxiety seems to be in respect to the growing crops and the condition of the money market. It is necessary to note that the money market shows in its widely extended credits and large foreign borrowings the effect of the measures taken to sustain securities values.

May 14, 1902

We have received an inquiry as follows:

"Do you consider the bull campaign at an end?" In the belief that the answer to this question may be of interest to others of our readers, we attempt a reply to it in some little detail.

The first thing that is necessary to note is that in dealing with the stock market there is no way of telling when the top of an advance or the bottom of a decline has been reached until some time after such top or bottom has been made. Sometimes people are able to guess when prices are at the top or at the bottom, but such guesses are of their nature of no particular value, and it is a proverb in Wall Street that only a foolish speculator hopes to buy stocks at the lowest and sell them at the highest. The speculator with experience knows that no one can do this with certainty or regularity. The first question, therefore, that we have to decide in attempting an answer to the question put to us by our correspondent is whether the market has recently made a new high point, and whether it has, so far, moved away appreciably from that point.

Curiously enough, as pointed out yesterday, our averages showed the high point in 1901 to have occurred on May 1, at 117.86 for the twenty active stocks, while on May 1, 1902, the high point for the year, so far, was made, the twenty stocks being at 121.86. It is noteworthy, however, that whereas on May, 1901, the twelve industrial stocks closed at 75.93, on May 1, 1902, they closed at 67.11, or close upon nine points off. If our averages are a true guide to the market for railroad stocks, as they have proved to be in the past, it follows that if the end of the bull campaign has been reached, it was reached on May 1, 1902, or less than two weeks ago. Now, it is very clear that two weeks is much too short a time in which to establish the fact of a permanent turn, more especially as at the close of last week there had been a decline from the top price of only about two points in the twenty stocks. In short, the only answer that we can make to the main question is that we do not know whether the bull campaign begun in 1896–97 is at an end or not. At this stage nobody can know. The best that anyone can do is to sum up the indications for and against and try to strike a balance.

There are some things in the situation that are beyond dispute and that point to the belief that the bull campaign is not over. Everybody knows that the volume of business in spite of last year's corn-crop failure is larger than at any time in the country's history. The railroad earnings, which are, of course, the final test of railroad values, continue to make a most satisfactory showing. In the third week of April, 51 roads reporting to *The Wall Street Journal* showed an increase in gross of 12.43 per cent, being the largest ratio of increase in many weeks. For the fourth week of April our final statement will probably show a ratio of increase of 11 per cent. There is no getting away from this fact, because earnings make values and values make prices. In the twelve months ending May 1, there was a larger increase in railroad values as measured by earnings than there was in railroad prices.

This increase in railroad earnings is the result of the extremely active business passing in every channel of trade. There is no need to go into the details of the various industries, for practically all, except where there are labor controversies, are in excellent condition. So much must be admitted by everybody. It is not possible to find anywhere in trade circles any definite indication as yet of a turn in the tide.

On the other hand, it must not be forgotten that in the past there has always been pulsation; reaction has followed action; depression has followed prosperity; decline has followed advance. For over five years, there has been steady growth in railroad earnings, reflecting the extraordinary rapid increase in the business of this country. For over five years, there has been almost uninterrupted expansion in all directions from territory down, and there has been a growth in public confidence almost unparalleled in the commercial history of this country. Signs are not wanting in the last twelve months that this confidence has resulted in a somewhat larger discounting of the future than usual, and in a willingness to make experiments in commercial and financial organization on a scale unprecedented in the history of the world. There has come with this an extension of banking credits on a scale that some people view with uneasiness. This extension of credit has affected very materially the foreign exchange market, and has placed this country in the position of being a large borrower in the money market of Europe. Of course, this in itself is nothing to worry about, provided that underlying conditions continue sound. Up to the present time, these conditions are sound, except for a congestion of securities in first hands at the financial center.

The whole thing seems to turn on the continuance of soundness in underlying conditions, because if this be assured, financial liquidation can be accomplished without much inconvenience. It is admitted by everybody that the growing crops this year will determine general conditions for the next twelve months. In a sense, therefore, the fate of the bull campaign, already five years old, may be said to depend upon the growing crops.

The only answer that it seems to us can be given to the query put to us, is that the matter largely depends on this year's harvest. If bountiful crops are assured, the indications point perhaps to higher prices with possibly some rather severe spasms of liquidation growing out of money market conditions. If, unfortunately, a disaster befalls the crops, the indications point to the setting of a general reaction in business which would, of course, result in the termination of the bull campaign. Hence, the next three months will be a period of the utmost importance to the financial world.

May 30, 1902

The market for stocks is apparently at a deadlock. For the greater part of the week transactions (with one or two exceptional cases) have reflected merely the operations of the room traders and the hardened speculators—the "regular customers" of the commission houses. And even in the exceptional cases the dealings have mostly been for the account of speculative cliques or combinations. Nothing approaching to large business for account of the public has been seen. Complete apathy is its present attitude, and nothing seems to dispel it.

Some days ago we recalled the various shocks that the market has encountered in the last twelve months without suffering any loss in quotations. Since that time, yet another casualty—the coal strike—has been added to the list, and, despite the fact that a great extension of this strike is threatened in the near future, the market remains apparently unaffected. It is difficult to imagine any particular form of trouble of which the Street has not had a taste in the last year. And yet prices keep their level, and there is clearly no general desire to sell.

The main reason is clear enough and has been described often enough in this column. Earnings make values, and values make prices; earnings have continued to increase, and hence values have increased; consequently, there has been no general force as yet operating against prices. Present earnings are more than satisfactory, and if there were any guarantee of their continuance, the general level of prices could not be called unduly high. As a matter of fact, measured by earnings, prices are relatively no higher today than they were in 1896, so far as railroad stocks are concerned. What people are waiting for is to see whether or not earnings will be maintained; that is why there is a deadlock in speculation at this time.

The country has conclusively demonstrated its ability to withstand one corn-crop failure without a wink, so to speak. But everybody knows that it could not stand another in quick succession, and that upon this year's crop depends practically the entire business of the country for the ensuing year. Last year the corn crop promised well in June, but was ruined by the middle of July. People remembering this say that while everything promises extremely well now, nothing is certain till July is out, at all events. In other words, the future of prices for the next twelve months cannot be determined until that time. Therefore, no one is justified at this time in entering upon large commitments. On the other hand, most people think that if the crops are all right this year, at least twelve months more of great prosperity may be looked for. Such matters as strikes are considered as of secondary and purely transitory importance.

There is much that is reasonable in this view of things. But there are other factors in the case that should not be forgotten. Assuming that the crops are all right, there is the money market to be reckoned with. Present indications are that an unusual strain will be put upon it some time this fall. We have borrowed heavily abroad in the last few weeks, and New York will in all probability have to ship as much money to the country this year as in other years. Meanwhile, our banking reserves are not as large as they should be at this season. This is something that should be borne in mind at this time.

Again, an immense mass of securities is now in first or second hands awaiting absorption by the public. It has been estimated that there are still in operation at least forty syndicates of various kinds in connection with new flotations, bond issues, etc. Some of these syndicates have made good progress with their operations, others have not. Their holdings are awaiting sale to the public, and the public is expected to take them all in time. No doubt it will do so—in time. But no one can doubt that there will be enough securities to go around.

Everything considered, the present deadlock is natural and healthy. Indeed, the strongest feature of the market situation is the absence of speculative fever on the public's part. This will give the market comparative stability if it has to face poor crops, and it will give it a broader basis for reasonable advance if the crops are good.

June 3, 1902

Whatever opinion may be held regarding the rights and wrongs of the war between the Boers and the British, there can be no difference of opinion respecting its conclusion. Both sides may well rejoice in the termination of a struggle lasting over two years and a half and involving a loss in lives and in money on an unexampled scale.

It is estimated roughly that the war has cost Great Britain, in round figures, $1,250,000,000 in money. It may well be that this is not an overestimate, everything considered. It is not an uncommon thing for people to argue that a war is good for trade and that it makes business active and, altogether, is not a bad thing for a country once in a while. This is not good economics. The plain fact is that war involves absolute waste of labor and material on a frightful scale, and cannot be regarded from any point of view as other than an evil. It may be a necessary evil, as when it is forced upon a country and that country must fight to preserve its independence. But an evil it is and will always remain to the end of time.

In the first place, it withdraws a large body of men from the peaceful pursuits upon which a country's wealth depends. The labor of these men is lost while [they are] in the army, and not merely is their labor lost, but they have to be fed and clothed and paid. In the second place, there is immense destruction of material of all kinds, and while a fictitious prosperity is produced in places where the munitions of war are manufactured, the result is unfavorable for other channels of trade.

It used to be estimated that Great Britain as a nation had a certain surplus income awaiting investment amounting to from sixty to one hundred million pounds annually. This represented income, as it were, on capital invested all over the world, in gold mines, plantations, railways, manufacture and shipping. Perhaps the smaller figure more fairly represents the truth in the above estimate. For the last three years this income has been absorbed either by new loans for the war or by taxation, and, what is more, the war has been the cause, directly or indirectly, of diminishing that income during the continuance of hostilities. For over two years Great Britain has been practically unable to invest surplus income because it has been compelled to throw it away in the cost of maintaining its army in South Africa. For many years to come the nation as a whole will have to suffer heavy taxation—which is in a sense enforced saving—to make good this loss.

A war, in fact, is like a crop failure over a country more or less dependent upon agriculture. Where a country is very rich and but little burdened with debt, as is the case with the United States, the drain and the waste are felt to a comparatively little extent, but they exist just the same. The process that went on in this country during the Civil War and in Great Britain during the war that is just ended is going on at this moment in this country in connection with the Philippine war, but we do not feel it because of our small debt and the comparatively small expenditures involved.

Those people who suppose that Great Britain will now proceed to branch out in a world-wide speculation are likely to be disappointed. There is no evidence that she has either the resources immediately available for that purpose or the inclination to any such purpose. No doubt the gold mines of the Rand will have to bear a large part of the taxation necessary to repair the losses of the war, but these mines could not possibly provide anything like the amount required, and for a long time to come Great Britian will be under heavy taxation. Moreover, it is extremely unlikely, in view of recent events, that British capital seeking investment—if there be much at this time, which is very doubtful—will turn to this country. In the last twelve months many things have happened which have aroused a certain amount of uneasiness with respect to our financial and speculative position, and the high level of prices now ruling serves rather to repel than to attract the foreign investor, whose distinguishing characteristic is that he likes to buy when prices are low.

If by the war Great Britain were coming into possession of a very rich country, which was susceptible of colonization to a large extent and which would produce for her wealth in other forms than those of the precious metals and precious stones, the process of recovery would no doubt be more rapid. But, in the opinion of the best judges, the new territory added to the British dominions is not a very rich country apart from its mines, nor is it a country that is likely to attract colonists on a large scale apart from those interested in mining ventures.

On the whole, so far as this country is concerned, there is little to expect in the way of added advantages from the conclusion of the South African war. The whole world, of course, gains by the cessation of any war, at all events, in a commercial sense, but beyond this it is difficult to see how we are to benefit much in the near future. It is a question, in fact, whether the stimulus that will be given in financial and commercial circles abroad by the announcement of peace may not result in an additional strain upon the money market some time this fall, owing to our large borrowing.

June 5, 1902

One of the distinctive features of the business situation in the last few months has been the restlessness of labor, resulting in strikes at many places and in many industries. It is clear, moreover, from what has happened in connection with the present coal strike that the attitude of labor in kindred industries is one of sympathy with the coal strikers, and it is by no means impossible that before the coal strike ends there may be considerable suspension of labor elsewhere.

It is fashionable in some quarters to represent the cause of this restlessness as being little more than a species of cupidity on the part of labor aroused by the general prosperity of the country and the sight of large profits being made by capital. This is not fair nor is it judicious. The plain fact of the matter is that a large part of the restlessness of labor arises from the fact that nowadays a given quantity of toil does not produce for the wage earner as much in commodities as it did three or four years ago. In other words, in the opinion of very careful observers, the advance in the cost of living has more than eaten up the advance in labor through increased wages or larger employment.

Everybody knows that the actual condition of a man on salary is better in times of depression than it is in times of prosperity. His money goes further. He gets more for his labor. A man with steady employment through the period of depression from 1894 on was able to save a good deal more money during the depression than he can save now. It is, of course, true that many men are now employed who were not employed at that time and that most of those who were employed at that time are getting more wages than they got then. Nevertheless, it is probably true, also, that in the exchange of labor for commodities the price of commodities in labor is higher today than it was then, and consequently there is diminution in the margin for saving.

Experience has shown that this is true of all booms and periods of great prosperity, and that one of the signs indicating the termination of such periods is usually a succession of strikes. The reason is simple enough. Employers feel themselves strong, and are less inclined to submit to what they conceive to be dictation at the hands of the unions, and the result is a fight. It not infrequently happens, moreover, that a prolonged strike will serve to check industrial prosperity in a certain line of business, and a succession of strikes will certainly tend to strengthen whatever factors there may be working in the situation to bring about a reaction. It may be so in the present case. Certain it is that if we are to have a prolonged strike in the anthracite coal industry and strikes of consequence in collateral industries, it is by no means improbable that confidence, upon which the present structure of prosperity so largely rests, will receive a considerable shock.

The more we consider the relations of labor and capital in this country, the more convinced we are that the principle of arbitration should be admitted as a last resort in settling disputes. Making all allowance for the very natural feeling on the part of the employer that he is and should be free from dictation at anybody else's hands in managing his own business, and making every allowance on the other hand for the principle of combination by labor for its own protection, the fact remains that all disputes between employer and employee in the long run simmer down to a question of dollars and cents, and it is difficult to imagine a question of dollars and cents that is not properly susceptible of arbitration.

The British colony of New South Wales has recently passed an act constituting an arbitration tribunal for the purpose of settling industrial disputes. This tribunal consists of a Judge of the Supreme Court, a representative appointed by the employers, and a representative nominated by the employees. The court has jurisdiction in the case of any industrial dispute, and a lockout or a strike before allowing a reasonable time for reference to the court or pending the proceedings of the court is illegal. The act provides for the registration and incorporation of labor unions. We are not prepared to say that such an act would be entirely suitable for passage in this country, and we do not even know whether it could be made effective under the Federal Constitution. Probably it could not. Certain it is, however, that the principle of arbitration is democratic in every respect and entirely suitable for the widest application in a community highly organized on democratic principles. For a strike is nothing but war, and war is of necessity anarchical at every stage. It is a confession that civilization and law no longer exist.

It is greatly to be hoped that the restlessness of labor now so evident may not develop into a general unsettlement in the various industrial centers. We believe this to be a time when employers of unskilled labor might wisely make concessions so far as they can do so without seriously prejudicing their position, for a good deal is at stake, and there is very little danger of losing anything thereby in the long run.

June 10, 1902

In speaking a few days ago of the unrest of labor as exemplified by the strikes in progress and threatened at various parts of the country, we spoke of the increase that has taken place in the cost of living owing to the advance in the prices of commodities, and stated that there was reason to believe that this increase in cost had been larger than the increase in wages. While we have no accurate statistics with respect to wages, Dun's *Review* contains a very interesting exhibit of the prices of commodities which it has compiled into an index number. This index number is composed of seven classes of commodities, namely, breadstuffs, meats, dairy and garden, other food, clothing, metals, miscellaneous. The index number consists of the sum of the index numbers in each of these classes. The movement in this index number is given in the following table, as of January 1 in each year:

1888	99.9
1889	99.0
1890	90.2
1891	98.2
1892	89.8
1893	94.1
1894	86.0
1895	81.0
1896	77.8
1897	75.5
1898	79.9
1899	80.4
1900	95.3
1901	95.6
1902	101.5

The index number on June 1 was 101.1, or substantially the same as on January 1. Comparing 1894 prices with those of 1902, there is an advance of about 17 per cent; between 1895 and 1902, an advance of about 25 per cent; between 1896 and 1902, an advance of about 30 per cent; between 1897 and 1902, an advance of 33 per cent;

between 1898 and 1902, an advance of 25 per cent; between 1899 and 1902, an advance of 25 per cent; between 1900 and 1902, an advance of 6½ per cent; and between 1901 and 1902, a similar advance.

Observing the movement more in detail, we may take the five classes of commodities first named above, leaving out meats and miscellaneous, and show the movement in these in the past seven years:

	Bread-stuffs	*Meats*	*Dairy, etc.*	*Other Food*	*Cloth-ing*
1896	11.4	7.5	10.9	8.9	12.8
1897	11.7	7.3	10.4	8.1	12.4
1898	13.5	7.3	12.3	8.3	14.6
1899	13.8	7.5	11.4	9.1	14.1
1900	13.2	7.2	13.7	9.2	17.4
1901	14.5	8.4	15.5	9.5	16.0
1902	20.0	9.6	15.2	8.9	15.5

Comparing 1896 with 1902, therefore, we have an advance of about 80 per cent in breadstuffs, close on 30 per cent in meats, nearly 40 per cent in dairy and garden food, other food about unchanged, and over 20 per cent in clothing. Taking these two dates, the sum of the index numbers on January 1, 1896 was 51.5 against about 70 on January 1, 1902. The total increase, therefore, appears to be about 36 per cent in the index number so constructed. Moreover, taking as recent a date as January 1, 1900, the increase in these items is 15 per cent, and taking 1901 with 1902, the increase is about 10 per cent.

It is surely safe to say that between 1896 and 1902 there has been no such increase in wages as is shown in the commodities given above. There can be very little doubt that our main contention, namely, that the cost of living has gone up more than has the rate of wages, and that the average unit of labor (if such a thing can be conceived) produces less commodities in the form of wages than it did in the 1893–97 depression, is correct.

Of course, averages are dangerous things, and we do not wish to draw conclusions too strongly even upon such a basis as that furnished above. Making all allowance, however, we think that the facts furnish a pretty reasonable explanation of the unrest that is beginning to manifest itself in labor circles in so many places. We think it would conduce to a better understanding on all sides of the situation if those who are compelled for one reason or another to regard themselves as enforced champions of capital in these matters would show themselves more willing to admit such arguments as can fairly be advanced for the other side. A good case was never helped by special pleading or weakened by frank recognition of the adversary's fair claims.

June 19, 1902

Experience shows that the market is rather more likely to advance in July or August, and particularly in August, than in any other month in the year. Good reason for this is that August shows crop certainties and probabilities for the year, and a good foreshadowing is one reason for the purchase of stocks on expected profits to come from the crop movement. The advance which frequently begins in July or August often culminates near the first of September, on account of a disposition to take profits, and because of the probability of dearer money in the fall.

We give in the table following the midsummer moves in the market since 1885, showing the duration and extent of each movement. The figures are the average price of twelve railway stocks in the earlier years, and the average of twenty railway stocks in the latter years:

Year	*Advance Begun*	*Average Price*	*Advance Ceased*	*Average Price*
1886	July 9	83.82	Dec. 3	94.25
1887	July 30	82.51	Aug. 16	85.63
1888	June 13	77.12	Oct. 1	88.10
1889	July 28	86.28	Sep. 11	93.67
1891	July 31	81.00	Sep. 21	92.95
1892	July 7	89.60	July 29	92.48
1893	July 29	63.72	Oct. 28	78.63
1894	July 10	71.60	Aug. 27	78.93
1895	Feb. 28	68.88	Sep. 4	84.23
1897	Apr. 17	48.12	Sep. 16	67.23
1898	July 19	64.30	Aug. 26	70.16
1899	June 1	77.38	Sep. 5	85.55
1900	June 23	72.99	Aug. 15	78.06

In each of the above specified fourteen years, there was advance in the market during a portion of the midsummer months. In twelve of the fourteen years the advance began in either June or July. Once it began in April, and once there was a very slow gain continuing from the end of February to the 4th of September. Five of these advances culminated in August, five in September, two in October and one each in July and December. The average rise was nine points; seven years showed eleven points or over; and only two years gave an advance of less than six points.

The year 1890 afforded an exception to the ordinary movement. Prices declined in July and until August 21. There was then a recovery from 91.78 August 21 to 94.70 September 3. The summer market was under the influences which culminated in the Baring failure.

In the year 1896 the market declined from 65.26 June 17 to 41.82 August 8. This proved to be the low point of the decade, and from August 8 the market rose from 41.82 to 50.21 by September 30. The movement was normal in August, but abnormal in July. The decline was produced chiefly by the anxieties connected with silver and the currency famine existing in July, 1896.

In 1901 the panic of May 9 dropped the average to 103.37, from which there was a recovery to 117.65 June 17. The steel strike and the great damage to corn caused a relapse to 105.36 August 6. This was followed by a recovery to 111.69 August 26, giving the usual August rise, notwithstanding the crop damage and the July weakness.

In sixteen of the past seventeen years, therefore, there was a substantial rise in the market during the whole or part of the month of August. The year 1890 afforded the most striking exception to the rule, and even in that year there was an advance of three points from August 21 to September 3. In 1896 and in 1901 the market declined in July for special reasons, but recovered in August.

In the present year, therefore, the market reached its high point April 29, with the average of twenty stocks 121.63. Prices declined until May 19, when the average was 117.46. There has since been recovery up to the present time.

June 20, 1902

The business of life insurance is founded upon the fact that out of a thousand people of a given class, approximately twenty will die each year. The scale varies with difference in ages and in surroundings, but the law in the case is beyond dispute.

Scientific speculation stands upon a condition somewhat similar. It is impossible to say what the temporary movement of a stock may be, but nothing is more certain than that prices respond in the long run to changes in values. Allowances must be made for discounting expected events, and for the effect of conditions that may be temporarily more powerful than values, but the investor finds that after a little time value reasserts itself, no matter whether stocks were pushed temporarily too high or too low. Other factors bearing on speculation are influential; value is essential.

Prices, as measured by the average value of twenty railway stocks, are at practically the highest point for many years. The average, which was around 42 in 1896, is around 120. On the surface this would seem to be a strong argument against buying stocks, but the fact is that values have risen to correspond with the advance in prices and, measured by earnings available for dividends, stocks as a whole, with prices represented by averages, are but little dearer now than they were at the low prices prevailing several years ago.

If it were certain that earnings would remain at the present level, stocks could not be considered especially dear. Whether earnings can be maintained at this level depends upon many causes, essentially the condition of general business. Opinions differ as to the outlook for general business, but agree that at present business is good and railway earnings are fully maintained.

A year ago gross earnings were showing gains ranging from 12 to 20 per cent over the earnings of 1900. It seemed improbable then that gains could continue after such an increase, but the current year shows improvement, although to a smaller extent. For the first week in June, the gross earnings of 46 roads increased 6.66 per cent. For the fourth week in May the gain was 11.69 per cent, and through May an average of nearly 9 per cent. Gross earnings of 89 roads in April increased 13.57 per cent, in March 5.7 per cent, and in February 3.1 per cent. For ten months ended April 30, the increase in gross was 10.85 per cent and in net 12.94 per cent.

There is nothing in this in the nature of going backward in values. If values continue to increase, prices will find higher levels, quite apart from the question whether prices seem high or low compared with previous times.

Holders of stocks can probably feel a fair degree of confidence in retaining them as long as values show so distinct an upward tendency. As long as values are maintained, stocks will probably be found a purchase on declines. Declines will come through realizing, manipulation or other causes, but prices will recover if values are maintained. The doubtful time in the market will be when values begin to decline and when it is uncertain whether they will recover or not.

The down-turn in the stock market did not come when it could have reasonably been expected, in 1901, because the reaction in business did not come when it might have been expected. Relapse will come, although the date will depend upon the time that it takes to exhaust the bull forces which have been and still are visible in their operations.

The point which we wish to impress is that it is not necessary for investors to be unduly anxious about prices as long as increases in earnings show gains in values. Such declines as come while values continue to improve will be temporary declines. They may, like the Northern Pacific panic, be enough to wipe out margins and cause widespread losses, but they will be followed by recovery, as was the decline of May 9, 1901.

A high level of prices is perhaps more dangerous than a low level on account of liability to larger temporary decline, but when investors and capitalists and syndicates are well assured of values, they are seldom backward about buying when stocks are temporarily made cheap. The time when they will not buy and when recoveries will not come will be when values are declining and when investors see no signs of an improvement in the general situation. With present conditions, trading cannot be regarded as extra hazardous.

NOTES

[1] Again Dow paraphrases Juglar's famous expression: "The only cause of depression is prosperity."

[2] In this editorial Dow sets forth, in broad terms, both the theory of the accelerator and of the multiplier. While it is interesting to note that he placed a multiplier of two upon railroad investment, it would be of much greater interest to know how he arrived at this figure. See George W. Bishop, Jr., "Charles H. Dow and the Theory of the Multiplier," *Financial Analysts Journal,* Vol. 21 (January–February 1965), pp. 39–41.

[3] Since statistics covering unemployment in the United States were not available in 1902, Dow was forced to use those of Great Britain. Mitchell complained, as late as 1913, that "systematic information upon this subject [unemployment] is exceedingly meagre in the United States." He likewise comments upon "the admirable British statistics of unemployment." See Mitchell, pp. 268–269.

The relationship of the prices of industrial stocks on the London Stock Exchange and the New York Stock Exchange from 1873 to 1939 may be found in Major C. B. Ormerod (Sir Berkeley Ormerod), *Dow Theory Applied to the London Stock Exchange* (London, 1939), pp. 85–90. This important contribution has been largely overlooked, no doubt due to the fact that the book appeared at the time of the outbreak of World War II and went out of print shortly after publication.

[4] It would be interesting to know if specialists, as a rule, revealed this information to manipulators. Most authorities hold that the specialist at the turn of the century was not an important figure on the New York Stock Exchange.

[5] There have been a number of estimates of the amount of "water" involved. Among others, see Benjamin Graham, David L. Dodd, and Sidney Cottle, *Security Analysis,* 4th ed. (New York, 1962), p. 728. The "water" is estimated at "no less than $769 million of written-up assets."

[6] This is in reference to the action against the Northern Securities Co.

CHAPTER EIGHT

July 8, 1902 — October 24, 1902

DESPITE the seriousness of the coal strike, the stock market in July, 1902, exhibited considerable buoyancy. John W. Gates fought in vain for control of the Colorado Fuel and Iron Company during July and August as stock prices in general continued to advance.

September witnessed a stock market decline which was the severest since the Northern Pacific panic in May, 1901, and in October, with the stock market under relatively heavy pressure, President Theodore Roosevelt was successful in securing a settlement of the coal strike.

The last editorials from the pen of Charles H. Dow appeared in October; he was seriously ill from that time until his death on December 4, 1902.

July 8, 1902

There is a widespread feeling that expansion in business in the last six years has resulted in absorption of the supply of money and that with high prices and activity in trade the coming fall money will be dear.

The relations of money and credit are such that it is impossible to decide this question by examination of the stock of money alone. Such an examination, however, throws light on one phase of the situation, and we give herewith a comparison of leading items in the national bank returns as shown by the reports of the Comptroller of Currency for May, 1896, and for April, 1902. The year 1896 was a period of depression in business, of lack of confidence and of curtailment in loans compared with some of the years immediately preceding. The present year, on the contrary, represents a period of almost unbroken expansion since 1896:

Returns	*May, 1896*	*April, 1902*
Number of banks	3,694	4,423
Loans	$1,982,886,364	$3,172,757,485
Deposits	1,711,661,270	3,231,795,057
Circulation	197,382,364	309,781,739
Specie	202,373,446	398,760,561
Legal tenders	118,971,652	159,484,226

Here is an expansion in loans amounting to $1,189,871,121, or an increase of 60 per cent. Deposits and loans move measurably together because the initial step toward deposit is generally a loan, which is transferred to the account of the borrower as a deposit. There are, of course, other deposits, and altogether deposits have increased $1,520,133,787, or 88 per cent.

The expansion represented by this increase in deposits must rest upon a foundation of cash. Bank circulation is not counted as cash in this sense. Specie, however, shows an increase of $196,387,115, or 97 per cent, while legal tenders, which are counted as cash, increased $40,512,574, or 34 per cent.

The total cash in 1896 was $321,345,098 against about 2,000 millions of loans and 1,711 millions of deposits. At present, the national banks have $558,244,786 cash against a little more than 3,000 millions of loans and a rather larger amount of deposits. The percentage of cash to loans in 1896 was 16 per cent and is now 17 per cent. The percentage of cash to deposits in 1896 was 18 per cent and is now 17 per cent.

The total increase in cash was 73 per cent compared with an increase of 88 per cent in deposits. An increase in loans of $1,189,871,121 rests upon an increase of $236,899,688 in cash. In other words, the increase in loans has been supported by an increase in cash amounting to almost exactly 20 per cent of the increased loans, or nearly up to the deposit requirement of the reserve cities.

This seems to be an approximate demonstration that the expansion in business, as far as it can be measured by national bank growth, has been normal and healthful. The cash foundation for loans is substantially as broad as it was at the depression in 1896. For every hundred dollars of expansion in loans, twenty dollars have been provided in specie or legal tenders as security. There is nothing in the figures to indicate that the basis of credit is less sound now than then.

Here, however, comes in another point of the greatest importance.

The true currency of commerce is credit. A part of this credit is represented by cash, but the larger part is represented by book entries on the ledgers of banks and merchants, representing the intangible credit of the borrower.

In times of prosperity credit tends to expand. Profits are capitalized; examinations are less strict; a feeling of hope pervades the business community. This all finds expression in larger credit given to borrowers as a class. A man believed to be worth $10,000 might in bad times be given credit for $5,000. In good times, on the same estimate of his estate, he could probably get credit for $7,500. When this expansion is multiplied by the millions of men engaged in business, the effect can be appreciated.

The property which is the basis of credit is not usually in cash. It consists of the stock in trade and the working assets of people in all lines of business. The farmer who adds a year's crops, less a reasonable outlay for cost, to his assets has an increased basis of credit just as effective as if his crop were sold and he had the cash therefor. There has been enormous addition to the actual wealth of the country in six years, and this has probably resulted in a far greater expansion of credit than would be indicated by the cash operations which have come to the surface through the national banks.

If there is danger at the present time, it lies not in the relations of loans and deposits to cash in the banks, but in the expansion of individual credits which may have gone too far and which may bring a strain upon resources should confidence be shaken. This may call for watchfulness, but the money situation as indicated by bank returns is not unsound, nor are loans unduly expanded, taking the country as a whole.

July 9, 1902

A correspondent writes: "Is it true that commercial or stock exchange panics are approximately periodic in their occurrence?"

The facts point distinctly in that direction, and there is reason back of the facts. The reason is that the business community has a tendency to go from one extreme to the other. As a whole, it is either contracting business under a belief that prices will be lower or expanding under a belief that prices will be higher. It appears to take ordinarily five or six years for public confidence to go from the point of too little hope to the point of too much confidence and then five or six years more to get back to the condition of hopelessness.

This ten-year movement in England is given in detail by Professor Jevons in his attempt to show that sun spots have some bearing upon commercial affairs. Without going into the matter of sun spots and their bearing upon crops, commerce or states of minds, it may be assumed that Professor Jevons has stated correctly the periods of depression as they have occurred in England during the last two centuries.

The dates given by him as the years in which commercial crisis have occurred follow: 1701, 1711, 1721, 1731–32, 1742, 1752, 1763, 1772–73, 1783, 1793, 1804–5, 1815, 1825, 1836, 1847, 1857, 1866 and 1878.

This makes a very good showing for the ten-year theory, and it is supported to a considerable extent by what has occurred in this country during the past century.

The first crisis in the United States during the nineteenth century came in 1814, and was precipitated by the capture of Washington by the British on the 24th of August in that year. The Philadelphia and New York banks suspended payments, and for a time the crisis was acute. The difficulties leading up to this period were the great falling off in foreign trade caused by the embargo and non-intercourse acts of 1808, the excess of public expenditures over public receipts and the creation of a large number of state banks taking the place of the old United States Bank. Many of these state banks lacked capital and issued currency without sufficient security.

There was a near approach to a crisis in 1819, as the result of a tremendous contraction of bank circulation. The previous increases of bank issues had promoted speculation; the contraction caused a serious fall in the prices of commodities and real estate. This, however, was purely a money panic as far as its causes were concerned.

The European crisis in 1825 caused a diminished demand for American products and led to lower prices and some money stringency in 1826. The situation, however, did not become very serious and was more in the nature of an interruption to progress than a reversal of conditions.

The year 1837 brought a great commercial panic, for which there was abundant cause. There had been rapid industrial and commercial growth, with a multitude of enterprises established ahead of time. Crops were deficient, and breadstuffs were imported. The refusal of the government to extend the charter of the United States Bank had caused a radical change in the banking business of the country, while the withdrawal of public deposits and their lodgment with state banks had given the foundation for abnormal speculation.

The panic in Europe in 1847 exerted but little influence in this country, although there was a serious loss in specie, and the Mexican war had some effect in checking enterprises. These effects, however, were neutralized somewhat by large exports of breadstuffs and later by the discovery of gold in 1848–49.

There was a panic of the first magnitude in 1857, following the failure of the Ohio Life Insurance & Trust Company in August. This panic came unexpectedly, although prices had been falling for some months. There had been very large railroad building, and the proportion of specie held by banks was very small in proportion to their loans and deposits. One of the features of this period was the great number of failures. The banks generally suspended payments in October.

The London panic in 1866, precipitated by the failure of Overend, Guerney & Co., was followed by heavy fall in prices in the Stock Exchange here. In April there had been a corner in Michigan Southern and rampant speculation generally, from which the relapse was rather more than normal.

The panic of September, 1873, was a commercial as well as a Stock Exchange panic. It was the outcome of an enormous conversion of floating into fixed capital. Business had been expanded on an enormous scale, and the supply of money became insufficient for the demands made upon it. Credit collapsed, and the depression was extremely serious.

The year 1884 brought a Stock Exchange smash but not a commercial crisis. The failure of the Marine Bank, Metropolitan Bank and Grant & Ward in May was accompanied by a large fall in prices and a general check which was felt throughout the year. The trunk-line war, which had lasted for several years, was one of the factors in this period.

The panic of 1893 was the outcome of a number of causes—uncertainty in regard to the currency situation, the withdrawal of foreign investments and the fear of radical tariff legislation. The anxiety in regard to the maintenance of the gold standard was undoubtedly the chief factor, as it bore upon many others.

Judging by the past and by the developments of the last six years, it is not unreasonable to suppose that we may get at least a Stock Exchange flurry in the next few years. This decade seems to be the one for the small crisis instead of the large one—a type of 1884 rather than a recurrence of 1837, 1873 or 1893.[1]

July 17, 1902

It is easy to see that the prices of stocks and commodities have had a large rise in the last six years. Explanation is afforded by large increase in railway earnings and by the growth of business as represented by bank loans and deposits and the increased volume of clearings. It is not, however, as easy to comprehend the causes and the force of this explanation without a comparison of statistics. Such a comparison is afforded by an address recently given by Mr. O. P. Austin, chief of the Government Bureau of Statistics. Mr. Austin said in substance:

"The year 1870 seems to have marked the beginning of a new order of things in the producing power of this country. From 1790 to 1870, imports exceeded exports by nearly 2,000 million dollars. Since 1870 exports have exceeded imports by over 5,000 millions. Since 1870 the production of corn has gone from 1,000 million bushels to over 2,000 millions; wheat from 235 millions to 535 millions; cotton from 3,000,000 bales to over 10,000,000 bales; the value of farm products from 2,447 million dollars to 5,739 millions; the production of petroleum from 220 million gallons to 660 millions; of coal from 33 million tons to 260 million tons; pig iron from less than two million tons to over 15 millions; and steel from 70,000 tons to over 13 million tons.

"Meantime, the railways of the country have grown from 53,000 miles to nearly 200,000 miles. The money in circulation has increased from 675 million dollars to 2,260 millions. The number of persons engaged in manufacturing has increased from two millions to over 5,500,000 and their earnings from 775 million dollars to 2,735 millions, the capital employed from a little over 2,000 millions to about 10,000 millions, and the value of the manufactured products from 4,250 millions to about 13,000 millions.

"The result of these developments has been that the United States has advanced to the head of the list of exporting nations. In 1870, England, Germany and France exceeded the United States in their exports. In 1901, the United States exceeded them. The principal requirements of man are food, clothing, heat, light and manufactures, and of these the United States is the world's greatest producer. They are supplemented by invention, communication, transportation, finance and energy.

"The genius of the American inventor is universally recognized. The number of patents issued in the United States since 1870 is half as great as the number issued in all the rest of the world during that time. The United States has more miles of railway than all Europe put together, and two-fifths of the mileage of the world. We have twice as many miles of telegraph as any other country, twice as many post offices, twice as many newspapers, and send more telephone messages than all Europe combined.

"The meaning of all this is that commerce must continue to expand. We hear threats of the exclusion of our products and rumors of European combinations against the United States, but neither experience nor the logic of the situation indicates that this will be realized. For years we have heard of legislation against American meats. Yet, exports of provisions were 50% greater in 1901 than in 1890, and this year will be the largest in the history of our foreign commerce.

"The growth of exports of manufactures has been so pronounced as to indicate that in this field the United States will be able to compete with Europe in both quality and price. In 1901, Europe took over 50% of our exports of manufactures, 90% of our exports of agricultural products, and 60% of all others. The field for growth here is large. We supply now only about 15% of those of Asia and Oceania, 1% of those of South America and 5% of Africa.

"In tropical products we have been hitherto absolutely dependent on other countries. We import enormous quantities of sugar, coffee, tea, cocoa and rice. Imports of rubber and silk also reach enormous figures. Imports of tropical and sub-tropical products have trebled since 1870. This clearly indicates that we should seek to pay in the products of our fields and factories for the increasing millions of tropical products which we import and must continue to import.

"Furthermore, a great amount of products of this kind can now be produced by American citizens using American capital in Porto Rico, Hawaii and the Philippine Islands. The Hawaiian Islands have increased their producing power more than twentyfold since we annexed them commercially by the reciprocity treaty of 1876, and have also increased their consumption of our products twentyfold. In the four years since the American flag was hoisted at Manila, exports to the Philippine Islands have increased tenfold, and those to Asia and Oceania have doubled."

Figures and facts like these brought out by Mr. Austin show the basis of the prosperity that has found its expression in the increased volume of general business, and the continued gains in railroad earnings. There could not be such an increase in the volume of foreign trade without corresponding advance in domestic trade. Indeed, the home demand has been so great in many lines during the past year as to lead manufacturers to suspend efforts to find markets abroad. We have been importing iron and steel through sheer inability to supply the home demand. This explains why, with the great damage to the corn crop last year, earnings of roads like Missouri Pacific and Atchison should have increased and why the Steel Comany is able to make its astonishing exhibit of earnings.

It is undoubtedly true that overtrading and overdoing will bring great reaction sooner or later. But it must be recognized that the forces which have been on the bull side in the past few years have been unprecedented in their breadth and strength.

July 19, 1902

No problem of the immediate future has a deeper interest for bankers at present than that involving the supply of money for the coming fall. The business of the Stock Exchange rests largely upon borrowed money. The speculative buyer of stocks puts up a margin of perhaps 10 per cent, the broker reinforces it with 10 per cent more, and the rest of the money required is provided by banks and trust companies on the security of the stock bought. The speculative foundation at best is small. Two thousand dollars purchase money on a $10,000 purchase makes ability to continue to borrow the needed $8,000 vital to customers and to brokers, and vital also to those whose plans rest upon the ability of the financial community to do business under ordinary conditions.

While it is of the utmost importance to be able to foresee the ability of borrowers to get money at normal rates, it is exceedingly difficult to measure the determining forces in view of the relations of cash and credit in determining this question. It is desirable to be able to judge something of the amount of cash that will be available for known requirements, but it is much more important to be able to judge whether anything is likely to produce general curtailment of credit or even special curtailment in the case of syndicates [of investment bankers] or large individual borrowers.

The part which the actual cash plays in carrying on the volume of business at any time varies greatly with varying conditions. When credits are good, a given amount of cash goes further than when credits are doubted. The contraction which is often an important factor in prices is much more in credit than in cash. Actual hoarding of cash is exceptional, but there can easily be shrinkage in credits running high into the millions.[2]

In periods of panic, or shortly after them, the cash holdings of the banks increase. The largest surpluses occur in dull times. Bank deposits are very largely credits founded upon loans, and while an increasing supply of cash goes with and supports an increasing volume of credits, the superstructure has a tendency to expand faster than the foundation.

With the idea of throwing some light on the present situation, we give in the table following a synopsis of the bank statement of this city [New York] at the middle of July in each of the last twenty years. The cash in hand is the sum of the specie and the legal tenders, and the surplus reserve is the excess of the cash in hand over the 25 per cent of deposits required by law.

Year	*Deposits*	*Cash on Hand*	*Surplus Reserve*
1883	$327,326,700	$ 90,349,600	$ 8,542,025
1884	299,512,000	98,740,820	23,852,800
1885	383,758,700	159,840,400	62,900,725
1886	379,142,200	107,947,000	13,161,450
1887	368,416,800	100,030,300	7,926,100
1888	400,642,800	120,624,400	28,863,700
1889	443,939,200	117,617,400	6,630,100
1890	415,933,300	110,266,400	6,283,074
1891	402,795,500	115,240,900	14,542,025
1892	523,862,600	151,172,800	20,207,150
1893	390,476,200	94,274,410	5,730,900
1894	589,224,500	221,322,500	73,941,375
1895	567,970,000	175,397,820	33,405,300
1896	503,488,100	148,109,300	22,237,275
1897	613,767,200	199,353,700	46,036,900
1898	757,786,300	238,812,400	49,365,825
1899	902,178,900	230,607,200	5,062,475
1900	882,174,000	224,625,400	24,081,900
1901	947,594,100	249,707,900	12,809,375
1902	942,198,000	247,776,400	12,226,900

The first thing likely to attract attention in this table is the growth of deposits from 327 millions in 1883 to 942 millions in 1902. This is an increase of nearly 616 millions. The cash in hand has increased during the same time $157,426,800. The amount of cash required to support the increase in deposits would be $153,717,825, showing that the situation, as far as the relation of cash to deposits is concerned, is as strong now as it was twenty years ago, when the amount of deposits was only about one-third of the present total.

The next point is that while the figures cover twenty years, the bulk of this growth, both in deposits and in cash, has occupied only ten years. The expansion of loans and cash from 1883 to 1892 was moderate, and the contraction which accompanied the panic of 1893 brought the loans down to near the level of 1883 and the cash to a point almost as low. The rebound, however, was rapid, showing that conditions in 1893 were abnormal. Nevertheless, the great growth has been since 1893.

The showing of the surplus reserve is suggestive from several points of view. It decreases when business is especially prosperous and increases when times are not good. In 1883 the surplus was 8½ millions, but after the stock market flurry of 1884 the reserve ran up in July, 1885, to about 64 [sic] millions. With the improvement that came between 1887 and 1890, the reserve dropped back to comparatively low figures. After the panic of 1893, the midsummer reserve was about 74 millions in 1894, and was nearly 50 millions in 1898.

The strain in the financial situation which became apparent in 1889 was reflected by a midsummer reserve of only about $5,000,000, but with the liquidation in the last half of 1899 and the first half of 1900, the reserve went back to $24,000,000. For two years, the situation seems to have undergone but little change. Deposits, cash and surplus are about the same as they were a year ago. The amount of surplus is small for midsummer, but last year there was money enough to go around, from which it may be argued that there will be enough this year also.

There are, however, some other points to be taken into account. The money required to carry stocks has increased in a ratio indicated by the fact that the average price of twenty stocks a year ago was about 110, while it is now 124. The price of commodities as represented by Dun's index number stands now at 101.91, compared with 91.50 a year ago. As this number reflects breadstuffs, meats, dairy products, clothing, metals and miscellaneous articles, it proves not only the advance in the cost of living and in the amount of money required to carry on the transactions that are settled daily in cash, but the amount that is represented by these commodities as against the stock of money in the country. Considering the position of the New York banks as typical of the situation throughout the country, the situation is less favorable than it was a year ago in view of the greater requirements made upon the supply of cash.

It must be remembered also that the process of converting floating into fixed capital has gone on at a great rate in the last twelve months, and that this has involved not only the conversion of capital, but has called for the employment of credit on a large scale by builders, manufacturers and, to no inconsiderable extent, by those who have pledged their credit to underwriting syndicates and to construction companies carrying on this work.

The fact that the money outlook is under constant discussion is important in itself. Nobody heard much talk of this kind two or three years ago. The fact that it is heard now, while partly inspired by high prices, must be inspired somewhat also by the personal knowledge by bankers of the financial position of companies, institutions and individuals. General discussion on this point means that there is greater or less disposition to scrutinize credits and to consider whether borrowing generally or particularly has been overdone. This is undoubtedly a corrective measure, but it contains the possibility of starting contraction.

We repeat what we have said before on this point. As far as the actual relations on hand to deposits or to loans is concerned, the situation seems sound. The danger, if there is danger, lies in the relation of confidence to credit, concerning which nothing is more important and nothing much more intangible.

July 29, 1902

The methods of financing a percentage of the business of the country have changed in the last five years. Up to 1896, a very large number of concerns carried on their business by loans obtained from local banks and secured to a very considerable extent by endorsed paper. Safety, from the standpoint of the money lender, lay in personal acquaintance with the borrower and more or less familiarity with the condition of the business on which money was being loaned.

The uniting of hundreds of such firms and small companies into large combinations has removed the financial management to business centers and changed the financing from borrowing small sums on notes to borrowing large sums on collateral. A good deal of the borrowing takes place at the large cities, but loans are sought not only by corporations, but by interests which are carrying industrial stocks at banks in smaller cities through the country. This prevents offering too much collateral of one kind at the city banks and gives smaller banks profitable employment for their money.

This system of borrowing rests, however, upon the quoted price of the stock at the New York Stock Exchange. A great deal hangs upon the integrity of this quotation. Conservative bankers, realizing this, do not like to lend much where the quotation consists chiefly of a bid and asked price. They want to see the size of the market, so as to be able to judge whether the stock which they take as collateral could be sold, if necessary, without too great depreciaton. Here is where manipulation becomes important from the position of the borrower and sometimes very misleading from the position of the lender.

The banker who sees in the papers that the transactions in X, Y, Z stock yesterday amounted to 15,000 shares within a range of three-quarters of a point, naturally believes that there is a fair market on which stock could be sold within a range of one or two points. This conclusion would be correct in many cases, but in others it would be far from the truth.

Any interest which wishes to borrow money on collateral can, at a moderate cost, give its stock the appearance of activity without its having any legitimate market whatever. If parties in interest order 10,000 shares bought and 10,000 shares sold, the record of business will be established and the price established, although there was not a genuine order for 100 shares executed during the day. The money lender who thought there was a 10,000-share market would find his impression entirely wrong should he try to sell 1,000 shares out of a loan.

We do not mean to say that this is a cause for special uneasiness at this time, although it is probably true that the market is more artificial than usual. In the opinion of very good judges, it takes the purchase of a thousand shares of stock in some of the more active stocks to sell 1,100 shares. When this is the case with stocks in which there is general trading, it is likely to be the case also in quite a proportion of the stocks in which general trading is usually small.

We have reason to believe that a great many loans have been made on stock collateral by out-of-town banks without very clear knowledge of the instability of some of the quotations. We took occasion some months ago to point out that a Wall Street interest was making loans with country banks under conditions which suggested that the banks were quite liable to become the owner of the collateral. Subsequent developments emphasized that warning.

We believe that conditions when times become unfavorable will emphasize the warning which we are giving now; which is, that money lenders, and especially out-of-town banks, should realize that Stock Exchange quotations do not necessarily mean that any considerable amount of stock could be sold at those prices, even if the records show that considerable amounts appear to have changed hands.

Stock Exchange quotations over considerable periods of time and taking one stock with another undoubtedly give a close approximation to value, but quotations can be made misleading, and lenders, especially on comparatively undistributed stocks, should protect themselves by knowing as fully as possible the facts in regard to the value of the property as well as the current quotations. The bank which accepts a quotation for what it is worth, but which requires in addition the particulars in regard to the business which it would have required had there been no quotation for the stock, will have reason at intervals in the next few years to congratulate itself upon the maintenance of a sound business policy.

If there is good value back of collateral, borrowers will have no hesitation in demonstrating the fact. Where there is hesitation and concealment and glittering generalities instead of solid facts, there are generally conditions which a conservative lender of money would rather learn before making a loan than to acquire his first information on the subject after he became the owner of the collateral through inability to close out his loan without loss.

August 5, 1902

. . . .

If the improvement in business and in prices has been a cycle movement, corresponding in character if greater in extent than the cycles in business which have left their record in quotations for two hundred years past, caution is needed, because the decline, when decline comes, will bear some relation to the extent of the rise.[3]

. . . .

August 6, 1902

We called attention in June to the fact that in sixteen years past there has been a rise in the market during the whole or part of the month of August, and showed by the records of those years that there was better than an average chance of some advance in prices during midsummer this year. The advance has been so continuous, however, as to raise the question whether the July move has not completed the ordinary midsummer rise and lessened the probability of the customary advance in August. In considering this question, we gave first the record of past years, showing when advances began and when they terminated, separating into groups the advances which ended in July, those which ended in August and those which ended at later dates:

Rise Ended in July

Year	*Rise Began*	*Price*	*Rise Ended*	*Price*
1892	July 7	89.60	July 29	92.48

Rise Ended in August

Year	*Rise Began*	*Price*	*Rise Ended*	*Price*
1887	July 30	82.51	Aug. 16	85.63
1894	July 10	71.60	Aug. 27	78.93
1898	July 19	64.30	Aug. 26	70.16
1900	June 23	72.99	Aug. 15	78.06
1901	Aug. 6	105.36	Aug. 26	111.69

Rise Ended in September

Year	*Rise Began*	*Price*	*Rise Ended*	*Price*
1889	July 28	86.28	Sep. 11	93.67
1890	Aug. 21	91.78	Sep. 3	94.70
1891	July 31	81.00	Sep. 21	92.95
1895	Feb. 28	68.88	Sep. 4	84.23
1896	Aug. 8	41.82	Sep. 30	50.21
1897	Apr. 17	48.12	Sep. 16	67.23
1899	June 1	77.38	Sep. 5	85.55

Rise Ended After September

Year	*Rise Began*	*Price*	*Rise Ended*	*Price*
1888	June 13	77.12	Oct. 1	88.10
1893	July 29	63.72	Oct. 28	78.63
1886	July 9	83.82	Dec. 3	94.25

It appears from the foregoing that only once since 1885 has a midsummer rise ended in July, and that year the advance was comparatively small. In five years the advance has culminated in August, and in no case before the middle of the month. In seven years, the rise came to an end in September, ranging from the 3rd to the 30th. In only three years has the rise persisted after the end of September, and in one of these it ended on the first day of October. In eight of the sixteen years, the rise began sometime in the month of July, and in a majority of cases after the 15th. In three cases it began in June and in three in August, showing that the probabilities favor expectations of a midsummer rise beginning around the middle of July and coming to an end around the middle of September.

The average time of the midsummer rise and the average extent are given in detail for sixteen years in the table following:

	Rise Lasted	*Amounted to*
1886	147 days	10.43 points
1887	17 days	3.12 points
1888	110 days	10.98 points
1889	45 days	7.39 points
1890	13 days	2.92 points
1891	52 days	11.95 points
1892	22 days	2.88 points
1893	92 days	14.91 points
1894	48 days	7.33 points
1895	188 days	15.35 points
1896	53 days	8.39 points
1897	152 days	19.11 points
1898	38 days	5.86 points
1899	97 days	8.17 points
1900	53 days	5.07 points
1901	20 days	6.33 points

It is apparent from the foregoing that the average time of the midsummer move for sixteen years has been seventy-one days and that the average amount of rise has been 8.75 points. In four years, the time of the advance has exceeded one hundred days and twice it has been less than twenty days. In six years, the average advance has been over 10 points, once being nearly 20, and in only three years has it been less than 5 points. The results thus far this year follow:

		Rise This Year		
Year	*Rise Began*	*Price*	*Top This Year*	*Price*
1902	May 19	117.46	July 26	127.16

Time of rise, 68 days; amount, 9.70 points.

It appears, therefore, that the rise which began on the 19th of May and reached its high point thus far on the 26th of July has been about an average in duration; and a little more than the average in extent. If the time of year were a month or six weeks later, there would be a probability that the rise was over. As it is, the time of the advance and its amount has to be offset against the fact that there is in every year strong probability of some rise in August.

This is not an arbitrary matter, but grows out of the fact that in August crops become sufficiently secure to justify some discounting of expected earnings [of the railroads] during the fall. This year the market has advanced in the face of somewhat unfavorable conditions. There has been too much rain, there have been gold shipments [abroad], a corn corner and a disturbing anthracite strike. Settlement of the strike, good weather in August, cessation of gold exports and assurances of business prosperity may make a basis for an August move. Against this is a question of whether the money situation is such as to cause market manipulators to endeavor to realize earlier than usual and on conditions that are expected to bring public buying.

We think it a market in which traders can best form their opinions by watching developments from day to day. If the market has a good undertone of strength for a week or ten days, it will probably go higher. If it gets weak and shows evidence of realizing, it will be an indication that the midsummer rise has culminated.

August 12, 1902

There are two periods when strikes predominate. The first is when the efforts of employers toward retrenchment cut down wages to a point where wage earners prefer the risks involved in a strike to the hardships involved in trying to live at lower cost. The second period is when times are extremely prosperous, but in which the cost of living advances out of proportion to the rise in wages.

At such times employees often say with truth that except in the matter of steady work, they are no better off than they were in bad times. They receive higher wages, but it all goes in the cost of living. Steady work is a real advantage, yet this does not neutralize the feeling that labor ought to have a larger share in the prosperity and the profits which sometimes come to employers.

The present unrest of labor is founded partly on this sentiment and partly on the increased cost of living. There is no way of judging accurately how great the advance in wages has been in the last few years. In some trades they have not advanced at all. In many establishments there have been advances of 10 per cent or perhaps more, following the increased demand for the output of the concern.

Railroad corporations have generally advanced wages somewhat. The average wages of engineers in Group 1 of the Interstate Commerce division in 1897 was $3.45 per day, and in 1900 $3.48. The pay of firemen rose in that time from $1.95 to $1.97; of machinists from $2.17 to $2.29, while the pay of switchmen fell from $1.49 to $1.48. In Group 6, the pay of engineers rose 1897–1900 from $3.65 to $3.68; firemen, $2.12 to $2.23; machinists, $2.14 to $2.18, and switchmen from $1.97 to $2.07. Other groups showed similar changes. There have been probably advances since 1900, but the changes have not been great. This means that railway employees as a class have probably not received an advance in wages averaging as much as 20 per cent.

A part of this, of course, is due to the labor unions, which, while aiming to secure advances in wages, actually keep wages immobile through interfering with the increase of pay of deserving employees. Employers naturally take the ground that if there is a union rate of wages there is no sense in going above that, which keeps all workmen at that level, no matter whether they are better or worse than their associates. Better value simply means a more stable position.

Where labor has been free, the advances in wages have been larger because the more valuable men have been able to make better terms for themselves individually where better terms would not have been made with the employees as a whole.

Assuming an advance in wages of from 10 to 20 per cent, it is evident that the position of wage earners, especially those having families to support, has not improved, except in the point of more constant employment compared with 1897. Dun's index number gives the average price of a large number of articles July 1, 1897, as 72.45. The average price of many quotations of breadstuffs was 10.58; of meats, including hogs, beef, sheep, provisions, etc., 7.52, of dairy and garden products, 8.71; of miscellaneous food products, 7.88; many quotations of woolen, cotton, and other textile goods, as well as leather and shoes, 13.80; metals, 11.64; and miscellaneous, 12.28, together producing what may be called the cost of the necessities of living, outside of rent, in the figures 72.45.

What is the index number now? Breadstuffs are up to 19.98, meats to 11.67, garden products to 11.34, other food 8.82, clothing 15.58, metals 16.23, miscellaneous 16.52, making the total index number 100.17, an advance of 27.72 or 38.26 per cent.

This means that the engineer of Group 7, who was receiving $3.65 per day in 1897 or $21.90 per week, who was getting $3.68 three years later and who, it may be assumed, is now getting $4 a day, or an advance of about 10 per cent, has to compare $24 a week and the index number representing the cost of living of 100 with wages of $22 a week and an index number of 72.45.

There can be no doubt that an advance only of 10 or 15 per cent in wages rankles in the minds of men who see the cost of living advanced 38 per cent, especially if there are evidences that employers are making abnormal profits. In many trades, the increase in the cost of raw material and in charges of one sort and another have made the percentage of profit very much smaller than would be supposed from the advance in the price of goods, and in cases of this kind larger advances in wages would have been impracticable. There is a tendency, however, on the part of both capital and labor to see their own difficulties and disadvantages without always perceiving the disadvantages of the other side. In a situation like that now existing, it behooves both sides to consider carefully the facts in every case so that equity may prevail.

August 13, 1902

While it is true that the business of the world is done to a very large extent on credit, it is also true that credit rests upon confidence that obligations will be settled in cash if cash is required. Hence the supply of money has a bearing upon credit, because too large an expansion of credit may create difficulties in getting cash.

There is some anxiety as to whether the available supply of cash in New York City banks is sufficient to meet the demands of commerce and of speculation during the coming fall. A considerable amount of this money belongs to individuals or institutions, who are liable to draw it for business purposes or for the crop movement in the West and South. The point has been made that the growing wealth of the country would have a tendency to lessen the demand upon this center for funds to move crops. This is probably true in a sense, but it is also true that business activity and prosperity have had a tendency to lock up money in enterprises at interior points as well as at the great centers. There are syndicates and schemes and operations requiring cash all over the country, and it is not at all impossible that the demand for money here this year may be rather larger than usual on this account.

Money is easy abroad, and interest rates have a tendency to draw money to the point of most profitable employment. Nevertheless, there is reason for thinking that this country is already employing its credit quite fully on the other side, and that, while dearer rates for money might stop an outward movement of gold, it would take considerable in the way of interest to bring gold this way.

It is said that the money situation always corrects itself and that high rates cause the liquidation of loans, a reduction in deposits and a cutting down of the reserve required to the normal ratio. This is true, and is the essential part of the whole question, namely, whether the present situation foreshadows liquidation of loans on a large scale, with the resulting depression in the market and decline in prices.

Let us look first at the bank statement as shown by the table following:

	August, 1902	*August, 1901*
Loans	$926,494,800	$886,455,600
Net deposits	959,643,000	965,381,000
Reserve required	239,910,750	241,345,250
Reserve held	248,942,000	262,298,200
Surplus reserve	9,031,250	20,052,950

With loans $40,000,000 greater than at this time last year, the surplus reserve is less than half as large. It is lower than it has been at this time in any recent years save 1899, when the reserve was low from the second week in July up to the end of the year, and in that fall prices declined.

Admitting the reserve to be small, the question arises whether the demands upon it can be seen to be larger than in other years. Clearings at all centers for the week ended August 2 amounted to $2,244,958,058, compared with $1,877,324,303 in 1901. Business generally, therefore, is on a larger scale than at this time last year. The average price of twenty active stocks is 126.51, compared with 106.38 at this time a year ago, showing that it takes approximately 5 per cent more money to carry stocks than it did last year. There has been a great addition to the securities to be carried. Listings for the six months ended June 30 amounted to $157,261,313 of bonds and $128,093,700 of stocks.

The price of commodities has, as a whole, advanced over five points in the year. The changes in the quotations of some important commodities are given in the table following:

	Aug., 1901	*Aug., 1902*
Wheat, No. 2 in elevator per bushel	0.7325	0.7587
Corn, No. 2 mixed, in elevator per bushel	.5875	.65
Oats, No. 2 mixed, in elevator, per bushel	.38	.65
Flour, straight winter, per bbl.	3.20	3.60
Beeves, native steers, per 100 lbs.	6.25	7.60
Sheep, prime, Chicago, per 100 lbs.	3.95	4.45
Hogs, prime, Chicago, per 100 lbs.	6.00	7.75
Eggs, New York State, per doz.	.18	.205
Bread, New York, per loaf	.04	.04
Butter, best creamery, per lb.	.205	.205
Coffee, Rio No. 7, per lb.	.0562	.0587
Sugar, granulated, per lb.	.054	.046
Tea, Oolong, per lb.	.235	.27
City, green salted, hides per lb.	.12	.14
Hemlock leather, No. 1, per lb.	.245	.25
Cotton, middling uplands, per lb.	.0806	.0893
Wool, Ohio, X, Boston, per lb.	.24	.24
Silk, No. 1, per lb.	3.70	3.95
Print cloths, Boston, per yard	.0262	.03
Iron ore, Lake Superior, per ton	4.92	4.92
Pig iron, No. 1, New York, per ton	15.50	25.00
Steel billets, Pittsburg, per ton	24.00	32.00
Tin plates, Pittsburg, per 100 lbs.	5.00	4.00
Copper	.165	.1187
Tin, spot, New York, per lb.	.275	.285
Brick, Hudson River, hard, per thousand	5.50	5.00
Pine, yellow, per thousand	21.00	22.00
Timber, hemlock, per thousand	14.50	16.00
Rubber, Para, new, per lb.	.85	.69
Tobacco, medium burley, Louisville, per lb.	.085	.097
Hay, Timothy, New York, per 100 lbs.	.95	1.00

Of the thirty-one commodities named, twenty-one have advanced in price, six have declined and four [remain] unchanged. The six that declined include copper, brick, rubber, sugar and tin plates. The advances in many cases are small, but when applied to the enormous volume of a commodity like corn or pig iron, the effect is material. There is no question that the business of the country requires more actual money than it did a year ago, assuming the ratio of cash to credit to be approximately the same.

There has been some increase of money in circulation. The volume reported by the government August 1 this year was $2,260,606,137, compared with $2,189,567,149 a year ago. The increase amounts to $71,-038,988, or to about 3.2 per cent, compared with an increase of over 5 per cent in the average cost of commodities, as expressed by index numbers, to say nothing of the demands for money growing out of syndicate and other operations, enlargement in the volume of business and the higher prices of securities and articles not covered in the commodity list.

September 6, 1902

One of the notable features of the last three years has been a development which has found expression in heavy speculation on the various markets where speculation is possible, and latterly in an outbreak of gambling, apart from stock and produce markets, which has been on a scale sufficient to attract the attention of many people who ordinarily take little interest in such matters. The recent season at Saratoga, for instance, is described by people who have seen it as having surpassed in the matter of heavy betting and high gambling anything that has been known since the palmy days of gold mining in the far West. From an economic point of view, too much importance should not be attached to this feature, but at the same time, taken in connection with other social developments which have found expression in what may be termed general extravagance, it is not without significance.

The development of large corporations in the industrial world has had, among other effects, the effect of placing large sums of cash or its equivalent in the hands of a large number of people who had heretofore not been in a position where the handling of very large sums of money for investment was the rule. It is unnecessary to offer instances of this, as the history of practically every large corporation formed within the last three years will furnish many examples to the point. There has been enough conversion of plants, factories, mines, etc., into cash to affect quite a large section of the population and to remove those who received it from the position of active factors in the industrial world into the position of capitalists. In some cases, the process resulted in turning over to individuals more money by a good deal than they could possibly have expected ever to possess. One of the results of this process has been to turn the thoughts of a great many people from methods by which a manufacturing business was slowly built up by a generation of hard work to methods whereby large sums of money were made in a short time. In other words, what is known as the "get rich quick" idea has in the last two or three years largely taken possession of the minds of quite a large number of people.

In the case of those who have not had plants or industrial enterprises to sell, the extraordinary speculation in the stock market, partly resulting from the operations of the new generation of capitalists, has had a great effect and has tended to turn popular thought in the same direction. The result is that by comparison with five years ago it may be said that there has been a general development of a tendency toward extravagance and speculation on the part of quite a large section of the people of this country. This is the secret of the present temper of the popular mind, and finds its expression partly in Wall Street, partly in other centers where gambling can be conducted and partly in those places where extravagance most naturally finds a vent.

In times past, periods of prosperity have always brought conditions of this kind, and it is natural that they should do so for reasons too obvious for mention. It has generally been found that such conditions mark the end of great booms and periods of great activity in business. It is natural that this should be so, because a tendency to extravagance and to excessive speculation contains within it the seeds from which grow financial disturbances and unsound commercial conditions. It must not be assumed, however, that the conditions underlying the appearances described are all necessarily evil. There is much in the present situation that can fairly be accounted for by the fact that this country has money to invest and that out of the process of investment has in a measure grown the great speculation. Nevertheless, all things considered, it cannot be denied that extravagance and speculation have reached a point in this country where they are entitled to the respectful attention of social and economic observers.

It may be argued that it costs more to live nowadays, and we have lately shown that this is so, but the fact is that the general standard of living has materially advanced in the past five years so far as a large portion of the population is concerned. Prosperity has created a new class of wants for many people, and the luxuries of five years ago have become the daily necessities of today. Again, it must be remembered that not all of this can be accounted as unjustifiable extravagance. Much of it may prove to be simply a permanent advancement in material conditions of life. Much of it, however, certainly is not. It has been so easy for so many people to make so much money in the past four or five years that they forget that the conditions under which the money was made were unusual and cannot be depended upon as a permanency. Thus, "windfalls" have been to a large extent regarded as regular income and largely spent. It is not without significance that careful observers have seen in the recent savings banks statistics in New England evidence that the saving habits of that thrifty community have undergone some change.

It is easy perhaps to attach too much importance to these things, but it is possibly easier to underestimate their significance.

September 23, 1902

The object of industry is the securing of income, and the measure of income is dollars and cents. Consequently, the object of industry is the securing of dollars and cents. The ultimate efficiency of any industrial machine representing invested capital must therefore be measured by dollars and cents. Not only is this the case, but it must be measured by the amount of dollars and cents that it annually produces in proportion to the amount of capital invested. In brief, the return per cent on capital is the final measure of efficiency of any industrial machine or enterprise.

Now it is clear that, taking a railroad for example, there are two kinds of efficiency. The efficiency of a car is directly measured in the number of units of transportation that it can turn out in a given time. The direct efficiency of a passenger car is measured by the number of passenger miles that it can produce per car mile, or per annum. In the same way, the direct measure of efficiency of a freight car is the number of ton miles that it can produce per car mile or per annum. The measure of a locomotive's direct efficiency is clearly the number of car miles that it can produce. Now, unless the ton mile is constant in its character and unless its selling price is constant, it is clear that the ultimate efficiency in dollars and cents of the whole plant does not necessarily vary with the actual efficiency as above described. We may call the actual efficiency the "absolute" efficiency and the ultimate efficiency as measured in dollars and cents the "relative" efficiency.

Practical railroad men as a rule see little or nothing of the relative efficiency of the property which they administer. They concern themselves mainly with the absolute efficiency of the plant under their control. This is practically a necessity of the case so far as rank and file are concerned, and it remains for the general officers and the auditing department to compare absolute results in the light of relative results. There are two classes of railroad expenses, viewing expense in a general way, namely, maintenance cost and transportation cost. The great difference between the two classes is that maintenance expenses must be canvassed in the light of absolute efficiency while transportation and other expenses must be canvassed in the light of relative efficiency.[4]

In analyzing annual reports, and in the attempt to estimate the net earning capacity of railroad properties, the method of procedure that we usually adopt is to reckon a certain sum of money as sufficient to maintain the plant and reckon a certain percentage of earnings as necessary to provide for other expenses. In the one case, we refer expenses to actual work done, and in the other we refer them to money received from sale of product. For instance, we will reckon that such and such a road requires an annual average expenditure of say $900 per mile for maintenance of way and say $500 per mile for maintenance of equipment. We will reckon in the case of the same road that 33 per cent of gross earnings should be enough to provide for conducting transportation expense. There is a vital difference in the units used as a test for both kinds of expense. The practical railroad man will not as a rule concern himself very much with transportation cost per ton mile; it is train mile cost that he chiefly regards.

We draw attention to these distinctions because people should bear in mind that nowadays dollars per mile spent in maintenance are not necessarily a real test of sufficiency of maintenance. A dollar does not go nearly as far as it did in many cases, owing to the increased cost of labor and materials, and it goes very much further in some places and under some conditions than it does under different conditions and in other places. We can make but very rough approximations of the amount of money per mile necessary to maintain a railroad nowadays. Consequently, when we make estimates of this kind, they must be taken in a very general way and with wide allowance for error due to different conditions of time, place and cost. Money that is spent hurriedly and in large quantities does not produce as much work as it would if spent carefully and in leisurely fashion. We do not wish to be understood at all as laying down any hard and fast standards for maintenance per mile. Such a thing, if it could be done at all, which we very much doubt, could only be done by those actually in charge of the physical work on the property and after an exhaustive study of all the conditions under which the work was done.

Furthermore, in making estimates of the relative cost of transportation, we can make only the same kind of rough approximate, and many allowances must be made in this case as well for various conflicting influences. In short, all such calculations are good only when taken in a very general way and as rough approximations. Readers will please remember this in studying over conclusions.

September 24, 1902

For some weeks there have been mutterings of growing discontent in railroad circles with respect to the matter of wages, and once or twice statements have been published to the effect that an important strike of railroad men for higher wages was impending. There appears to be some truth in the statement that in railroad circles generally labor is getting restless—as it is, in fact, everywhere—and it is not at all impossible that it may formulate articulate demands in the near future.

We think it will be very unfortunate for the general interests of people in this country if railroad men decide to make large demands upon the railroads in a general way at this time. No doubt, there may be cases where individual grievances exist, and it is proper that these should receive attention, nor is there any doubt that they will be promptly adjusted if brought to the notice of employers. It may well be questioned, however, that there is any great general grievance on the part of railroad employees in the matter of wages. Two things should be remembered.

The first is that in times of depression, following 1893, railroad managers strained every nerve to avoid reducing wages to any large extent. We know of cases where the general officers called the representatives of the men together and told them that it was their intention to cut everything else before wages. They exhorted the men to lend assistance by every means in their power to making economies in other directions, and in a number of cases a cut in wages was avoided in this way. Moreover, where wages were cut, they have, of course, since been restored in practically all cases, and it is fair to say that railroad men, as a whole, are receiving pay as high today as at any time in the history of the industry. It should further be remembered that as a class railroad men are well paid, and they stand very high as representatives of intelligent labor.

The next thing that should be remembered is that, taking a period including the last ten years, labor has had at least its fair proportion, considering the movement of commodities. If a chart were drawn giving the course of labor prices as measured by wages and commodity prices, it would be found that starting both lines together, ten years ago, the line of commodities would rule well below the line of wages until within a year. In other words, by the decline in the price of commodities up to within a year or so, the position of employed labor showed a material improvement as compared with the period previous to the 1893 panic.

Now, it is admitted on all hands that within the past twelve months, the price of commodities has risen relatively more than the price of labor. The position of a man on regular salary is not as good today as it was five years ago, assuming that salary has not been raised. On the other hand, the position of a man employed on salary five years ago was undoubtedly very much better than it was ten years ago, when the country as a whole was prosperous.

In a word, the railroad men may fairly be said to have been taken care of during the late depression, and to have suffered less than the men employed in most other lines of industry. Furthermore, the railroads are face to face now with greatly increased expenses for materials of all kinds, and it is very certain that the cost of transportation will in the next twelve months be materially higher per service unit than it has been in the past. It should further be remembered that owing to the great improvements in railroad operations and plant, more especially in the matter of grade reductions and curve eliminations, the work of railroad men has been facilitated so that the day's work for which the day's pay has been given has probably on the whole been diminished. The freight engineer and fireman, for example, have undoubtedly averaged faster time on their run than they did.

For these reasons, it is to be hoped that railroad labor will take an enlightened view of the situation at present, and will not lend itself to any policy of agitation on general principles. Cases of individual hardships will surely be remedied, and remedied willingly, for railroad employers are among the most enlightened in the land. Moreover, there is between railroad employers and their employees probably more real sympathy than may be found frequently elsewhere. We believe that it will be the wisest course for labor employed on railroads to co-operate with railroad managers in the next year or two. They will lose nothing in the long run by doing so.

October 9, 1902

The stock market is always sensitive to the condition of the money market. This is because a large proportion of speculative stocks are carried on borrowed money. The ordinary trader buys stocks on a margin ranging from 5 to 25 per cent. In buying Union Pacific he puts up from $500 to $2,500 for the purchase of one hundred shares, and the remainder, of at least $7,500, is borrowed of the broker or by the broker for account of customers.

A broker having $100,000 or $200,000 capital carries oftentimes quite a large amount of stock on the money which he borrows from banks or which he obtains by lending the stock carried [to short sellers]. In such a case, however, his margin of safety is small, and anything which interferes with borrowing money is serious. A house which has difficulty in borrowing money is sure to endeavor to induce its customers to sell their stocks, partly, no doubt, in good faith, but partly in order to relieve the house of embarrassment in making loans. Dear money, therefore, operates against the stock market, not only in the sense of increasing the cost of carrying stocks, but in the sense of bringing pressure to bear upon those who have stocks on margin to induce them to lighten the broker's load.

The dear money which affects speculation comes generally in one of two forms. It is either a quick flurry, very high rates and great scarcity of money due to a panicky feeling, or it is a slow hardening of money rates resulting in continued difficulty in obtaining loans.

The first condition is brought about by special causes, and seldom lasts more than two or three days. It is almost always wise to buy stocks on the second day of a dear-money squeeze of this kind, because the anxiety is soon dispelled, money comes in and stocks recover.

The dear money which is the result of changed conditions is a very different affair. It comes usually at the end of a period of prosperity, and is the result of absorption of the supply of loanable funds. It means the conversion of floating into fixed capital, and the tying up of money in so many ways as to reduce the floating supply at practically all points. Dear money has marked the approaching end of every period of great expansion which this country has seen. It was a feature of 1837, of 1857 and of 1873. It was present, although not so conspicuous, prior to 1893.

Dear money, after a period of prosperity, does not always mean an immediate turn in the tide. It is sometimes a feature of current business a year before the turn comes, but after dear money has once come, it usually recurs until it has its effect. The effect is always the same in the end. It means contraction, curtailment and lessened demand for funds. The more money has been tied up, the longer it takes to secure adequate liquidation. The sounder the situation, the less the unfavorable effect, but permanent relief from money absorption must come through lessened demand.

Take the stock market at this time. We have had six years of advance; six years of business enlargement, with all the requirements for money that have come with the great change that has taken place since 1896. There has been great expansion in the available money supply, particularly in the holding of gold, but for months past there has been evidence that money would become dearer. This has been shown by the foreign exchange situation, by the foreign trade statements, by the recognized commitments of syndicates and others, and by the great volume of work under way requiring the use of capital.

We are now having a period in which money is comparatively scarce. In the opinion of competent judges it will remain comparatively dear for some time. The effect has been to bring liquidation in stocks, and if money continues dear, it will stand against any large rise in stocks. Rallies will be more likely to bring realizing than fresh buying. This will have a tendency to keep the market within a comparatively narrow range of prices, except when liquidation may bring temporary declines. As this goes on, the stock market will tend to adjust itself to the money market, and, after a time, normal conditions will be restored, and there will be money enough to support speculation at the level established.

Then will come again the question of values, and this is the point every operator needs to watch this fall. Prices may be forced down by dear money without loss of value, in which case there will come certain recovery in prices when money rates again become normal. But the conditions which make dear money may also lessen stock values by lessening railroad earnings. If that occurs, the tendency will be toward further depression in stocks and against more than partial recovery.

The difference between decline in a bull period and decline in a bear period is this: In a bull period stocks go down in response to special conditions, but values go on rising and stocks recover. In a bear period stocks go down in response to special conditions, but, while these local conditions are adjusting themselves, values have fallen also, and there is nothing to give stocks recovery. Hence, they drop again and establish successively lower levels in response first to special causes and later to reduced value.

The money market is essential in its bearing upon the stock market at present, but whether values go on increasing or begin to decrease is the great question for the next three months.

October 17, 1902

The statement that "Wall Street is the only blue spot in the country" is often made at a time like the present and is familiar to all who have had experience of past depressions. It is a very favorite "argument" with a certain class of superficial critics and has generally involved a fallacy apparent to all who are able to look below the mere surface of things.

Nevertheless, there is sometimes truth in the saying, and at present there is rather more truth in it than is usually the case.

The great boom of 1877 to 1881 has many points of similarity with the boom that began in 1897 and has continued with intermission since that time. Nevertheless, there is an important difference between the two periods of expansion which ought not to lack attention. Twenty years ago, the distinguishing characteristic of the prosperity period was tremendous competitive building of railroads, factories and mills. The prosperity of existing enterprises irresistibly attracted fresh capital, which was practically all borrowed money, so that when the period of expansion ceased, all lines of industry were practically overcrowded, and profits which had heretofore gone to one man had to be divided by him with another—when there were any profits. Borrowed money was largely sunk in rails, rolling stock, bricks, mortar and machinery, which when they became unproductive practically ruined their owners. The characteristic of the 1878–81 boom was duplication of existing industrial enterprises.

Now, the essential characteristic of the present period of commercial prosperity has been the combination, consolidation and increased capitalization of existing industries, with very little competitive building. For ten years, there has been little or no construction of railroads in a competitive sense. What construction there has been is to be found mainly in the opening up of new territory, such as in the Southwest, or in filling up the gaps in existing systems. Practically the only competitive railroad built within the last ten years is the Kansas City Southern, and that became a bankrupt in the middle of great general prosperity. In the case of industrial enterprises, there has been a tremendous tendency toward consolidation in practically all important lines by the formation of so-called trusts. Competitive building of mills and factories has not thus far assumed extraordinary proportions. The building that has been done is mainly in the line of extensions to existing plants, and, while there has been great overcapitalization in the case of the so-called trusts, there has also been a good deal of very conservative extension of enterprises by investment of surplus profits. The result is that so far as the commercial situation is concerned, the position of manufacturers and merchants has not been sapped at the base as it was in the last boom. In the case of the railroads, the position has been greatly strengthened in a strategic sense by the absence of competitive construction and by the concentration under very strong management of a large portion of the formerly independent mileage.

Now, the unfavorable features in the present boom are essentially indigenous to Wall Street. There has been a quantity of injudicious promotion in the matter of industrial enterprises, and there has been a good deal of unsound finance in the case of the railroads, chiefly exemplifying itself in the increase of capitalization by splitting, and in the purchase of stocks of one road with bonds of another. This process, however, has in no way impaired or prejudiced the ultimate values of railroad and industrial property which have been unquestionably strengthened and solidified by the process described in the preceding paragraph. Hence, there is a great deal of truth in the statement that the troubles at present lying on the surface—excepting, of course, the labor situation, which is a problem standing alone—are troubles which largely concern Wall Street exclusively and which are likely to be settled without serious detriment to the ultimate conditions that make industrial and railroad values. Of course, serious trouble in Wall Street is always a disturbance to the whole country, and at times it may dislocate—at all events temporarily—commercial conditions. Unless, however, causes are in operation directly affecting commercial conditions, trouble in Wall Street is more or less transitory in its effect upon the business of the whole country.

Making all allowance for the influence of railroad betterments and industrial extensions upon the general prosperity, and pre-supposing that the labor situation will not at once develop dangerous qualities, it is perhaps fair to say that the chances somewhat favor Wall Street being able to adjust its position without greatly prejudicing general conditions of business. Barring crop failure next year, and barring very serious labor conditions, there is much to be said in favor of the statement that no permanent check to business prosperity has as yet developed in this country. In other words, there is as yet no evidence that ultimate values have begun to recede—unless it be furnished by the lately noticeable tendency toward increase in railroad expenses, although as against this the continued large gain in gross earnings is of much importance.

October 24, 1902

The reports of national banks and the comptroller of the currency showing their condition September 15 make it very clear that the ability of the banks to increase loans from this point is comparatively small. In the fall of 1900, the proportion of cash to deposits of all banks was 29.67 per cent, and a year ago the proportion was 27.65 per cent, showing in each case a fair margin for expansion.

Now the proportion of reserve to deposits is 25.74 per cent or within about three-quarters of one per cent of the limit, although some allowance can be made on account of the fact that in practice reserve is not required against government deposits. This, while a considerable sum, is not large in its relation to total deposits, and the indisputable fact is that the national banks of the country, as a whole, are very near the limit of their issue as long as 25 per cent of deposits is held in cash as a margin of safety.

The development of the past year has been in the direction of expansion of loans and deposits. Loans are 261½ millions greater than a year ago and deposits 271½ millions greater, while cash is 31½ millions less. This means that the activity in business and in speculation has made further demands upon credit, carrying both loans and deposits to the highest point on record. . . .

The true basis of loans is not cash, but credit. There may be great increase in the credit of a community and in its borrowing power, without any increase in the amount of actual cash. But as long as cash is made the basis of national bank loans, through the required holdings of 25 per cent of deposits in reserve cities, the supply of cash acts as a check upon the ability of such banks to make loans, no matter what the credit of borrowers may be. . . .

. . . .

NOTES

[1] S. A. Nelson included this editorial as Chapter XIX in *The ABC of Stock Speculation,* one of fifteen chapters designated as "Dow's Theory." In printing the depression years stated by Jevons, an error in Nelson's volume occurred. The year 1721 is given as 1712, which probably confused many of Nelson's readers, since the listing was in support of a ten-year periodicity in commercial crises.

[2] Note that Dow is aware that "actual hoarding of cash is exceptional" and that "in periods of panic, or shortly after them, the cash holdings of the banks increase." Mitchell agrees, p. 333: "Money has flowed into their vaults in large amounts" in times of depression.

[3] It is important to note that Dow does not say that the decline will equal the extent of the rise, but that it will bear "some relation to the extent of the rise."

[4] Cf. Veblen, *Theory,* pp. 316–318.

EPILOGUE

Dow's Place in the History of Economic Thought

INSTITUTIONALISM, or institutional economics, is essentially American and a product of the twentieth century. The names of Thorstein Veblen, John R. Commons and Wesley C. Mitchell are connected with this pragmatic school of economics.

There is no doubt that Dow's theory of business cycles as presented in the foregoing chapters places him among the early Institutionalists. It should be remembered that these selected writings of Dow antedate Veblen's *Theory of Business Enterprise,* which was published in 1904, and Mitchell's *Business Cycles,* which appeared—more than a decade later than Dow's editorials—in 1913.

Dow was familiar with the statistical work of John R. Commons, since he used the index numbers prepared by Commons and published in the *Quarterly Bulletin of the Bureau of Economic Research,* July 1900, in his editorials of September 13, 1900, and October 1, 1901.

Mitchell considered his 1913 volume, *Business Cycles,* as "an analytic description of the complicated processes by which seasons of business prosperity, crisis, depression, and revival come about in the modern world." He likewise described Chapters X through XIII, inclusive, in Part III of *Business Cycles,* as a "descriptive analysis of the process of cumulative change by which a revival of activity develops into intense prosperity, by which this prosperity engenders a crisis, by which crisis turns into depression, and by which depression, after growing more severe for a time, finally leads to such a revival of activity as that with which the cycle began."

Mitchell also wrote in the 1913 volume (page 570) with reference to the scope of this famous work the following lines:

"This analysis rests primarily upon an elaborate statistical enquiry into the phenomena of recent cycles in the United States, England,

France, and Germany. The statistical line of attack was chosen because the problem is essentially quantitative in character, involving as it does the relative importance of divers forces which are themselves the net resultants of innumerable business decisions. The selection of statistical data, the methods of presentation, and the co-ordination of the results were determined in large part by ideas borrowed from theoretical writers or from financial journals. But all the tables of figures and all the borrowed ideas were fitted into a framework provided by a study of the economic organization of today, which showed that the industrial process of making and the commercial process of distributing goods are thoroughly subordinated to the business process of making money."

There is no doubt that Dow provided his readers with both an "analytic description" and a "descriptive analysis of the process of cumulative change." A comparison of Dow's editorials with Mitchell's classic 1913 volume shows a similarity of thought and methodology. In both we find attention paid to business annals and statistics. Likewise, in both, little attention is paid to orthodox economic theory.

This should come as no surprise as far as Dow is concerned. He was not an academician, but a journalist and businessman. Like all financial journalists, he was concerned with the problem of the simplification and explanation of complex events. As a businessman he was an entrepreneur of note, as his work with Dow Jones & Company attests. Thus, Dow was an active participant in business as well as a viewer of the economic scene. It is interesting to note that Mitchell also worked for a short period of time as a newspaperman with the *Chicago Tribune*. Five articles on the steel strike published in the *Chicago Tribune* during the summer of 1901 are listed in Mitchell's bibliography.

Professor Paul T. Homan has noticed that "the introductory chapters of *Business Cycles* cannot be intelligently read without perceiving that they rest upon a groundwork of ideas incompatible with any variant statements of orthodox economic theory."

Professor Alvin H. Hansen wrote concerning Mitchell's work:

"The 1913 volume took business cycles out of the ivory tower and made them the 'stock in trade' of every financial writer and businessman. It was phrased in the language of the market place. The man of affairs at once recognized that here at last was a competent account of what goes on in actual economic life. And for the professional economist all discussions of 'crises' became at long last obsolete. The concept of the cycle had indeed been advanced long before by many, but it was nonetheless Mitchell who put it over. Henceforth the phenomenon to be studied was the *cycle* [italics in original], an unfolding integrated movement which had to be looked at as a whole."

Dow's writings on business cycles are also pragmatic and he was not concerned with the various schools of economic thought. It seems reasonable to assume that Dow was familiar with the work of William Stanley Jevons, as evidenced by his editorial of July 9, 1902, and probably that of Walter Bagehot and Clement Juglar as well. All were available in American editions.

Dow's writings on business cycles are likewise "phrased in the language of the market place." He certainly viewed the cycle as "an unfolding integrated movement which had to be looked upon as a whole."

Dow's editorials contain the following observations, which form the basic framework of his theory of business cycles, although many other principles were established as well:

1. The business community is either engaged in reducing business activity, believing prices will be lower, or increasing activity because it is of the opinion that prices will rise. Rising prices normally mean increased profits, while falling prices denote falling profits.
2. The process of expansion and contraction described above is a continuous one.
3. Business moves in cycles because businessmen attempt to make profits when business activity is expanding and to "decline as strongly as possible" when business is contracting.
4. Business of all kinds moves in periods of alternate expansion and contraction.
5. Although all business moves in this fashion (as in 4 above), all lines of business do not share equally. Declines may be limited to a single industry with much less effect on the economy than declines in general, i.e., declines in many industries.
6. The "great indicators of the rise and fall in business" and the stock market in their turning points at crests and troughs keep close company. The stock market usually leads at turning points due to its discounting function.
7. The fabric representing general business is so intertwined that decline or advance in one great industry cannot fail to affect others.
8. The process of revival from depression starts when some one industry begins to improve and others gradually follow. Raw materials and partly finished products advance in price. Inventories are increased on a cumulative basis.
9. The process of decline from prosperity occurs when the economy

experiences a "check in the prosperity of one industry after another resulting in a loss of profits."

10. During periods of prosperity and depression great psychological changes take place as the mass of the people change from being optimistic to pessimistic, and vice versa.

11. While changes in business activity in many single industries may not be great, the cumulative influence exerted is enormous.

12. Technology plays a role in the process. When iron and steel prices are falling, "the best way of reaching bedrock is to curtail production and take antiquated furnaces out of blast."

13. The character of the movements in the expansion and contraction of business activity is slow at the turning points, becoming quicker as progress is made in line with the existing trend, and usually quickest of all before the cyclical movement ends.

14. There are at all times forces in the economy working for and working against continued prosperity or depression.

15. The momentum of business activity will overcome obstacles that would present greater difficulty at a different stage of the business cycle.

16. Businesses which buy and sell again are not concerned with prices, but are vitally concerned with the margin of profit.

17. The prices of finished goods are vital to the ultimate consumer, since he uses the products and does not offer them for resale.

18. Costs of materials increase during prosperity, causing a decline in net earnings (of railroads).

19. When the costs of materials increase during prosperity, certain ultimate consumers suspend "all work requiring much material until supplies can be obtained at a lower figure."

20. Modern business is done chiefly on credit.

21. Wages lag during a period of revival.

22. The economy never stands still. The times are always becoming a little better or a little worse.

23. The element of time is important with respect to changes in general conditions. "The great manufacturing and mercantile interests of the country are not going in a single month from great prosperity to depression."

24. The loss of confidence and curtailment of demand in the contraction phase of the cycle "is a kind of flame which creates the fuel which is burned."

Thus, Charles H. Dow presented a modern view of business cycles in the years 1899 to 1902. Only by viewing Dow's editorials on business cycles as a whole is it possible to visualize the scope of his work.

In all fairness, we should consider Charles H. Dow as one of the early members of the school of institutional economics, and a forerunner of Wesley C. Mitchell. As such, his name should be included in histories of economic thought, and his work recognized as a pioneering accomplishment in the theory of business cycles.